MW00532545

ENDORS

"Richard Parrott has vividly reminded us that the life of faith is neither simple nor easy as some preachers might represent it. In doing so, he helps us see that the patriarchs are not characters in a fictional novel but real people who encountered life much like the rest of us. Most importantly, he has not let us forget that in the uneven journey of life with Christ, we are not alone."

H. Ray Dunning
Professor Emeritus of Theology, Trevecca Nazarene University, and author of *Grace, Faith, and Holiness*.

"I encountered this book on my own 'reluctant journey' during a difficult transition in my career. Richard's work is a wise and helpful guide for anyone whose life has taken an unexpected turn. This is not a safe or easy journey we are on together with Christ, but we must press forward; the final destination is indescribable."

Rev. Brent E. Tallman
Director of Campus Spiritual Formation, Trevecca Nazarene University

"The patriarchs, Abraham, Isaac, and Jacob, are compelling biblical characters, exemplifying how God established a special, covenantal relationship with his creatures. Parrott not only surveys their historical and literary background, but also shows how they are exemplary for those with whom God is establishing such a relationship today. His study is not satisfied with analyzing the 'then' of the biblical stories of these called but flawed men; he seeks to apply their lives in relation with God to our 'now' as we, equally flawed, seek to serve out our own call."

David W. Baker
Professor of Old Testament, Ashland Theological Seminary

"Who among us has not taken a RELUCTANT JOURNEY . . . many miles that were much too long, traveling toward a less than desirable location, or even worse, having to make the journey with those who should have stayed at home. Using this insightful and effective metaphor, Dr. Parrott explores such a challenge, but at the heart of this candid text is the author's fundamental question, 'Can God be trusted?' as all of us undertake these inevitable "spiritual" pilgrimages. I deem this book's multiple "paths" to be a credible and potentially life-redirecting journey itself for both believer and seeker alike!"

Gary W. Streit PhD
Special Assistant to the President/Interim Dean, Arkansas Baptist College

"As Rev. Dr. Richard Parrott's pastor for several years, I have had the privilege of not only reading his work and hearing him speak, but watching his life and sharing his heart. Richard has lived the 'reluctant journey.' He's felt what it's like to be 'homeless with God.' This is not just words on pages: this is a biblically-based, theologically-sound journey Richard has experienced, and is now helping thousands of others take their own journey. I heartily endorse it for your life, your small group, and your church. People need guidance in this area, and this book is an excellent source."

Dr. Kevin M. Ulmet
Senior Pastor, Nashville First Church of the Nazarene

"Following the petitions of the Lord's Prayer, this book weaves the broken, heroic, faltering, and victorious stories of the patriarchs not only as examples for us but as demonstrations of the lengths to which God will go to partner with each one of us. Through the stories of Abraham, Jacob, Joseph, and others, Richard Parrott has unpacked the grace of God in word pictures that will renew the heart and inspire the reader."

Dr. Stan Toler, bestselling author & speaker

"Richard Parrott is smart, educated, talented, and experienced. It is the "experienced" that makes me want to hear a speech or read a book. Dr. Parrott's book delivers and is absolutely worth your time to read, reflect, and find strength for your real life experiences. The truth and insight of the book will serve you well."

Dr. Jim Van Hook
Retired Music Executive and Dean of the Mark Curb School of Entertainment, Belmont University

THE RELUCTANT JOURNEY

FULFILLING GOD'S PURPOSE FOR YOU

RICHARD LESLIE PARROTT

THOMAS NELSON
Since 1798

NASHVILLE MEXICO CITY RIO DE JANEIRO

Published in Nashville, Tennessee, by Thomas Nelson. Thomas Nelson is a trademark of HarperCollins Christian Publishing, Inc.

Page design and layout: Crosslin Creative

Images: VectorStock

Thomas Nelson titles may be purchased in bulk for educational, business, fundraising, or sales promotional use. For information, please e-mail SpecialMarkets@ThomasNelson.com.

* Note: Italics in quotations from *The Voice* are used to "indicate words not directly tied to the dynamic translation of the original language" but that "bring out the nuance of the original, assist in completing ideas, and . . . provide readers with information that would have been obvious to the original audience" (The Voice, preface). Author emphasis in quotations from *The Voice* is indicated with the use of **boldface** type.

ISBN: 978-1-4016-8038-1

Printed in the United States of America

14 15 16 17 18 19 RRD 6 5 4 3 2 1

The book is dedicated to Dr. Esther Swink and Mr. Eddie Hales for their authenticity, inspiration, and partnership; each has joined with Christ on a reluctant journey; each has walked the path with grace, faithfulness, and dignity.

He who made us without ourselves,
will not save us without ourselves.
—John Wesley[1]

CONTENTS

ACKNOWLEDGMENTS

A book evolves and grows in the heart of an author and through the support of a community:

I want to express deep appreciation for the rich counsel and mentoring of Mark Maish.

I also want to thank Dr. Esther Swink for her careful and thoughtful reading of the manuscript.

In addition, I express my appreciation to Eddie Hales who has provided deep encouragement as well as the technical support for my blog and social media.

In addition to those who shared direct involvement in this project, there are several individuals and groups that have listened and provided feedback as I shared evolving ideas and insights:

First among these groups is the Koinonia Sunday School class I have the privilege of teaching each week. Also, thank you to students in my classes who heard and responded to early versions of these chapters, which they received as devotional material during our coursework.

I especially appreciate my marvelous group of first-year teachers who prayed with me and for me throughout the year of writing: Julie Dimick, Erin Holt, Preston Hunt, Mary Kirby, Haley Laborde, Erin Lintzenich, Erin Miller, and Elise Sirois.

There is also a rich intellectual and scholarly underpinning for this practical volume:

I am indebted to Dr. Jerry Flora and Dr. Dee Freeborn for their personal teaching and modeling of Christian spiritual formation.

I also want to express my heartfelt appreciation to Dr. Ray Dunning and his theological and biblical writing and teaching.

In addition, there are two professors I have never met, but would be remiss not to express in writing my deep respect and appreciation for their combined work that shapes my own thinking: Dr. Walter Brueggemann and Dr. N. T. Wright.

Finally, to my wife, Shirley, my partner for every journey in life: thank you for guarding my time, talking through the ideas, and listening each time I had one more version of a chapter to read aloud. You make the reluctant paths bearable and the open road wondrous.

INTRODUCTION

"Lead us not into temptation, but deliver us from evil."

—Matthew 6:13

Begin with the word **TRUST**—to rely on and place confidence in someone. Now, turn the word over and read what is underneath it—**RISK**. There is a risk in every act of trust.

Move on to the word **HOPE**; on the underside of the word, you find the shadow word—**FEAR**. We experience optimism and anxiety simultaneously when staring into an unknown or uncertain future.

Again, for every meaningful **PROMISE** you can count on the presence of **PAIN**. Stand at an altar and say, "I do," and you understand that promise and pain are wed. There is pain in fulfilling the promise as well as receiving the promise.

Finally, within every **CALL** you find a **TEST**. Whether you are called to a new level of responsibility on the job or to an expanded ministry in your church, you can count on the fact that the call will test you and teach you.

Line the words, side by side, as if on opposite edges of a winding path:

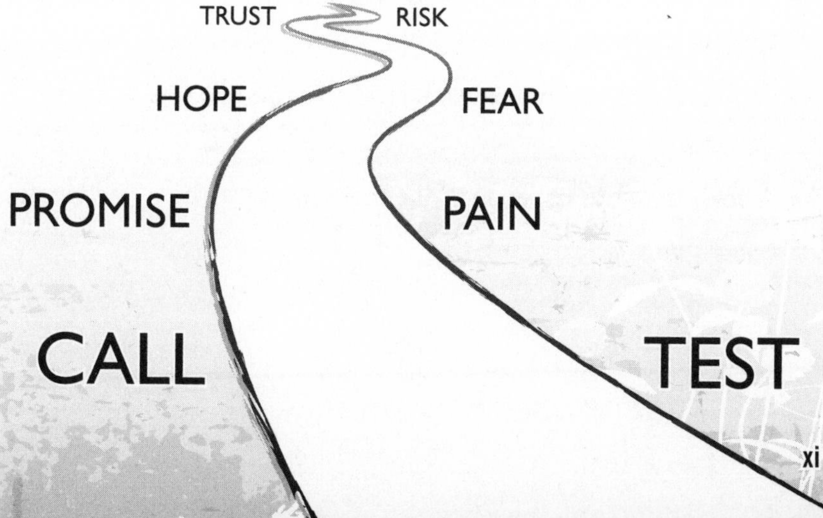

The winding trail between the two sides of the path mark the reluctant journey. This is a journey to which we are committed yet cautious. We are dedicated but wary. We are obligated but anxious. Everyone faces a reluctant journey:

- A wounded vet looks at the pain-filled path toward uncertain healing.
- A young schoolteacher discovers the terrors of the first year.
- A retiree faces uncertain years in an uncertain era.
- A college graduate examines the hardships of finding work.
- An angry son knows he should make amends with his parents.
- A couple's call to full-time ministry means life will change forever.
- A mother holds a baby with Down syndrome and considers the future.
- An addict knows she needs help, but the way forward is hard and long.
- A new believer discovers resistance and ridicule at his fresh faith.
- A wealthy business owner struggles with the call to give sacrificially.
- An agnostic battles her doubts as she desires to believe.
- An employee in a toxic organization determines to live true to Christ.
- Parents hurting with a prodigal child struggle to know what to do next.
- A complacent Christian feels the prod to move into a deeper life in Christ.

THE SAVIOR'S STRUGGLE

The reluctant journey is the struggle our Lord validated in the prayer He taught His disciples: "Lead us not into temptation, but deliver us from evil" (Matt. 6:13). We repeat the words so easily and debate them so intellectually that we miss the deep, spiritual dynamic that these ten words carry.

"Lead us not into temptation" voices a cry from the soul, a lament in the heart, as we gaze on the path ahead and tremble. We trust, but we know there is risk. God's promise is sure, but there will certainly be pain. Hope and fear fold into one another like colors in the finest marble. The reluctant journey is a calling and will test everything about us.

Put yourself in the sandals of Moses, who when summoned by God to return to Egypt and confront Pharaoh said, "Please, Lord, *I beg You to* send *Your message through* someone else, *anyone else*" (Ex. 4:13).

Isaiah responded to his call with confidence and obedience; yet when he understood the message he was to deliver, he cried out, "How long, Lord?" (Isa. 6:11).

The Psalms lament the reluctant journey: "There's no way out of here; no one cares about *the state of* my soul" (Ps. 142:4). And, "I only asked, 'When I stumble *on the narrow path,* don't let them boast or celebrate *my failure*'" (Ps. 38:16).

Our Lord's prayer for His disciples became our Lord's personal lament in the Garden of Gethsemane. He knew the reluctant journey; it was before Him:

> He took Peter, James, and John with Him; *and as they left the larger group behind,* He became distressed and filled with sorrow.
>
> **JESUS:** My heart is so heavy; I feel as if I could die. Wait here for Me, and *stay awake to* keep watch.

He walked on a little farther. Then He threw Himself on the ground and prayed for deliverance from what was about to come.

JESUS: Abba, Father, I know that anything is possible for You. Please take this cup away so I don't have to drink from it. But whatever happens, let Your will be done—not Mine. (Mark 14:33–36)

THE PARTNER'S PRAYER

We also pray, "Deliver us from evil" (Matt. 6:13). When confronted with God's full demand on our lives, we experience a bit of foot-dragging, hesitation, and caution. Your personal trail of reluctance may involve moving from . . .

Guilt to confession,

Wound to healing,

Resentment to forgiveness,

Complacence to surrender,

Self-focus to sacrifice,

Sorrow to new life,

Sinner to saint.

The spiritual challenge is daunting. Imagine unpacking your gear at the base camp of Mount Everest as you look at the climb ahead of and above you. Put yourself on a beach in Normandy with a plan to take the plunge and swim to the White Cliffs of Dover. The spiritual calling of God is formidable. Oh yes, we may declare our unwavering commitment before the assembly of believers. Yet, tucked in the shadows of the soul, we are squeamish, guarded, and circumspect. We will make the journey, but we are going to ask if it is at all possible for the cup to be removed.

We struggle with the wish that God might eliminate the journey and put us in the jet stream to heaven! Where did we develop the false impression that following Jesus was a stress-free boulevard? Jesus does not promise to save us from the struggle. Neither does Jesus abandon us in the struggle. First, Jesus has blazed the trail. He made the journey and conquered the journey.

> Though He was in the form of God,
>   He chose not to cling to equality with God;
> But He poured Himself out *to fill a vessel brand new;*
>   a servant in form
>   and a man indeed.
> The very likeness of humanity,
> He humbled Himself,
>   obedient to death—
>   a merciless death on the cross! (Phil. 2:6–8)

Second, Jesus takes the journey with us. He leads the way and calls us to partner with Him, to join Him as His allies, companions, and joint-heirs. "God's Spirit confirms in our spirits that we are His children. If we are God's children, that means we are His heirs along with the Anointed, set to inherit everything that is His. If we share His sufferings, *we know that* we will ultimately share in His glory" (Rom. 8:16–17).

We enter the struggle with Him. He continues the battle through us. Therefore, "adopt the mind-set of Jesus the Anointed. *Live with His attitude in your hearts*" (Phil. 2:5).

As in any partnership, you must take up your responsibility. "Continue to work out your salvation, with great fear and trembling, because God is energizing you so that you will desire and do what always pleases Him" (vv. 12–13). The reluctant journey is God's way to transform us and bring His transformation to the world. We are called to "shine like stars across the land" (v. 15).

And so, more than once, we heave a sigh, return to our purpose, and give all to God again. "Whatever happens, let Your will be done—not Mine" (Mark 14:36).

A JOURNEY OF PARTNERSHIP

The purpose of the reluctant journey is to spread the light of God. "The God who spoke *light into existence,* saying, 'Let light shine from the darkness,' is the very One who sets our hearts ablaze to shed light on the knowledge of God's glory *revealed* in the face of Jesus" (2 Cor. 4:6). The call rings with inspiration and challenge.

The next verse begins with the catch *but*. But there will be struggle as well as strength. There will be pain as well as power. There will be shame as well as the glory of God's presence. The purpose of the partnership in suffering is revealed. "But this beautiful treasure is contained in us—*cracked* pots made of earth and clay—so that the transcendent character of this power will be clearly seen as coming from God and not from us" (v. 7).

Make the verse personal: God places His treasure, the Spirit of Jesus (Acts 16:7; Phil. 1:19), in you. Yet, you have faults, flaws, and failures. Surely it is the wrong setting for such a diamond, yet, that is the point. Attention is drawn to the glittering light rather than the humble setting. You are evidence, the verification, the proof, and the living reminder of God's work in the world. And God answers our prayer; He leads us and delivers us.

> We are cracked and chipped from our afflictions on all sides, but we are not crushed by them. We are bewildered at times, but we do not give in to despair. We are persecuted, but we have not been abandoned. We have been knocked down, but we are not destroyed. We always carry around in our bodies the reality

> of the brutal death *and suffering* of Jesus. As a result, His *resurrection* life *rises and* reveals its wondrous power in our bodies as well. (2 Cor. 4:8–10)

The reluctant journey of Christ, His brutal death and suffering, is alive and at work in us. His death was a direct confrontation with the unholy trinity: sin, death, and the Devil. His work continues in us. We are His partners in the continuing battle. Thus, His resurrected life shines out through us.

PATHWAYS OF PURPOSE

The purpose of this book is to explore the reluctant journey, specifically three paths God calls His partners to walk. The different paths comprise the three parts of the book:

Part One: Homeless with God: The Path of Wandering

Part Two: Troubled by God: The Path of Wounds

Part Three: Hidden from God: The Path of Wisdom

To explore these three pathways, we will follow the journey of three men and their families: Abraham, Jacob, and Joseph. Each one embarked on a reluctant journey that embodied a petition of the Lord's Prayer.

Homeless with God: The Path of Wandering. Abraham left country, family, and his father's house upon hearing the Voice call him. He left all to find a heavenly Father and a glorious kingdom. Abraham embodied the prayer of our Lord: "Our Father in heaven, let Your name remain holy. Bring about Your kingdom" (Matt. 6:9–10).

Abraham was not a model of virtue. He struggled with fear, deception, and, on one occasion, cynicism. Because Abraham and his wife, Sarah, were well past the time for bearing children, he struggled to believe God's promise that a son would be born to them.

Nevertheless, Abraham believed, and this established a right relationship with God.

God's promise of a son to Abraham and Sarah foreshadows God's gift of Jesus. When God called Abraham to wander after Him, God was thinking of Jesus, who would later say, "Foxes have dens *in which to sleep*, and the birds have nests. But the Son of Man has no place to lay His head" (Matt. 8:20).

Abraham's story is for those of us who cannot quite find our place in this world, or who have been called to give up our place in response to God's voice. It is not an easy journey to move from trusting in a home on earth to staking all we have on our Father in heaven.

> Some people store up treasures *in their homes* here on earth. *This is a shortsighted practice*—don't undertake it. Moths and rust will eat up any treasure you may store here. Thieves may break into *your homes* and steal *your precious trinkets*. Instead, put up your treasures in heaven where moths do not attack, where rust does not corrode, and where thieves are barred at the door. For where your treasure is, there your heart will be also. (Matt. 6:19–21)

Troubled by God: The Path of Wounds. God is a troublemaker precisely because the values of His kingdom are opposed to the values of the world system. When you pray, "Manifest Your will here on earth, as it is manifest in heaven" (Matt. 6:10), you pray for trouble.

Jacob personified the conflict of heaven and earth. He understood the values of this world—hard bargaining, deception, resentment, and fear. Every point in his life was full of trouble. Yet, he saw the heavens opened and angels ascend and descend. He saw the place where heaven and earth meet.

God laid a foundation in Jacob. In that foundation we see Jesus, the ultimate meeting of heaven and earth, fully God and fully human. Jesus described Himself and His journey with His disciples: "I tell you the truth: *before our journey is complete,* you will see the heavens standing open while heavenly messengers ascend and descend, *swirling* around the Son of Man" (John 1:51).

Jacob lived out the Lord's Prayer for heaven's will on earth. He became Israel, the name God gave him, which the Scripture interprets as the one who struggled with God and his own humanity, yet overcame (Gen. 32:28).[1] He limped away with a wound and a blessing.

Jacob's path is for those who do not know what to do with a life full of wounds and trouble. Jacob escaped his dysfunctional family and lived among those who did not understand his faith, and the sins of his past caught up with him. Nonetheless, at each point God used his troubles to lay a foundation for the will of heaven on earth.

God has plans for your troubles, your wounds, and your failures. God's tactics are at work in your trials. He wants you to have new eyes to see heaven's will at work in the world's woes. "The eye is the lamp of the body. *You draw light into your body through your eyes, and light shines out to the world through your eyes.* So if your eye is well *and shows you what is true,* then your whole body will be filled with light" (Matt. 6:22).

Hidden from God: The Path of Wisdom. Joseph, like many of us, did not hear the Voice or see the portal open between heaven and earth. Joseph dealt with family and famine, the everyday events of daily living. He learned to discern the wisdom of God in daily bread and belonging. For most of his journey, God was hidden. He lived the prayer of Jesus, "Give us each day that day's bread—*no more, no less*—And forgive us our debts as we forgive those who owe us something (Matt. 6:11–12).

Joseph received a hint from God in a dream that resulted in a series of seemingly bad breaks in life. He was abused by his brothers, sold into slavery, falsely accused, and abandoned in a prison. Yet, as he faced inequality and injustice he slowly but certainly found God's wisdom.

The Lord set up a harsh curriculum for this young man. It was what Joseph needed to prepare him for the position God had in mind, viceroy over Egypt. Pharaoh's nightmares became God's moment to fulfill the dream of so many years before. The famine in the land made Joseph famous. Joseph had prepared the nation for lean days during the days of abundance. The famine also brought his cruel brothers back into his life. In the intense struggle to reconcile the resentment in his heart, Joseph found the wisdom to see God's hand at work. He learned to forgive.

Just as God's plan was revealed to Joseph, God's grand scheme for the world was revealed through Jesus. God has always been at work, choosing His way to bless the whole world. "What was hidden for ages, generations and generations, is now being revealed to His holy ones. He decided to make known to them His blessing to the nations; the glorious riches of this mystery is the indwelling of the Anointed in you! The very hope of glory" (Col. 1:26–27).

Joseph's tale is for those of us who find life unfair and do not hear a word from heaven concerning our plight. We feel hidden from God. Can we learn to spy God in the ordinary moments of life? Can we seek God in the inequalities of life? In a world full of worries about what we eat and what we wear, Joseph's story teaches us to look for God's hand.

> So do not consume yourselves with questions: What will we eat? What will we drink? What will we wear? Outsiders make themselves frantic over such questions; *they don't realize that*

> your heavenly Father knows exactly what you need. Seek first the kingdom of God and His righteousness, and then all these things will be given to you *too*. So do not worry about tomorrow. Let tomorrow worry about itself. Living faithfully is a large enough task for today. (Matt. 6:31–34)

"COME TO ME"

In my private study, I have a small, old farm instrument—a double yoke used for training young cattle. The yoke was made in Tennessee, the state where my grandfather and father were born, as well as the place I make my home. The yoke is meaningful to me because it hung on the wall behind my father's desk for as many years as I can remember.

The fact that it is a double yoke reminds me of my partnership with Jesus. Jesus offers us partnership. The invitation is found in the last verses of Matthew 11. We often lift the invitation out of its proper setting in Scripture. In doing so, we separate the invitation of Jesus from the authentic, painful, and personal experience He was facing. The context of His invitation is in the midst of trouble and suffering.

- John the Baptist, cousin of Jesus, had been imprisoned and was uncertain, filled with questions. He wondered if Jesus was the one they were waiting for. John faced a reluctant journey (Matt. 11:2–6).
- The cities where Jesus traveled had rejected Him. On every side, there was misunderstanding, accusation, falsehood, and denunciation. Despite mighty miracles, people did not believe (Matt. 11:16–24).
- Jesus prayed. His prayer reveals His own sense of homelessness, trouble, and the hidden mystery of His true identity. He

was wandering, wounded, and thanking God for wisdom (Matt. 11:25–27).

It is at this place on the path, here on the trail of the reluctant journey, that Jesus invites you to be His partner: "Come to Me, all who are weary and burdened, and I will give you rest. Put My yoke upon your shoulders—*it might appear heavy at first, but it is perfectly fitted to your curves*. Learn from Me, for I am gentle and humble of heart. *When you are yoked to Me*, your weary souls will find rest. For My yoke is easy, and My burden is light" (Matt. 11:28–30).

When I look at the double yoke in my study, I often imagine Jesus inviting me to join Him. He slips His head in one side of the yoke, and He invites me to place my head on the other side. We are bound together, side by side. Whatever burdens we carry, whatever cross we bear, we do so together as partners in the reluctant journey.

Richard Leslie Parrott
February 21, 2014

PART ONE

HOMELESS WITH GOD

The Path of Wandering

"Our Father in heaven, let Your name remain holy. Bring about Your kingdom."

—Matthew 6:9–10

The opening of the Lord's Prayer reads like the prayer of a homeless man searching for a home he has never seen. This is the story of Abraham who left his family when he heard the voice of a new Father, a Holy Father who promised him a family as numerous as the stars of the sky.

Abraham left his country, his kinsmen, and his father's house to partner with God. He believed God's promise that stated, "All of the families of the earth will find their blessing in you" (Gen. 12:3; Gal. 3:8). Abraham anchored his life on the promise that God's kingdom would come through Abraham's legacy. He is the example of one being made righteous by faith: "Abram believed

God *and trusted in His promises,* so God counted it to his favor as righteousness" (Gen. 15:6; Rom. 4:3, 22; Gal. 3:6; James 2:23).

Abraham walks the first path of the reluctant journey, the path of wandering. His path was demanding—to trust the Voice and leave all that is familiar, to trust the promise as years slipped by without a child, and to offer the promised child back to God in sacrifice.

THE CALL TO THE UNKNOWN

How Do I Know This Is God's Voice?

My soul *is dry and* thirsts for You, True God,
as a deer thirsts for water.
I long for the True God who lives.
When can I stand before Him *and feel His comfort*?
—Psalm 42:1–2

"What shall we create out of your life? What shall we create out of this world?" God offers this invitation for you to join Him in creating your life and changing the world. He invites you to live in authentic partnership with Him. Respond in faith by trusting the voice of God and stepping into a new life. Abraham accepted God's invitation; God chose Abraham as His first human partner in the mission of salvation for the whole world.

It was a cool afternoon in late spring, common in the Northwest. My oldest son was a member of a Little League team, the level of Little League where they actually pitch the ball. I sat in the stands as he took his place in the dugout.

Clouds filled the sky, threatening rain. Parents and grandparents crowded into the stands, calling out their cheers and jeers as the game progressed. Watching the boys play, I saw them float between

THE STORY IN SUMMARY
Genesis 12:1–13:18

Abraham is living in Mesopotamia (modern Iraq) when the voice of God calls him into a partnership through which all people on earth will be blessed. Remarkably, Abraham believes the voice of God and moves to the land of Canaan, the promised land, with his wife, Sarah, and nephew, Lot.

When famine comes to the land, they go to Egypt, the breadbasket of the ancient world. There, he fears Pharaoh and asks his wife to lie and say she is his sister. Despite his lapse in integrity, he returns from Egypt with great wealth.

The expansion of the flocks creates conflict between the servants of Lot and the servants of Abraham. Abraham offers to divide the promised land with Lot, but Lot chooses to settle in the valley of Sodom and Gomorrah.

high intensity and unintended boredom. My son struck out his first time at bat, walked his second time at the plate, and struck out again the third time he was up to bat.

As the game progressed, the excitement grew. This was not a one-sided contest, but a real struggle for victory. In the final inning the teams were tied. My son's team was at bat. There was one out and a runner on first. A second out followed. Then came a strong hit that put runners on second and third. My heart skipped a beat, and I gasped for air; my little boy was at bat with two outs, two on base, and a tied score.

A swing and a miss! What else could I do but pray, "Lord, help him get a hit, or help me help him work through the disappointment." The next pitch was a ball. Another swing and a strike! The tension was too much for this young father to endure. I looked at my little boy standing beside the plate. The pitcher wound up and threw with all his might. I must confess to you I closed my eyes. I could not bear to watch.

With my eyes closed, my ears were open to receive the sound of a distinctive ping as the ball and bat met. Without time to think, my eyes flashed open, and I saw the ball flying high and far and over the left field fence. The crowd broke out in jubilation. The boys on the bench leapt out of the dugout and ran with my son as he circled the bases. They carried him across home plate, making sure he touched the plate.

When I gathered him up as all the other parents were taking their children, I said, "I think we need a little ice cream to celebrate." He smiled. Sitting at a favorite ice cream spot in town, we talked about the game and his amazing home run. It was a moment of bonding. It felt right to confess, "Andrew, you know, I was so nervous when the last pitch was thrown that I actually closed my eyes."

"So did I, Dad," he replied with a big smile on his face.

A blind swing of the bat is not recommended for a baseball player. Today, my son is a grown man. He can swing at a pitch with his eyes wide open. But that day, in his childhood, at the very beginning stages, he closed his eyes and swung the bat.

In a sense, a deep and true sense, we all begin with blind faith, a leap to faith.[1] Without full understanding or perception, we stake our lives on God's promise. This is the way of faith. So it was with the father of our faith, Abraham.[2] He had no mature pastor or church members to guide him. He had no study group to surround him and pray with him. He did not have a Bible for guidance. All he had was a voice, an inner voice that asked him to stake his life on following God. In the way that we hear an inner voice and follow, so it was with Abraham. Abraham heard the Eternal One.

ETERNAL ONE: *Abram,* get up and go! Leave your country. Leave your relatives and your father's home, and travel to the land I will show you. *Don't worry—I will guide you there.* I have plans to make a great people from your descendants. And I am going to put a *special* blessing on you and cause your reputation to grow so that you will become a blessing *and example to others.* I will also bless those who bless you *and further you in your journey,* and I'll trip up those who try to trip you *along the way. Through your descendants,* all of the families of the earth will find their blessing in you.

Without any hesitation, Abram went. He did exactly as the Eternal One asked him to do. (Gen. 12:1–5)

God's promise was fulfilled in Jesus. When God called Abraham, He had Jesus in mind.[3] The Voice came to Jesus when He and His cousin, John the Baptist, stepped into the Jordan River. There, the last prophet of the kingdom's promise baptized the God-man who embodied the kingdom of God in Himself. At that point the heavens opened, the Spirit of God descended on Jesus, and He heard a voice from heaven say, "You are My Son, My beloved One, and I am very pleased with You" (Mark 1:11).

The Voice came to Abraham while he was still in Mesopotamia and instructed him to leave his country, his people, and his father's house and go to a new land. God's plan was to make Abraham's family a great nation, out of which would come a blessing for the whole world (Gen. 12:1–3). Abraham received the promise that he would be the father of a nation, a great kingdom. God's promise to Abraham wound and waned its way through the generations until the day the promise was fulfilled in Jesus when He declared,

In a sense, a deep and true sense, we all begin with blind faith, a leap to faith.

"It's time! The kingdom of God is near! Seek forgiveness, change your actions, and believe this good news!" (Mark 1:15).

God's strategy is to partner with people. With Abraham, God began a new strategy in the salvation of the world.[4] In Abraham, God invited a human being to be His partner. Adam[5] was called to enjoy the world as God created it. Noah[6] saved his own family under God's direction. However, in the call of Abraham, God chose a human partner[7] so the whole world would be blessed.

Just as God promised to take on Abraham as a partner, that same promise extends to the legacy, the seed, of Abraham, Jesus Christ. Through faith, we are the legacy of Christ. The call of Abraham is our call (Acts 3:25). God wants to bless us so that the whole world is blessed.

Note two things about God's invitation. First, God takes the initiative. God called Abraham, and Abraham responded. God calls you, and you respond. The call starts with God. Second, answering the call requires trust, a leap of faith. Abraham's response to God's invitation helps us understand how to genuinely respond to God's call. For Abraham, responding to God's call required listening, trusting, struggling, and praying.

LISTEN: GOD CALLS YOU TO BE HIS PARTNER IN THIS WORLD

We might ask, why did God call Abraham? The question seems reasonable and a good place to begin. However, it may be the wrong question. Rather than assuming the invitation was offered to Abraham alone, it might have been that God was calling the whole world. God's plan has always been and continues to be the salvation of the world. So was Abraham the only one who received the call? Or could it be that although God was calling everyone, Abraham was the only one listening and responding?[8] Authentic partnership with God begins with listening.

The New Testament is clear and consistent; you may know with certitude that God calls you into a deep, life-changing relationship with Him.[9] You begin your journey when you listen for God's voice.

Listening is not as easy as it sounds. The world is full of voices clamoring for attention. Your inner life may be deaf to God's voice because of the brassy voices of demands, the past, fear, pride, shame, pain, or promise.

How do you know you are hearing the voice of God? The voice of God will always point toward Jesus. The voice of God will invite you into relationship with Him and His mission, into a life of love and purpose.

The Voice invites you to join Him. How do you listen? God often speaks into our current situation, our stillness, our pain, or our confusion. God's word to us often comes through the good words of others, an inner nudge of the Holy Spirit, and in the holy Scriptures. God's Word to us is real.

In his book *The Captivating Presence*, minister Albert Day wrote:

> God is present in reality no matter what unreality our practices and our ponderings imply. He is forever trying to establish communication; forever aware of the wrong directions we are taking and wishing to warn us; forever offering solutions to the problems that baffle us; forever standing at the door of our loneliness, eager to bring us such comradeship as the most intelligent living mortal could not supply; forever clinging to our indifference in the hope that someday our needs, or at least our tragedies will weaken us to respond to his advances. The Real Presence is just that, real and life transforming. Nor are the conditions for the manifestation of his splendors out of the reach of any of us! Here they are; otherness, openness, obedience, obsession.[10]

TRUST: THE BLESSING AND BURDEN OF BEING GOD'S PARTNER

Listening with openness to the otherness of God requires faith. Faith is a verb, an action. A while back I was offered an opportunity, a calling, to provide in-depth leadership development for a national company. Answering the call would mean starting my own business. At the time I had a position with an organization that provided stability, health insurance, a regular salary, and support. Nonetheless, the opportunity to step out of the past and into a new entrepreneurial calling was before me. I could think about it, talk about it, and be grateful for it. None of that mattered, however, until I was willing to step into it. That was faith.

God calls you and me into partnership with Him. God initiates the call, but we must respond with trust, the action form of faith. We may praise God for our call, study it in depth, and consider all the ramifications of living a life according to God's calling. However, until we step out of the old life and into the new life, it is all talk rather than trust.

Abraham stepped out of his old life and into a new life. What did he leave? God provided a list of things he was to leave, and God provided the list in a specific order: "Leave your country. Leave your relatives and your father's home" (Gen. 12:1). In short, he left everything.

Partnering with God requires change. Trusting God results in physical and measureable change. Some things are left behind. New paths are out ahead of us. Trust changes our choices, attitudes, and patterns of behavior as well as patterns of thinking.

God's plan has always been and continues to be the salvation of the world.

Trust also changes who we are. Note the order of what God told Abraham to leave:

1. your country,
2. your relatives,
3. your father's home.

The geography in this list is backward. If you follow a map, you leave a house (your father's home), then the people of your city or region (your relatives), and finally your country of origin. God's list reverses the order.

What does the reversal of the list mean? It means that leaving is from the outside in.[11] The periphery is the culture of your country. Partnering with God means parting with any tradition that takes priority over God.

The next level of leaving involves your relatives, your people, and the relationships that sustain you. God requires you to put the people in your life in proper perspective. Anchor in God your need to belong.

Finally, your core level is your identity, your father's house. God created a new identity for Abraham, compelling him to place his identity in God.

God's call makes you a new person. We are all attached to the security of our families, our traditions, and our familiar ways. Abraham walked away from all of it. He gave up tradition, belonging, and identity. What are you willing to walk away from to be a partner with God?

Partnering with God is a blessing and a burden. The blessing of a new life in God resulted in the burden of being uprooted in the life of Abraham and

A sense of homelessness is part and parcel to partnering with God.

Sarah. Blessing and burden are attached at the hip. Oh, the blessing of partnering with God; oh, the burden of leaving everything for Him. God asked Abraham to be a homeless wanderer (Deut. 26:5).

A sense of homelessness is part and parcel to partnering with God. Jesus was also a man without a home, as He said in Matthew 8:20: "Foxes have dens *in which to sleep*, and the birds have nests. But the Son of Man has no place to lay His head."

Paul, a great follower of Jesus, reported, "Up to this very minute, we are famished, we are thirsty, and our clothes are shabby, *practically rotted to pieces*. We are homeless, *hapless wanderers*" (1 Cor. 4:11).

As you learn about the lives of Abraham, Jacob, and Joseph, you will discover that each of them experienced personal and physical homelessness. Abraham was called to leave his home. Jacob escaped from his home and went into exile as a fugitive. Joseph was sold into slavery and taken to Egypt.

There is something about the spiritual nature of homelessness that connects us with authentic partnership with God. What does spiritual homelessness mean for us? God is not asking or expecting that we wander the streets as homeless people. Abraham had tents, treasures, and trusted servants. Jacob and Joseph eventually had homes and families. A network of friends and Christians supported Paul. Jesus was supported in His ministry (Luke 8:3). Yet, each of these partners of God knew an inner, spiritual homelessness.

The call to spiritual homelessness with God is also extended to us. It is natural to attach our identity to home. Here we are talking about a matter of priority and commitment to God. By using the words *home* or *father's house*, God was pointing at our core identity. God sent Abraham in search of a new identity, an identity in God. We are to find our home in God. He asks you to trust Him with not only all you have but also with who you are.

Let goods and kindred go, this mortal life also.
The body they may kill, God's truth abideth still.[12]

STRUGGLE: LIVING INTO THE PROMISE WITH GOD'S HELPING HANDS

I like happy beginnings. We have such a happy beginning in Abraham and Sarah. They hear the call of God, leave everything, and faithfully follow Him. Let us naively imagine our hero and heroine living out unfailing faith without flaw or failure, passing every test, and setting a perfect example that none of us will ever match. It would be nice to leave it there, as if the beginning was also the end.

Such naivety is false to their experience and dangerous for ours. Faith is not easy. To present it as easy is deceptive and perilous. The Scripture presents the story in messy and scandalous authenticity. Abraham and Sarah stumble and struggle. Further, they stumble and struggle again and again and again. The first incident of struggle shadows God's call.

Abraham responds to God's invitation by faithfully doing all the Lord told him to do, leaving family and country to follow God. Following his wholehearted commitment, Abraham is caught in a scandalous failure (Gen. 12:10–20). and then shines in a moment of compassion and grace (Gen. 13:1–18).

Disgraceful fear and duplicity. In the first incident (Gen. 12:10–20), under pressure of famine, Abraham leaves the land of promise and journeys into Egypt. In Genesis and Exodus, Egypt serves as a living symbol of the evil empire, the kingdom that opposes God's kingdom. The evil kingdom turns the faith of Abraham into fear. He discovers that Pharaoh wants Sarah for his harem. The evil empire knows the power of terror and intimidation.

Abraham convinces Sarah to lie for him: "Tell them you are my sister so that nothing will happen to me because of you. In this way you can save my life" (Gen. 12:13). Abraham turns his wife over to Pharaoh; he "pimped out"[13] his wife. Sarah is carted off to the harem of Pharaoh. Pharaoh certainly expects to conceive a child with Sarah. However, God has promised a legacy to Abraham and Sarah, not Pharaoh and Sarah. By giving Sarah to Pharaoh, Abraham places the whole promise and plan of God in jeopardy, and God intervenes. The Lord captures the attention of Pharaoh with a plague of illness, a foreshadowing of things to come (Ex. 7:14–11:10). God intervenes and saves the mission and the relationship, the plan and His partner, Abraham.

Let me draw out the point. It is God's way to offer two hands. With one hand He comforts—"I love you as you are." With the other He challenges—"We can do better than this." In our stumbling, God offers the same helping hands—"I love you just as you are, but together we can do better than this."

Graceful generosity and humility. In the second incident (Gen. 13:1–18), Abraham matures. Conflict flares between the servants of Lot and the servants of Abraham. There is not enough water or grazing room in the land.

This time Abraham follows the lead of his partner, the Lord, rather than rely on his own strategies. Abraham stands with his nephew, Lot, on a mountain where they look over the land God has promised. The land stretches far to the north and deep into the south, from the Mediterranean Sea to the jagged mountains.

God promised all this land to Abraham and his family. Lot is family. With conflict rising and enemies creeping into the land, Abraham

It is God's way to offer two hands. With one hand He comforts—"I love you as you are." With the other He challenges—"We can do better than this."

and Lot needed a peace agreement. This conflict was an opportunity to possess more of the promised land. Abraham must have felt that this was the beginning of fulfillment. He would take half the land, and Lot would take the rest. With humble generosity, he gives Lot the choice, north or south.

Lot takes neither the northern nor southern stretches of the land of promise. Why? The evil empire strikes again; Lot learned a worldly lesson in Egypt. "Lot looked around, and he noticed the *grassy plains in the* Jordan Valley looked well watered *and fertile,* just as *he imagined* the Eternal One's gardens might be or *as he knew* the land of Egypt in the direction of Zoar *to be*" (Gen. 13:10).

Lot was gazing on the valley of Sodom and Gomorrah. He turns his back on God's promised land and moves to the cities of opportunity, fortune, and decadence. Lot walks out on Abraham's generosity.

Lot's decision crushed Abraham. He offered his nephew, his living relative, a heritage and a legacy in the land of God's promise. Yet, Lot would have none of it. At that moment of discouragement, God intervened again. The Lord came to the aid of His partner:

> **ETERNAL ONE:** Look around you now, as far as you can see to the north, south, east, and west. All of the land you see is for you and your descendants to possess forever. I will make your descendants as many as there are specks of dust on the earth. If anyone could count the dust of the earth, then he could also count how many descendants *I'm talking about*! Go on now, and walk the entire expanse of the land, for *you need to see* what I am giving you! (Gen. 13:14–17)

Again, God offered both hands to His partner—"I love you like you are; together, we can do better than this." Whether we fail others or others fail us, God is there with open hands to love us and lead us.

Abraham learned to live into the promise. It is one thing in a moment of zeal and determination to fully trust God mentally, physically, emotionally, and spiritually. It is something else to learn to live into the promise of God as each new circumstance captures our attention, distracts our faith, inflicts its pain, wears us down with disappointment, and challenges us to grow in our partnership with God.

PRAY: EMBRACE GOD'S PURPOSE AS GOD'S PARTNER

Jesus taught his disciples to pray, "Our Father in heaven, let Your name remain holy. Bring about Your kingdom" (Matt. 6:9–10). This is certainly the prayer of a human being in search of a home (Father) and a homeland (kingdom).

Abraham did not know these words when he returned to an altar he had built and, there, called on the name of the Eternal (Gen. 13:4). However, he lived the prayer of Jesus, the prayer of a homeless man seeking to make his home in God. He left everything. He placed his identity in God, our Father in heaven. Abraham answered the call to be the first human being to partner with God in the coming of the kingdom, the salvation of the world.

In Jesus Christ, the call to Abraham is now our call. The Lord's Prayer calls us to make God our Father and God's kingdom our homeland. Our loyalty and identity are found in Him. This call challenges us to make God our life's source and resource in all things.

Many years ago, as a college student, I sat alone in an empty church after a Christmas Eve service drinking in the decorative lights that remained on while the sanctuary was dark. Hearing a noise behind me, I turned with a start. There sat a young man about my age. I didn't know him, nor did he know me. What happened in his heart was so moving; he was willing to talk to a stranger in a dark church. In the silence of that late Christmas Eve moment, he said, "I need to tell this story; will you listen?"

I turned fully to face him, and he went on sharing. "This afternoon I was listening to Billy Graham on the television. I had heard him before and wasn't that impressed. He said what he always says and what I thought he would say, 'God loves you.' But something happened this afternoon. For a moment, just a moment, it was not Billy Graham speaking, but God speaking to me. It was God saying, 'I love you, I love you.'"

He sighed with emotion welling up within him. And then he looked up and fixed his eyes on mine as he said, "I think this has changed my life."

SUMMARY: Whose Voice Is This?

How do you know the voice of God? Here is the answer: The voice of God always has Jesus in mind. He calls you to partner with Him in bringing His way of life ("Your kingdom come") to the world now. God invites you to partner with Him in creating your life and changing the world. You respond by trusting the promise and living into the promise. God, your partner, offers His helping hands—"I love you as you are; together, we can do better than this."

THINK: Conversation and Reflection

1. What did you find most comforting and most challenging in this chapter?

2. Consider the term *partnership with God*. In what ways is this partnership like other partnerships in life? In what ways is this partnership different from other partnerships?

3. Look at the four dynamics mentioned in the chapter: listen, trust, struggle, and pray. Which one best describes your spiritual life at this moment? Why?

4. Dealing with practical matters of authentic partnership with God:
   - When did you first put your trust in God? What happened? In what way was it blind faith?
   - In what ways do you hear the voice of God? How do you test and know it is God's voice?
   - This chapter suggests that following God is both a blessing and a burden. Is this your experience? In what way?
   - Living into the promise of God often includes moments of failing others and others failing us. How has God used those moments in your life?
   - How does the term *spiritual homelessness* connect or disconnect with your life in God?

Looking Ahead: In the next chapter we will see how Abraham's faith confronts deep and lingering disappointment.

FACE THE DISAPPOINTMENT

Can God Be Trusted?

> Some people store up treasures *in their homes* here on earth. *This is a shortsighted practice*—don't undertake it. Moths and rust will eat up any treasure you may store here. Thieves may break into *your homes* and steal *your precious trinkets*. Instead, put up your treasures in heaven where moths do not attack, where rust does not corrode, and where thieves are barred at the door.
>
> —Matthew 6:19–20

Sometimes life just does not make sense; it does not work out as it should. Life feels like a collection of disjointed bits and pieces gathered from different puzzles. We rush through our days; duties call, troubles come, and unexpected knocks come to our door. In the rush and worry, life in God loiters in the background rather than leading the direction for life.

The same is true for Abraham and Sarah. In the next chapter of their story, they face a barrage of disjointed events—a war of retaliation, the kidnapping of Lot, a successful rescue attempt, a battlefield victory, a blessing from a king, and an offer of wealth from another king. None of these things seem to fit together in a story (Gen. 14:1–24).

We also juggle the misfit fragments of life. Not all the shards fit quite right, yet each bit belongs to our lives. A good novelist would know what to toss out of the story and what to embellish. We do not have that option. We take life as it comes, make our decisions, and reflect on our successes and failures. Through the relentless flow of events, we try to maintain our trust in the promise of God.

THE STORY IN SUMMARY
Genesis 14:1–15:21

After Lot chooses to settle in the valley of Sodom and Gomorrah, Abraham and Sarah remain in the promised land without a family.

In the valley, Lot becomes a victim of the wars of retaliation as five kings descend on the valley. When word comes of Lot's kidnapping, Abraham could have said, "He had it coming." However, Abraham mounts a rescue party and saves Lot and his family. Abraham is a hero.

Two things happen following the war: First, a strange character, Melchizedek, king of Salem (the city would become Jeru-Salem), gives Abraham bread and wine (a distant hint of the Last Supper) and a blessing. Second, the king of Sodom offers plunder to Abraham for his heroic action in the war. Abraham will not accept even a thread or a strap of leather from him.

After the gallant rescue by his uncle Abraham, one would think that Lot, in gratitude, would return to the promised land. He does not.

Again, Abraham and Sarah are without family, childless, and wondering how or if God will keep His promise. At this moment, God returns to Abraham and repeats the promise. Abraham trusts God, even in the face of disappointment. God renews His covenant with Abraham in a vision of mystery and wonder. Abraham's trust becomes the foundation of New Testament faith in Christ.

Here is an unpopular truth: Inevitably, disappointment will come. An assortment of clichés expresses it: for Pete's sake; you gotta be kidding; for cryin' out loud; that's a tough pill to swallow; they don't make 'em like they used to; and what's the world comin' to?[1] The experience of disappointment intrudes on our lives in a variety of ways:

- I am disappointed because something I hoped for never happened.
- I am disappointed because what happened didn't live up to my expectations.
- I am disappointed because someone I believed in and counted on let me down.
- I am disappointed because someone treated me unfairly.
- I am disappointed because I could have done better and didn't.

Disappointments fester in unmet expectations. During the years I directed a doctoral program at a seminary, I witnessed the discontent of shattered hope in ministers. Young pastors enter ministry enthused and energized, ready to do great things for God. They often mistakenly believe that the members of the church are also ready to do great things for God. Such is not the case. Almost all ministers go through a time of deep disappointment because the people did not meet their expectations.

We all often experience the disappointment of unmet expectations. Disappointment may come after we start a new job or relationship. When something is new, our hearts create great space for hope and possibility. This heart space fills with expectations. We may root our expectations in reality. However, unrealistic expectations also take up residence in the heart. Dealing with the disappointment of unmet expectations, either well founded or unrealistic, weaves its way into the journey of marriage, career, friendship, ministry, and faith in God.

Here is a second unpopular truth: Facing disappointment is the path to mature faith. Abraham walked the path of disappointment. God made a promise. Abraham left everything because he believed the promise. The promise was land and a family that one day would grow into a nation. Years later, he and Sarah have no family in a land where they are nomads who do not own enough land for a grave.[2] After all the faith and faithfulness, the promise was unfulfilled. At this point in his journey, Abraham is not the father of a nation; he is not even the father of a child.

Abraham's God watched over him, and God knew this was the moment for His human partner to walk into a deeper understanding of faith. Out of disappointment, Abraham would emerge with a profound sense of God and His promise.

GOD'S ASSURANCE

After leaving his homeland, after Lot's desertion, after rescuing Lot, after victory on the battlefield, after turning down a handsome reward, after all this:

> Some time passed. One day, the word of the Eternal One came to Abram through a vision—*a kind of waking dream.*
>
> **ETERNAL ONE:** Do not be afraid, Abram. I am *always* your shield *and protector.* Your reward *for loyalty and trust* will be immense. (Gen. 15:1)

How did God's voice come to Abraham? No one knows for sure. The translators of *The Voice* suggest "*a kind of waking dream*" (Gen. 15:1). One may think it was an audible voice. Perhaps God's voice entered Abraham's outer ears, traveled over the auditory nerves into his brain, and from there, descended into his soul. God may have used an audible voice with Abraham. However this is not the way God speaks with us.

Every Christian at some point has wished that God would use an audible voice to make His wants and plans plain. If God would just send a daily e-mail, even a text message or tweet, into the physical world to make His presence and plans known, we would appreciate it. But God's voice does not come to us that way.

An internal voice. I remember four specific times when God spoke inside me with such certainty that it startled me, shook me, and set me on a new path. The first word shaped my ministry within the church. The next two assured me at deep, lonely, and precarious moments. The last lifted my ministry beyond the church. These events changed my life. However, God never spoke in an audible voice.

If God spoke in an audible voice, which is possible, Abraham's story is far removed from our struggle to hear God. I am more inclined to think that God's voice came to Abraham in the way His voice comes to us. We hear the voice of God as an inner nudge, an inspiration, a silent whisper, or a thought that surprises us because it could not be our own thought. God's word speaks silent inner assurance we cannot explain in scientific terms.

For followers of Christ, we most often hear God's voice in Scripture, through other people, in circumstance, and in a still, small voice. The small voice speaks peace, rest, and assurance. Elijah, a prophet and

Dealing with the disappointment of unmet expectations, either well founded or unrealistic, weaves its way into the journey of marriage, career, friendship, ministry, and faith in God.

partner of God, needed the Lord's assurance and challenge. God's voice came in the quietness:

> The Eternal passed by him. The mighty wind separated the mountains and crumbled every stone before the Eternal. *This was not a divine wind, for* the Eternal was not within this wind. After the wind *passed through*, an earthquake *shook the earth. This was not a divine quake, for* the Eternal was not within this earthquake. After the earthquake was over, there was a fire. *This was not a divine fire, for* the Eternal was not within this fire. After the fire *died out*, there was *nothing but* the sound of a calm breeze. *And through this breeze* a *gentle, quiet* voice entered into Elijah's ears. (I Kings 19:11–12)

Like the psalmist, in the presence of quiet waters, God's presence renews us (Ps. 23:2). When life is unjust and does not meet our expectations, "Be still. Be patient. Expect the Eternal to arrive *and set things right*" (Ps. 37:7). In trouble and war, such as Abraham experienced, the Lord instructs, "Be still, *be calm, see,* and understand I am the True God" (Ps. 46:10).

Make the challenge personal. How do you make time and place for stillness in a swirling world of conflicting values and demands? What do you wish you could do to experience stillness in God? Why don't you do it?

An external link. God's inner voice links to the outside world of experience. God assures Abraham, "I am *always* your shield *and protector.* Your reward *for loyalty and trust* will be immense" (Gen. 15:1).

Our last glimpse of Abraham was when he returned from the battlefield. It had been a long time since Abraham had heard from God, but the story leads us to believe that Abraham had just stepped off the battlefield when God spoke to him again.

The shield and reward God references to Abraham are images taken directly from the wars of retribution described in the previous chapter, Genesis 14. A prisoner escapes from the enemy and tells Abraham that Lot has been taken. Abraham raises a force of over three hundred men from his own camp. He plans the battle and divides his troops for a midnight attack. The troops rout the enemy and chase them north of Damascus where "Abram recovered all the spoils *the enemy had taken* and brought them back *with him*. He rescued his nephew Lot and brought him back, along with his goods; there were other captives, too, including some women whom he rescued" (Gen. 14:16).

With a modicum of imagination, we can see how God used Abraham's recent experience to give him an inner word: "I am *always* your shield" (Gen. 15:1). Perhaps Abraham still held his battle shield when God spoke a silent word of assurance. Notice that the outward symbol, the shield, became a message of God's protection and compassion. Soon, Abraham will take up the shield of faith (Eph. 6:16) in deeper commitment to God.

In addition to the shield, God assured Abraham of his "reward" (Gen. 15:1). Abraham had just turned down a great reward in the name of God. Offered plunder from the war, Abraham addressed the king of Sodom: "I have pledged a solemn oath to the Eternal One—the Most High God, Creator of the heavens and earth. I promised that I would not keep *any shred of* what belongs to you—not a thread *of a garment* or a strap of a sandal. That way you could never take credit for any wealth of mine" (Gen. 14:22–23).

We hear the voice of God as an inner nudge, an inspiration, a silent whisper, or a thought that surprises us because it could not be our own thought.

Abraham chose wisely; it is best not to be beholden to the king of Sodom. Abraham showed courage on and off the battlefield. He was not frightened by the warring kings, nor was he seduced by the treasures of the king of Sodom.

Now, the battle is over and the troops go home, disappointed at receiving no treasure since Abraham turned it down. No doubt Abraham was struggling with his own inner confusion. I wonder if Abraham was rethinking his decision to turn down the reward. (God often speaks when we engage in inner moments of authenticity.) God uses the moment to speak a word to his heart and remind him of the Lord's loyal reward.

Here we find a truth about hearing God's word: The symbols of the outside world bring new and different meaning to the soul. Reward is a profound example of how a term in the outside world takes on a different meaning in your relationship with God.

The way you understand the term *reward* shapes your life in Christ. Reward in the outer world means bargain and bribe. Think of bank cards, hotel chains, or restaurants that offer rewards for loyalty. You grew up with this type of motivation—rewards for good grades, prizes for winning, and accolades for excellence.[3]

What motivates your life in Christ? The way you understand reward makes a difference.

- Either secretly or openly, do you relate to God as if you were striking a bargain or earning a reward?
- Do you find yourself thinking that if you say your prayers and stay out of trouble, you can bribe God?
- Do you secretly feel that God owes you because of all you have given up, all you have done for Him?

- Do you fear you won't live up to the grace God gives—that you can never keep up your end of the bargain?

There are many faithful but frightened Christians whose drive to serve Christ is based on rewards and punishments. Jesus reveals a different meaning of reward. Jesus understood the inner meaning of reward as the treasure of heaven. The treasure of heaven is "Our Father in heaven" (Matt. 6:9). God Himself is our reward, our treasure:

> **JESUS:** Some people store up treasures *in their homes* here on earth. *This is a shortsighted practice*—don't undertake it. Moths and rust will eat up any treasure you may store here. Thieves may break into *your homes* and steal *your precious trinkets*. Instead, put up your treasures in heaven where moths do not attack, where rust does not corrode, and where thieves are barred at the door. (Matt. 6:19–20)

Life does not need to be driven by fear of punishment or greed for reward. Abraham would not store his treasure with the king of Sodom. He trusted the Eternal One. It is not the kingdom of Sodom that will enrich the life of Abraham. Abraham finds his reward in the kingdom of God.

A personal bond. God's Word is both universal and personal. The shield and reward are pictures of protection and hope for all, but these images, these silent words from the Lord, were personal for Abraham. At moments of disappointment, our Father in heaven touches us with a personal word of assurance.

Reward is a profound example of how a term in the outside world takes on a different meaning in your relationship with God.

ABRAHAM'S CANDIDNESS

God's word of assurance did not take immediate hold of Abraham's soul. Abraham needed more than one-way communication; he needed to confess his disappointment to God.

Abraham voices his prayer. God wants to hear your concerns even though "your Father knows what you need before you ever ask Him" (Matt. 6:8). So why do you (and why did Abraham) need to express your pain and disappointment?

Here is a truth about prayer: God works through your candidness to meet your need and strengthen your relationship with Him. In a moment of genuineness, you name the elephant in the room, share the pain you feel, declare the disappointment, or reveal the anger in your heart. Deep relationships require such moments of courage and forthrightness. Now, raise the stakes to the level of your relationship with God. God knows what is in your heart, but He knows you need to express it to Him.

Abraham has no child, no heir. He has no legacy. Abraham left the security of his homeland on the risk of God's promise. After a decade, it seems that hope has abandoned him. Abraham had hoped God would fulfill His promise. He is disappointed in God and sincerely names the pain in his heart: "Eternal Lord, what could You *possibly* give to me *that would make that much of a difference in my life*? After all, I am still childless, and Eliezer of Damascus stands to inherit all I own. Since You have not given me the gift of children, my only heir will be one *of the servants* born in my household" (Gen. 15:2–3).

Let me rephrase the lament of Abraham in contemporary language:

> Lord, I believed You could do anything. You just don't keep Your promise in my life. Your grand plan and promise has crashed and

> burned. In case You hadn't noticed, I do not have a child. Also, in case You don't know, that means that my servant will get everything. That servant lives in Damascus. I was up there recently and spoke with him about it. He's elated. I'm utterly discouraged. Lord, this just isn't going to work. You will have to find someone else. Sarah and I are old, worn down, and ready to quit. So much for Your promise, Lord. My servant will take it all.

Are you surprised that I dare write such words in a prayer? Here is another truth about dealing with disappointment: Prayer is the ultimate place for free speech. Many Christians do not know this because they hear only high and mighty prayers delivered on Sunday mornings. At times of disappointment, we do not need polished Sunday morning prayers. We need the middle-of-your-darkest-night prayers. The book of Psalms teaches a broken heart to pray with utter authenticity. As you read these psalms of prayer, look for phrases that reveal the secret pain, anger, or disappointment in your heart:

> For my days *come and go*, vanishing like smoke,
> and my bones are charred like *bricks of* a hearth.
> My heart is beaten down like grass withered *and scorched in the summer heat*;
> I can't even remember to eat.
> *My body is shaken* by my groans;
> my bones cling to my skin, *holding on for dear life.*
> I am like a *solitary* owl in the wilderness;
> I am a *lost and lonely screech* owl *at home* in the rubble.
> *I stare at the ceiling*, awake in my bed;
> I am alone, a *defenseless* sparrow perched on a roof.
> (Ps. 102:3–7)

I cry up to *heaven*,
"My God, True God," and He hears.
In my darkest days, I seek the Lord.
Through the night, my hands are *raised up*,
stretched out, *waiting*;
And though they do not grow tired,
my soul is uneasy.
I remember the True God and become distraught.
I think *about Him*, and my spirit becomes weak.
(Ps. 77:1–3)

My God, my God, why have You turned Your back
on me?
Your ears are deaf to my groans.
O my God, I cry all day and You are silent;
my tears in the night bring no relief. (Ps. 22:1–2)

Something happens to you and to your relationship with God when you truthfully open your heart to God. Look at the result of the prayer in each of the psalms quoted above:

- The one who "stares at the ceiling" in Psalm 102:7 resonates the hope Abraham received:

  In the beginning, You laid the foundation of the earth
  and set the skies above us with Your own hands.
  But while they will someday pass away, You remain
  forever;
  when they wear out like old clothes,
  You will *roll them up and* change them into something
  new, and they will pass away.
  But You are the same, *You will never change*;
  Your years will never *come to an* end. (Ps. 102:25–27)

- The confession of the darkest night in Psalm 77 breaks into confidence, "You led Your people as a flock *tended* by the hands of Moses and Aaron" (Ps. 77:20).
- In Psalm 22, the forsaken one finds new life and hope and "will tell the generations to come of the righteousness of the Lord, of what He has done" (Ps. 22:31).

God answers Abraham. Abraham receives an answer from God. But the answer is not what you might expect. God does not provide Abraham with logic, argument, or evidence. Instead, God points to the stars. He gives Abraham a vision. Somehow a picture of the stars and the heavens touch the disappointment in the soul of Abraham, and faith is revived.

> Immediately the word of the Eternal One came to him.
>
> **ETERNAL ONE:** *No, Abram,* this man will not be your heir. No one but your very own child will be an heir for you.
>
> God took him outside *to show him something.*
>
> **ETERNAL ONE:** Look up at the stars, and try to count them all if you can. *There are too many to count!* Your descendants will be *as many* as the stars.
>
> Abram believed God *and trusted in His promises,* so God counted it to his favor as righteousness. (Gen. 15:4–6)

A PARTNERSHIP OF FAITH

"God counted it to his favor as righteousness" (Gen. 15:6). Before this verse became the watchword of Paul[4] and Luther,[5] Abraham experienced righteousness with God. Righteousness, at its core, means putting things right, doing the right thing, and being in right relationship.[6] Abraham's experience of righteousness, again, comes out of his recent experience. God meets us where we are and brings us what we need to partner with Him. Moses' recent experience with war creates a mind ready to consider God's righteousness.

Abraham returned from wars of retaliation. In war the plan is simple: make things right by exacting revenge. Our world relies on vengeance, payback, and reprisal to make things right again. Against the world's way of retribution, God offers Abraham a different way to make things right. It is not righteousness by reprisal, but righteousness by faith.

Faith is not the self-generated stuff of our culture. Faith in American culture often means believe it and receive it.[7] We say we want something. We set our hearts on it. We get it. We call it faith. There is no such thing in Scripture. In the Bible, faith means a wholehearted response to the promise of God. You reorder your life as if you believed that God's promise was true. "The story of how faith was credited to Abraham was not recorded for him and him alone, but was written for all of us who would one day be credited for having faith in God, the One who raised Jesus our Lord from the realm of the dead. He was delivered over to death for our trespasses and raised so that we might be made right *with God*" (Rom. 4:23–25).

God's Covenant with Abraham. Following Abraham's expression of faith in God, the Lord seals His promise with a covenant of death and life. God enacts a promise with Abraham, a promise in which all is at stake. The ritual of the covenant is profound and mysterious:

ETERNAL ONE: Bring to Me *the following*: a three-year-old cow, a three-year-old female goat, a three-year-old ram, a turtledove, and a young pigeon.

> Abram brought God all of these animals and cut them in two, laying each half next to the other, *making two rows*. Only the birds were not cut in two. (Gen. 15:9–10)

Envision the bloody trail between the halves of slaughtered animals. In an era before formal written contracts, making a promise needed to be memorable. You would never forget this trail of blood.

In a covenant between two people, they both walk the trail together. If you and I are to enter into agreement, into partnership, we take arms and walk together down this blood trail. In doing so, we stake our lives on the promise. If one or the other should fail in keeping the promise, that one will die. This is intensely serious. God wants Abraham to know the authenticity of their partnership.

With Abraham and God, we do not have a normal situation. The story contains an incredible and unexpected turn of events: "As the sun was setting *in the west*, Abram fell into a deep sleep. A terrifying darkness descended upon him. . . . When the sun had gone down and darkness had fallen, a smoking firepot and a flaming torch passed between the halves *of the animal carcasses. With this ritual and* on this day, the Eternal One made a covenant with Abram" (Gen. 15:12, 17–18).

On that day, God alone walked the trail of blood and death. In every other partnership, each partner makes a promise to the other. Each partner is responsible for his or her part of the promise. Here, in sheer wonder and grace, God takes responsibility for the whole promise, the full covenant.

God's gift of grace. The story of God's walk through the bloody trail is an act of grace. Partnership with God is a gift of grace. You do nothing. God

Partnership with God is a gift of grace. You do nothing. God does all. It falls on you to simply exercise faith.

does all. It falls on you to simply exercise faith. Yes, exercise! Faith is a verb. You respond to God's grace by believing the promise. You believe by reordering your life in alignment with God's promise. God's grace invites you to partner with Him. If you believe this promise, your life cannot remain the same.

Our lives on this earth may feel like a detached and disjointed flow of events—meals, text messages, babies, jobs, betrayals, friendships, shopping, sleep, lack of sleep, bills, debts, car repairs, church events, school events, family, more family, and on and on. In the dissonance of jumbled experiences, there is one certainty upon which we stake our lives—the promise of God.

SUMMARY: Can God Be Trusted?

Yes! But, let us get down to specifics. Put the question in terms of expectation, your expectations of God. Do you call it faith if you expect God to find a parking place for you on a busy shopping day? Is it biblical faith to expect God to save you from all disappointments? Should you expect God to spare you and your family from all tragedies? God cares about your tragedies, disappointments, and even parking places. Biblical faith is not rooted in expectations. Yet, it is good and right to invite God into your expectations. "Since God cares for you, let Him carry all your burdens and worries" (1 Peter 5:7).

Ask the question again, this time in terms of righteousness: Can God be trusted to embrace you in a right relationship with Him? You can stake your life on it. Can God be trusted to use "all things" to advance His purpose? Yes! "We are confident that God is able to orchestrate everything to work toward something good *and beautiful* when we love Him and accept His invitation to live according to His plan" (Rom. 8:28). God is love. Can God be trusted? Yes!

THINK: Reflection and Conversation

1. Everyone deals with expectations and disappointments.
   - First, how would you characterize your style of dealing with expectations and disappointments? Do you have high or low expectations? Do you take disappointment in stride, or does it knock the wind out of you?
   - Second, what expectations and disappointments are you dealing with right now?
   - Third, what expectations and disappointments have you encountered in your life with God?

2. How does God speak to you? Has God spoken to you in an audible voice? Do you hear God's voice in Scripture, circumstance, or other people?

3. What is your experience in being honest with God? Do you find it difficult to be genuine and open? Do you find yourself cleaning things up or leaving things out when you talk with God? What would it take for you to be more honest with God?

4. What has been your experience with the grace of God?

Looking Ahead: In the next chapter, we will see how Abraham and Sarah learn to live without the fulfillment of God's promise.

3

FAITH ISN'T EASY

Is Anything Too Hard for God?

JESUS: *What do you mean,* "If there's anything?" All things are possible, if you only believe.

FATHER *(crying in desperation)*: I believe, Lord. Help me to believe!

—Mark 9:23–24

We build our lives on promises.[1] We relate to one another by making promises, keeping promises, and managing promises. Promises create commitments and expectations concerning who does what, when, where, and how. We place faith in the promise and the promise maker. God promised Abraham and Sarah, "I have plans to make a great people from your descendants" (Gen. 12:2). Abraham and Sarah aligned their lives with God's promise, "*Without any hesitation,* Abram went. He did exactly as the Eternal One asked him to do" (Gen. 12:4).

I AM CHANGED WHEN I TRUST GOD'S PROMISE

The story of Abraham and Sarah is a journey of faith. Once again, let us clarify what the Bible means by faith. We use the word *faith* in two different ways. First, there is doctrinal faith, meaning accepting the doctrines and beliefs of the church. There are a few places in the Bible where faith, often translated as "the faith,"[2] is used in this way, but not many. Second, there is trusting faith, meaning faith that results in action, life choices, and aligning your life with God's

THE STORY IN SUMMARY
Genesis 16:1–18:15

Abraham received God's promise that he would have a son. It had been more than a decade since God first gave His promise. Yet, the old couple does not have a baby. Abraham and Sarah live with the tension and incongruity of God's promised child when no child is born.

In a practical response to the problem, Sarah suggests an ancient custom of asking her husband to sleep with her handmaid, Hagar. The child, Ishmael, is considered Sarah's child by tradition. Rivalry between the two women erupts. God intervenes and rescues Hagar and Ishmael.

More than a dozen years pass when the Lord appears to Abraham and renews the promise of a child for Abraham and Sarah. Abraham laughs at the possibility. God requires Abraham to symbolize his commitment to the covenant through the ancient practice of circumcision.

Within a short time after enacting the ritual, three visitors arrive at Abraham's camp. The strangers bring the Lord. The Lord gives the birth announcement. Sarah will be with child within a year. Sarah overhears the conversation and laughs. The Lord asks, "Is anything too difficult for the Eternal One to accomplish?" (Gen. 18:14).

promises. This is the meaning of faith in most of the Bible. This is faith in the life of Abraham and Sarah.

In May 2012, my wife and I celebrated our tenth anniversary. More than a decade ago, I asked Shirley to marry me. I shared my heart with her and said, "You are the one I love, and I want us to build a life together under God's blessing."

She could have responded with doctrinal faith: "I have faith that what Richard says is true. His statements are accurate. I would like to invest time discussing the implications of his promise. I will create a group to gather together once a week and talk about this promise. We will discuss how his promise might form the foundation of our life together."

Discussing God's Word is a worthy enterprise. No doubt, Shirley discussed my promise of marriage with others. However, discussion and intellectual exercise was not enough. If she believed the promise, her life would have to change.

I am happy to tell you that Shirley responded with trusting faith, faith that changed her life and mine. She believed the promise of marriage. Because she believed, she made plans to move. She sold many of her possessions, and she quit her job. She left the city of her family. She sent her furniture to the house we were to occupy once married. She even sold her car and bought an airline ticket. Within a short period of time, she relocated to the small town where I was living. Why did she do all these things? She had trusting faith. She believed my promise of marriage. Thus, she rearranged her choices and her life to align with the promise.

Note the order in which her life changed. First, there was the promise of marriage. Second, she rearranged her life to get in step with the promise. Selling her possessions and moving across the country did not create the promise of marriage. In fact, should someone sell her possessions and move across the country in an effort to secure a promise of marriage, we would call that an act of desperation, not an act of faith. Such behavior would be presumptuous. The promise invites and creates the possibility of faith. Biblically, faith does not create God's promise; faith responds to God's promise.

The story of Shirley believing in a promise of marriage is a simple illustration of our relationship with God. First, God makes the promise. Second, we rearrange our lives to get in step with God's promise. God graciously promises a right relationship with Him, a partnership with Him. God's promise is a gift of grace. Trusting faith aligns our lives with God's promise. In a phrase, your life finds your home in God.

God promised Abraham, "Your very own child will be an heir for you" (Gen. 15:4). Abraham "believed God *and trusted in His promises,* so God counted it to his favor as righteousness" (v. 6). In the New Testament, the birth of Isaac symbolizes the gracious promise of God—a "son was born through a promise *from God*" (Gal. 4:23). God makes the promise. God keeps the promise. Our part is to align our lives with the promise.

Abraham and Sarah fumbled faith. As time passes, Abraham and Sarah struggle to believe, to align their lives with God's promise of a child. They devise an alternate plan for producing the promised baby. They learn to live without the promise. Finally, they laugh in the face of God's announcement that Sarah will have a son within a year. In their struggle to trust, we see our own struggle to believe.

God faithfully keeps His promise. The story, ultimately, is not about Abraham and Sarah's struggle. The story is about God's faithfulness in keeping His promise despite their lapses, doubts, and disappointments. The story does not display the shining faith of Abraham and Sarah. The story reveals one genuine truth: God keeps His promises. "In Jesus we hear a resounding 'yes' to all of God's many promises" (2 Cor. 1:20).

I AM CONFUSED WHEN GOD DELAYS HIS PROMISE

God promised Abraham a legacy and destiny, but God delays and time passes, year after year. God gave the promise again, this time specifically stating that the son would be Abraham's flesh and blood. And, again, a long delay follows the promise: "*Despite God's promise, years went by.* Still Abram's wife Sarai[3] remained childless" (Gen. 16:1).

Can you distinguish the difference between a delayed promise and a broken promise? When you are in the middle of it, it is difficult to tell the difference. We live in an age of shallow and thoughtless promises. Imagine you have been promised a new job. You quit your current job only to discover that the job you were promised did not materialize or, worse, was given to someone else. Broken promises generate pain, anger, and a threat to our identity.[4]

Let me tell you of a child I know who lives under a broken promise. She was only twelve when her daddy fell out of the attic and was rushed to the hospital. In the waiting room, surrounded by family and friends, everyone wanted to ease her fear and suffering. People offered words of comfort and promised, "I know your dad is going to be okay." Her daddy died.

Some weeks later, in a quiet moment, the two of us were talking about what had happened. With as determined a look as a twelve-year-old can conjure, she asserted, "They said my daddy would be okay. He died. It was not right for them to promise me."

Wait or act? From Abraham and Sarah's perspective, the thought that God broke His promise must have drifted through their minds. From our perspective, we know that God did not break His promise to them; He simply delayed it. Imagine what it was like for this elderly couple. As each year goes by, the possibility of having a child decreases. God promised, but nothing happens.

Abraham and Sarah faced a dilemma we understand personally. Do we simply wait for God to act, or do we act in order to bring about God's plan? How do you know when to wait or when to act? Both can be expressions of trust. Either can be a means of trusting God or taking over for God. To wait can be a means of frustrating God's plans. To act can be a method of getting ahead of God's plans.

Sarah decided to act. It is hard to know her motives, even as it is hard to understand our own motives. It had been ten years since Abraham and Sarah rearranged their lives to follow God's promise. They left family and moved. Talk of the promised baby had been going on for years. Eventually, people whispered and Sarah, no doubt, felt foolish, old, inadequate, and abandoned.

We feel foolish when we believe a promise that never comes. The saying goes, "Fool me once, shame on you; fool me twice, shame on me."[5] Sarah was not going to be a fool.

Sarah turned to an accepted custom of her culture and time. Her servant, Hagar, could have a child with Abraham. The child would be considered Sarah's baby. This is the first but not the only time the custom was applied in Abraham's family.[6] Abraham agreed, and soon Hagar was pregnant. One could make a case that the child was actually Abraham's seed, his own heir, as God had promised. One could say that Abraham and Sarah worked out a way to fulfill God's promise.[7]

The result of the alternative plan was a pregnancy in the house of Abraham. It looked like things were moving forward at last. Here is a lesson to grasp: taking over for God may seem to make things better for a while.

The strategy was not an issue of morality,[8] but it did result in complication. Abraham's life was made problematic. Hagar's attitude became haughty. Sarah would have none of it, and she blamed Abraham. She declared that her own plan was Abraham's blunder: "This is all your fault. I allowed my servant girl to be intimate with you, and as soon as she saw she was pregnant *with your child,* she started behaving arrogantly and disrespectfully toward me! *I have done*

Do we simply wait for God to act, or do we act in order to bring about God's plan?

nothing to deserve this. Let the Eternal One judge who is in the wrong here—you or me!" (Gen. 16:5).

Calling down the judgment of God quickly drove Abraham out of the rivalry between the two women. He let Sarah do whatever she wanted with her servant. Sarah clamped down on Hagar, mistreating her harshly. The young woman, carrying a child in her womb, ran away.

When do our actions or inactions complicate God's plan and our lives? Did Sarah's alternative strategy further delay God's plan? We simply do not know. We do know that God cared for Hagar's child, rescued her in the desert, promised greatness for her baby, and brought her back to Abraham's care.[9]

When trying to align our lives with God's promises, we do not always make good decisions. Our motives are mixed, our relationships complex, and our knowledge incomplete. Yet, we must make choices. Trusting God is not an intellectual exercise but a plan for life. Note that God did not allow Sarah's strategy (with Abraham's full support) to destroy either His plans or Hagar's baby. God was still in control.

We understand Abraham and Sarah's predicament. We struggle making our own decisions.

Reuben Welch[10] was a wise and seasoned man I deeply admired. In a sermon he gave on the campus where I attended college, he startled all of us when he declared, "If missing God's perfect plan gives me God's second best, then by this time in life, I must be on God's 347th best."[11]

Be wary when you measure your faith by the perfection of your decision.

I'M STUNNED WHEN GOD'S PROMISE IS TOO BIG FOR ME

Hagar gives birth to little Ishmael, and Abraham becomes the doting father. He loves him. And, God delays the promised baby as another dozen years roll by. In a dozen years, life settles into a comfortable and conventional routine. Sarah and Hagar manage their differences. Ishmael looks up to Abraham as the ninety-nine-year-old man struts through his camp bursting with pride. Suddenly, without warning, God shows up with the grandest promise of all:

> The Eternal One appeared to him *again, assuring him of the promise of a child yet to come.*
>
> **ETERNAL ONE:** I am the God-All-Powerful. Walk before Me. *Continue to trust and serve Me faithfully.* Be blameless *and true. If you are true and trust Me,* then I will make *certain* the covenant with you that I promised. I will bless you with a throng of descendants.
>
> Abram bowed low, his face *and body flat* on the ground. (Gen. 17:1–3)

Unexpectedly, God shows up. In the biblical record, it had been more than twelve years since Abraham had heard from God. Now, as Abraham is looking toward his one hundredth birthday, old and worn, weary and weathered, settled and secure, God shows up with a call to arms: Trust me, serve me, be blameless and true! God speaks as if He were calling a twenty-year-old, not a man completing his first century of living.

God again promises that Abraham will have a multitude of descendants, nations of descendants. God calls Himself by the name *El Shaddai*, God Almighty (Gen. 17:1). It is the first time we hear this name. It is a magnificent name that is heard again and again in the lives of the generations to come—Isaac, Jacob, and Joseph.[12] After a dozen years of silence, God seems to have gathered a second wind in regard to His plans for Abraham. Abraham responds as if the wind had been knocked out of him.

God does not even slow down His announcement long enough for Abraham to catch his breath. The Mighty One continues to declare His promise louder and longer than He did at any previous time in Abraham's life. He speaks of a family tree, descendants, and children's children, naming Abraham the father of a great multitude of nations (Gen. 17:4–8).

Completing His pronouncement of promise, the Lord requires a symbol of agreement, of covenant—the ancient ritual of circumcision. He declares that this will be a sign of their relationship for all generations. It will be the external mark of the internal covenant between God and Abraham's family (Gen. 17:9–14).

The Mighty One concludes declaring His plans for Abraham with an intimate promise, a birth announcement, for Sarah: "She will receive My *special* blessing, and she will conceive a son by you. With My blessing on her, she will become the founding *princess* of nations to come. Kings of *many* peoples will be *counted* among her children" (Gen. 17:16).

Unpredictably, God moved forward. God, once again, disrupts Abraham's life and sets it spinning. God rarely appears on the side of the comfortable, the status quo, the conventional, the expected, or the unimaginative. God sweeps in with the wind of change: "The wind blows all around us as if it has a will of its own; we *feel and* hear it, but we do not understand where it has come from or where it will end up. Life in the Spirit is as if it were the wind of God" (John 3:8).

A friend of mine attended a denominational meeting for a group of ministers and their leaders. The group was discussing the placement of pastors for various churches and ministries. The leadership carefully considered skills, knowledge, experience, and a reasonable prediction of success.

My friend naively asked the question, "But what part does the Holy Spirit play in placing the right person in the right ministries?"

The answer he received was clear and shocking. "We don't consult with the Holy Spirit in these matters. If you let in the Holy Spirit, you never know what might happen."

When God showed up, Abraham did not know what to think. Has that happened to you? I remember the first church I pastored in a full-time capacity. We prayed and prayed for renewal, revival, and growth. It happened! All kinds of people, and I mean all kinds of people, started attending the church. Some of the members from years gone by found it disconcerting. I could almost read their thoughts in their faces: We prayed for revival, but we didn't know God would send revival like this.

Dumbfounded, Abraham responded. How does Abraham respond—or more accurately, react? He does three things. First, to the promise of having a child, he does not praise, bless, glorify, or thank the Lord. Instead, he falls to the ground laughing:[13] "Abraham fell on his face and erupted into laughter *in a moment of private absurdity,* as he thought to himself, '*Yeah, right!* How can a centenarian father a child? Am I supposed to believe that Sarah, *my* 90-year-old *wife,* is going to have a baby?'" (Gen. 17:17).

It is not exactly an image of unflinching faith in the face of God's awesome impossibility. In fact, we have to ask, to what degree did Abraham believe at that moment? Did he believe at all? Did he believe he needed to overcome his skepticism, his unbelief?

I don't know the answer, and the Bible is ambiguous. The story questions our own faith as much as the faith of Abraham. It is certainly a reminder that faith is relational, not just intellectual. Faith rests on a promise and the promise giver. At one moment, years before, Abraham believed (Gen. 15:6). In this moment, Abraham laughs in incredulity. Yet, God was true to His promise. The promise is not dependent on the steadiness of our trusting faith but the steadiness of God's faithfulness.

Second, Abraham retreats to what he knows and loves; he puts his heart around Ishmael. Gathering himself from laughter, he seemingly ignores the entire declaration of God's promise and asks for only one thing, "May *my son* Ishmael *be blessed and* live a long life beneath Your watchful eye" (Gen. 17:18). Abraham seems to have missed the point—Isaac, the baby yet to be born—and is instead choosing to hold to the past—Ishmael, the alternative child (whom God also blesses in Genesis 17:19–20).

Here is a question to consider: When God's thoughts are so big, when God reveals more than our imaginations can take in, do we retreat to what we know best and hold dearest? In partnership with God, the immensity of His purpose and plan can overwhelm us. It is easy and tempting to reduce the God of the universe to a household God, to what God has done or will do for the people I love. Our God is King of the world. We must act in support of His purpose and think beyond ourselves as partners in His plan.

Third, Abraham obeys God's command. He immediately implements the rite of circumcision among all those in his care, including Ishmael. In the face of an overwhelming promise that Abraham could not control, God gave him a specific command to obey. Abraham's actions raise another question: Is it sometimes easier to clench our

Faith rests on a promise and the promise giver.

teeth and obey with our actions rather than genuinely trust with our whole heart?

God presented a promise to Abraham that was seemingly impossible for him to imagine. Yet, without being able to confidently embrace God's promise, Abraham immediately obeyed God's command. In Abraham's obedient response, we find a word of faith, as well as a word of danger. In faith, Abraham was obedient in what he knew to do. We have every reason to believe that his heart was with God even though his head could not get around God's plans. There is a picture of faith here. We may not know or be able to get our thoughts around all God is going to do, but we can faithfully carry out what we know He wants us to do. We can love our neighbor and our enemy, support those who carry the gospel, and live in the spirit of Jesus even if we cannot envision God's grand plan.

A word of danger is also found in this same act of obedience. For Abraham, obedience came from the heart. Across the generations and the centuries after Abraham, however, the rite of circumcision changed in meaning. Rather than adherence to God's plan to bless all people through Abraham's family, the act came to mean separation and rejection of all people outside of Abraham's family.[14] This brings us to another question to consider: Is it possible to use acts of obedience as a means to personal power and prestige? We must watch our inward commitment and outward obedience carefully.

I GROW COMFORTABLE WITHOUT GOD'S PROMISE

Abraham and Sarah have learned to live with an unfulfilled promise. The promise of a baby is in the back of their thinking, but not their planning. The couple settled in by the oaks of Mamre, a place of worship and comfort (Gen. 13:18; 14:24; 18:1). Years ago, under these great trees, Abraham built an altar to God after his cowardice in Egypt. It was here he received the call into battle and returned as a war hero. Under the shade of these trees, their life was good, predictable, and without vision.

For a period of time, I worked under the direction of a leader who touted the latest leadership lingo. A favorite phrase of his was "think outside the box."[15] The staff was fully capable of thinking outside the box. As ideas flowed, the leader's anxiety surged. A pattern emerged: 1) we were instructed to think outside the box; 2) we came up with ideas outside the box; and 3) we were told to make the idea fit back inside the box. Abraham and Sarah had built a beautiful box, a lovely life. They were the power couple in the hill country of Canaan.

Abraham and Sarah had left their home twenty years previously to make a new home built on God's promise. The promise had not yet been fulfilled. Over the years, they learned to build a home without God's promised child. Into their complacent, quiet life God would announce that the delay is over. God announces the birth to Abraham: "Sarah is going to give birth to him at this very time next year" (Gen. 17:21). Imagine the conversation between Abraham and Sarah when he shared the announcement with her. God's next visit will push their life outside their box of comfort and ease.

Sarah, in the biblical text, does not encounter God directly until God makes the birth announcement. Now, she overhears God, and God confronts her. Out of this confrontation, God reveals the heart of trusting faith.

Calm gives way to chaos. The story opens with Abraham "resting at the entrance of his tent in the middle of a hot afternoon" (Gen. 18:1). Such a peaceful picture of security invites our own fantasies of leisure and comfort. When dealing with His partners, God frequently interrupts afternoon napping. C. S. Lewis provokes this painful point in a paragraph you may wish to question: "I didn't go to religion to make me happy. I always knew a bottle of Port would do that. If you want a religion to make you feel really comfortable, I certainly don't recommend Christianity . . . If you think of this world as a place intended simply for our happiness, you find it quite intolerable: think of it as a place of training and correction and it's not so bad."[16]

Three strangers arrived at Abraham's camp. Suddenly, a sleepy old man became a commander on a mission: "He ran from the entrance of the tent out to where they were standing. . . . Let me send *someone* for water . . . for some bread" (Gen. 18:2–5). He pulled Sarah into the fray: "Abraham hurried . . . to Sarah. 'Sarah, *we have guests.* Quickly prepare . . . knead . . . and make cakes" (v. 6). Servants were ordered: "Then Abraham ran to *where* his herds *were pastured.* He took a tender calf and gave it to one of his servants, who rushed off to prepare the choice meat" (v. 7). The frenzy concluded with the strangers served, and the old man, Abraham, "stood nearby under the tree while they ate *to their fill*" (v. 8). Whew! Makes one dizzy to read it.

Promise gives way to skepticism. The story aims at Sarah when the strangers ask, "Where is Sarah, your wife?" (v. 9). Discovering she was in the tent with her ear pressed to the flap, one of the men makes the announcement loud enough for Sarah to overhear: "I will return here to you when life emerges from the womb of your wife, Sarah. She will give birth to a son" (v. 10).

Sarah's brain was whirling with thoughts. The thought of having a baby at her age was ridiculous. She knew she was well past her use-by date. The thought of having a child was overtaxing, and her mind's filter shut down. Out came the words, "At my age—old *and decrepit,* as is my husband—both of us long past having any desire *to engage in lovemaking*?" (v. 12).

I wonder if she immediately thought to herself afterward, *did*

The priority of nothing-is-impossible-faith puts hope and confidence in God above everything.

I say that out loud? That is a frightening question to ask yourself. It means words passed out of your mouth that you wish had stayed buried in your brain. But we can understand her response, even her skepticism. Sarah could not imagine that she would have a child within the year. For her, it was an impossible thought. Children and mad men may believe the impossible, but not Sarah. She knows how the world works. She knows the limits. The possibility of giving birth at her age leaps far beyond the bounds of reason and nature.

In response to her skepticism, the Eternal One, the Lord of creation appears: "Why does Sarah laugh and say *to herself, 'There's no way* I'm going to give birth at my age!'" (v. 13). We know why she says there is no way she can give birth. Because it is impossible at her age; at least it is impossible from any human evaluation.

Delay gives way to impossibility. Now we know why God has delayed fulfilling His promise for these many years. God is dealing with His first human partners in Abraham and Sarah. God is laying the foundation for all partners in the generations and centuries to come, including us. He has waited and waited, wearing down the faith of this old couple, reaching the point of no return on the promise. It cannot be. Yet, it will come to pass. God makes it clear for all time that our faith does not produce His promise, and His promise is not dependent upon our faith. He is God!

> For it's by God's grace that you have been saved. You receive it through faith. It was not *our plan or* our effort. It is God's gift, *pure and simple.* You didn't earn it, *not one of us did,* so don't go around bragging *that you must have done something amazing.* For we are the product of His hand, *heaven's poetry etched on lives,* created in the Anointed, Jesus, to accomplish the good works God arranged long ago. (Eph. 2:9–10)

IS ANYTHING TOO HARD FOR GOD?

God speaks, "Is anything too difficult for the Eternal One to accomplish? At a time that I will determine, I will return here to you when life emerges from her womb. *I'm telling you,* Sarah will give birth to a son" (Gen. 18:14).

Was it the confidence in the voice? Was it a movement in her soul? How does she know she has heard from God? Sarah knew this was no ordinary stranger. Embarrassed, she covers her tracks in the vain hope that she can convince the stranger she did not laugh. Too late. God knows. "That is not true, *Sarah.* You did laugh" (Gen. 18:15).

The strangers move on, and Abraham follows. Sarah is left alone. She carries the echo of her laughter and the pain of her lie. She also carries the great question of faith: Is anything too hard for God?

Perhaps it was an act of faith, beautiful and tender faith, when this aged couple found the courage, passion, and intimacy between them to make love again. Dare they hope against hope, trust against trust, that all things are possible? Morning sickness, emotional swings, and then movement within her womb, and she knew it was true. Nothing is impossible for God.

The promise of Jesus. Jesus was born through God's impossible promise. To a virgin, Mary, the angel of God promises she will conceive and give birth. This holy child will be the Son of God.

How can this be? The promise will be fulfilled through the Holy Spirit, the Spirit of the Most High. The angel provided evidence that the impossible was possible when he told Mary the story of Zacharias and Elizabeth, a story that harkens back to Abraham and Sarah. In the New Testament, Zacharias and Elizabeth were also an elderly childless couple. The angel explained: "*It sounds impossible,* but listen—you know your relative Elizabeth has been unable to bear children and is now far too old to be a mother. Yet she has become pregnant, *as God willed it*. Yes, in three months, she will have a son. So the impossible is possible with God" (Luke 1:36–37).

The Faith of Jesus. Jesus believed that nothing is impossible with God. The wealthy who struggle against the snares and tentacles of their possessions can be set free in the kingdom of God: "Remember, what is humanly impossible is possible with God" (Luke 18:27, also Mark 10:27). Jesus knew that God could free anyone tangled in the snares of Satan's possession: "All things are possible, if you only believe" (Mark 9:23, also Matt. 17:20).

For Jesus, nothing was impossible for God except one thing. Jesus confronted the one impossibility in the Garden of Gethsemane. For Jesus and for us, trusting faith aligns life with God's purpose. Only one time did Jesus ask for the possibility of stepping outside God's purpose. He prayed for release, to let the cup pass. Yet, He knew, trusted, and followed God's plan to the bitter end. "Father, *this is the last thing I want*. If there is any way, please take this *bitter* cup from Me. Not My will, but Yours be done. . . . Father, if there is no other way for this cup to pass without My drinking it—*then not My will*, but Yours be done" (Matt. 26:39, 42).

SUMMARY: Is Anything Too Hard for God?

The question addressed to Sarah and Abraham forms the core question of faith. It is not a question about what God will do, but about who God is. The priority of nothing-is-impossible-faith puts hope and confidence in God above everything. First, this kind of faith changes your view of God. He is the Almighty One, El Shaddai, who claims all power and authority and who is completely free to do as He chooses. Second, this faith alters your view of life. Faith pushes you out of your comfort zone and challenges you to align your life with God's purpose. Third, faith places you in proper perspective.

To trust a God of impossibilities means to be ready for what He is about to do, whatever that may be.

THINK: Conversation and Reflection

1. When you read of Abraham and Sarah's struggle with faith, are you shocked, unnerved, disturbed, discouraged, comforted, enlightened, or encouraged? Why?

2. Faithfulness calls for action and inaction. Sometimes we need to act as a faith response to God. At other times we ought to be still and wait for the Lord to act. How do you sort out when to respond one way or the other?

3. Trust and obey is at the core of the Christian walk. Is it possible to trust and not obey? Is it possible to obey without trust?

4. There are some practical concerns when trusting the Nothing-Is-Impossible-God:

   - If our faith is flawed, what can we do to mature in faith?
   - When are we trusting God's promise? When are we presuming God will work on our behalf?
   - Faith is relational. How can we bolster each other's faith, especially in moments of doubt and confusion?

Looking Ahead: In the next chapter we will look at the deep and soul-challenging conversation between God and Abraham as they debate the destiny of Sodom and Gomorrah.

CHALLENGE THE PROMISE GIVER

Will God Do What's Right?

> Had I gone to Sodom and worked miracles there, *the people would have repented, and* Sodom would still be standing, *thriving, bustling.*
>
> —Matthew 11:23

More than one bride or groom has awakened some months or years after the wedding to wonder, "What happened to the person I married?" Abraham had such an experience in his relationship with God. The Lord told him of the plan to destroy Sodom and Gomorrah. The news left Abraham questioning God—not God's existence, but God's character: "Surely it can't be Your nature to do something like that—to kill the right-living along with those who act wickedly, to consign the innocent to the same fate as the guilty. It is inconceivable to me that You, *my God,* would do anything like that! Will not the "*Merciful and Loving* Judge" of all the earth do what is just?" (Gen. 18:25).

The destruction of Sodom and Gomorrah is out of character for God. It is a story of fire and brimstone, moralizing and retribution, violence and disaster. It has all the stuff of modern entertainment. The story is a long way from the love of Christ and the God of love we know and trust.

THE STORY IN SUMMARY
Genesis 18:16–19:29

After they announced the birth of Isaac, the three men get up to leave Abraham's tents. Abraham walks with them. In the valley below, they see Sodom and Gomorrah. The Lord thinks about His long term plans for Abraham. In doing so, He decides to discuss His immediate plans for Sodom and Gomorrah.

The cities represent great sin, injustice, and violence. The men walk toward the city, but the Lord remains with Abraham. Abraham wants to know if God will destroy the righteous with the wicked. He challenges God. How could the judge of all the earth do such a thing?

God moves ahead with His plans to destroy the cities. What follows details the violence, perversion, and final destruction of Sodom and Gomorrah. However, there is one note at the end of the story that indicates the influence of Abraham on God. We are told that when God destroyed the cities, He remembered Abraham. This is why He saved Lot from the catastrophe.

Even people who have little knowledge of the Bible know the story of the destruction of Sodom and Gomorrah. The story is the stuff of blockbuster movies: a threat of homosexual gang rape, the rescue of Lot and his family, the rain of fire and brimstone, and turning Lot's wife into a pillar of salt.

Our attention is riveted by the violence and destruction. The event has more in common with the Flood or the Tower of Babel than with the stories of Abraham. However, for us who seek to partner with God, the more significant portion of the story is the conversation between God and Abraham prior to the destruction of the cities.

This is an important conversation for people of faith and partners of God. Abraham questions God. Part of partnership involves questioning God and His plans and character. Read again. This is our question in the face of unexplainable horror and tragedy: "Abraham confronted him, 'Are you serious? Are you planning on getting rid of the good people right along with the bad? . . . I can't believe you'd do that, kill off the good and the bad alike as if there were no difference between them. Doesn't the Judge of all the Earth judge with justice?'" (Gen. 18:23, 25 THE MESSAGE).

The Lord who promises a child and the God who destroys cities leaves us wondering how to understand "the *'Merciful and Loving* Judge' of all the earth" (Gen. 18:25).

TWO GOSPELS: RETRIBUTION AND RECONCILIATION

God's kingdom is righteousness, making things right, making the creation new (2 Cor. 5:17). Much in the world needs to be made new. Much needs to be made right. Something is very wrong in the human heart. This wrong creeps into our homes, our places of work, our houses of worship, our government's transactions, and every human endeavor.

A famous story is told of G. K. Chesterton. *The Times* once sent out an inquiry to famous authors, asking the question, "What's wrong with the world today?" and Chesterton responded simply:

> Dear Sir,
>
> I am.
>
> Yours,
>
> G.K. Chesterton.[1]

There is something wrong in the human heart and in the world. The question is, how do we set things right? Two different paths hold promise. The first path, retribution, promises a better world by destroying wicked people. The second path, reconciliation, promises a better world through right relationships with God and one another. Is it more effective to inflict retribution on the wicked or to make wicked people righteous, to be reconciled?

Retribution. The first and most commonly practiced means of creating a better world is the path of retribution, vengeance, and reprisal. Destroy the wicked, curse the sinner, and annihilate evildoers. The story plays in our action heroes and violent films.[2] The plot line promises salvation by getting even, by destroying the bad people. The myth of salvation by vengeance goes like this: when the action hero destroys enough wickedness, goodness will win and reign.

A reasoned and rational approach to retribution is embedded in the talion principle. Found in early Babylonian law, *lex talionis* declares that criminals should receive punishment with exactly the same injuries they inflicted on their victims.[3] We know the law as eye for an eye and tooth for a tooth. "The standard for the punishment is *reciprocal justice*: a life for a life, an eye for an eye, a tooth for a tooth, a hand for a hand, a foot for a foot, a burn for a burn, a wound for a wound, a bruise for a bruise" (Ex. 21:23–25, also Lev. 24:19–21 and Deut. 19:20–21).

The law reins in unbridled vengeance. Without the law, the person who loses one eye might, in the passion of vengeance, take both eyes of his assailant. The law limits retribution. In modern societies, we limit the law of reciprocal justice by placing it in the hands of the government. Citizens who take the law into their own hands are vigilantes.

In the minds of most people in the world, God's role is to dish out what evildoers deserve. We jest about God as the avenger.[4] If someone gets a bit out of line, we humorously take a step to the side and look up as if waiting for lightning to strike. According to salvation by retribution, God is in the business of settling scores, balancing the books, and raining down a bit of hellfire as needed.

The myth of the divine retaliator permeates many primitive religions.[5] Years ago I took a group on a mission trip to Peru. Before heading into the jungle to work with missionaries, we enjoyed a few days in Lima, the capital city. There, we visited the *Museo de la Nación*[6] (Museum of the Nation). Artifacts of various eras and different parts of the country were displayed.

In one display room there was a large stone carving under glass. As explained by our guide, the carving depicted a vicious crocodile. Beneath the tail of the crocodile was a woman, and above the tail was a man. The teeth of the beast held a suffering priest. The carving represents a godlike figure that separates lovers and makes a meal of those who serve him.

I stared at the carving. It had a mesmerizing effect on me. Emotions welled up inside, and I could not control them. I stood and wept. I thought about the millions of people who envision God as an angry, vicious creature, bent on finding an excuse to destroy them. I felt the pain and fear of living under that horrible image of a pagan god. I wept because there is another way, the way of the merciful, compassionate, and just God of heaven. "For God expressed His love for the world in this way: He gave His only Son so that whoever believes in Him will not face everlasting destruction, but will have everlasting life" (John 3:16).

The siren call of retribution is tantalizing, seducing us into twisting God's gospel into payback.

When I finally drew my face away, I noticed I was the only one left in the room. The rest of the group had moved on.

Reconciliation. The alternate promise for making the world right is a better gospel, a gospel rooted in the power of love. This is the gospel of Jesus and the New Testament writers. The gospel of God's grace promises salvation by reconciliation by making relationships right again. Rather than destroy the wicked, the wicked are made new, right, holy, and like God:

> If you have heard Jesus and have been taught by Him according to the truth that is in Him, then you know to take off your former way of life, your *crumpled* old self—*that dark blot of a soul* corrupted by deceitful desire and lust—*to take a fresh breath* and to let God renew your attitude and spirit. Then *you are ready to* put on your new self, modeled after the very likeness of God: truthful, righteous, and holy. (Eph. 4:21–24)

Salvation is the way of forgiveness, of being made new, and of the character of God. Salvation, being reconciled with God, changes the foundation of our relationship with God. Rather than fear of retribution, our relationship with God is anchored in love: "We have experienced and we have entrusted our lives to the love of God in us. God is love. Anyone who lives *faithfully* in love also lives *faithfully* in God, and God lives in him" (1 John 4:16).

How wonderful is this way of love, love that makes the world right, and love that reconciles us to God. Nonetheless, the siren call of retribution is tantalizing, seducing us into twisting God's gospel into payback. I have seen and heard the great truth of grace perverted into a pseudo-gospel of reprisal and retaliation clothed in Christian words.

When I was a child attending Sunday school and church camp, the Christian words of God's love came through again and again. Yet, the stories told to explain God's love delivered a different message through the plot. I heard many stories that are a version of the following:

> God is the angry Judge on the bench, and He is angry with you. Fortunate for you, Jesus comes to stand at your side. When God's terrible sentence is pronounced, Jesus steps up to take your punishment. With fierce and bloody blows, God brings pain and suffering on Jesus. The cross displays God's hateful revenge. Yet, Jesus takes the blows, and all the while He shelters you from the savage vengeance of an all-powerful and angry God.

The meaning of the story was plain to any child who heard it—God is so angry with you that He must crucify His own son to get over His anger and accept you. The closing line of the story was always the same: God did this because He loves you so much.

Do you see the inconsistency in the story? At its heart, this version of the Christ story repeats the crocodile god story. It is the pagan story of retribution disguised in the trappings of Christian images. This telling of the story is wrong.

Let me provide a proper version and understanding of the gospel story. The accurate understanding of the gospel begins with God's love. God is a Trinity of love—Father, Son, and Spirit. The triune God has a purpose: to make the world right again. The members of the Trinity, operating in various tasks but as one God, combine their efforts to make a new and right relationship of love with you. Let me retell the story:

God occupies the judgment seat. Sin destroys the world He created. The outcry breaks His heart and stirs His anger. God knows that you, also, are trapped in the vengeance, injustice, and evil of the world. Sin, death, and the Devil hold you. God in the second person of the Trinity, Jesus Christ, moves from the bench of judgment to stand with you. He will fight the battle for you. He will take the punishment and brutality. On the cross, He wins the day and defeats the enemy. Now, God in the Holy Spirit enters your life bringing the true essence of God to you and in you. You are truly right with God. You are made different, a new creation in love. This is the path of salvation by reconciliation.

Love wins the day and declares the victory. The triune enemies of sin, death, and the Devil fight on, but final victory is guaranteed. We live as if we have won, are winning, and will win the battle over the evil prince of this world.

THE PATH LESS TRAVELED: RECONCILIATION

You face a decision in your Christian life: Will you put your faith in a God of retaliation or reconciliation? If you choose retaliation, there are enough texts in the Bible to cobble together an argument for a God of vengeance. If you trust in the vicious god of retaliation, eventually you will become a person of revenge.

In the first weeks following the terrorist attacks of September 11, 2001, I felt in myself and heard from friends feelings of anger, thoughts of vengeance, and a desire for retribution. In a class I was teaching at the time, students argued for God's destructive action. They were full of anger and grief. The argument for a destructive God began with debasing the enemy. At this point, they called for payback from God. This summarized their thinking: First, dehumanize the enemy, and then demand retribution.

Against this all too common way of reasoning, a quiet and low voice from the back row of the classroom spoke. At first, no one understood what was said. I asked him to speak up. He said, "You think just like the terrorists think."

The ancient Greeks named their goddess of retribution Nemesis,[7] referring to the hot fire of vengeance, the spirit of justified anger, and the righteous revenge that smolders in us. Vengeance promises a quick and final response to the evil. Destroy the enemy. The enemy is not human,[8] or at least not as human as we are. What could be more convincing?

The disciples seethed with the fire of vengeance. When rejected by a Samaritan village, they asked, "Lord, do You want us to call down fire from heaven to destroy these people who have rejected You?" (Luke 9:54). But Jesus turned and rebuked them: "You just don't get it" (Luke 9:55).

The disciples and Jesus were not the first to discuss the conflict between vengeance and reconciliation. The first recorded conversation on this subject was between Abraham and the Lord. The two discussed what should be done with Sodom and Gomorrah. The conversation exposes the relationship between them. Each respects and listens to the other: In this exchange, the sides of the argument are oddly reversed. Abraham, on behalf of Sodom, bargains for mercy, while God plans for total destruction. The conversation tells us how God works with Abraham and with us.

The Lord confers with Abraham. On His way to Sodom and Gomorrah, the Lord pays a call on Abraham. The poignancy of the moment is clear: Abraham's family lives in harm's way because Lot's family (Abraham's nephew) lives in the cities of destruction. The Scripture reveals the Lord's private thoughts concerning Abraham:

> I wonder if I should hide from Abraham what I am about to do. After all, Abraham will become *the father of* a great and powerful nation, and all the other nations of the earth will find their blessing in him. I have chosen him *for a reason, namely* that he will carefully instruct his children and his household *to keep*

> *themselves strong in relationship to Me and* to walk in My ways by doing what is *good and* right in the world and by showing *mercy and* justice *to all others. I know he will uphold his end of the covenant,* so that he can ensure My promises to him will be fulfilled and upheld as well. (Gen. 18:17–19)

God's purpose and promise to bless the whole earth through Abraham's legacy do not change. God's desire is that Abraham's descendants will live in the way of God and do what is just and right. God knows that the way of Sodom and Gomorrah is destroying the earth He created. Abraham and his seed will live a different way of life. God considers hiding His plans to destroy the cities, but upon further reflection He chooses to be open and confer with Abraham: "*I have heard terrible things*—urgent and outraged calls *for help*—coming from *the cities of* Sodom and Gomorrah, and their sin has become a serious problem. I must go down and see *for Myself* whether the outcries against them that My ears have heard are really true. If not, I will know" (Gen. 18:20–21).

Abraham questions the Lord. Because of His relationship with Abraham, God revealed His plans for destroying the cities. The text says that Abraham stood before the Lord. There is an alternative reading of the verse in a few ancient texts of the Bible. The alternative reverses the position of the two; the Lord stands before Abraham. Is it possible that God has come to learn from Abraham? Dare we believe that God is interested in and considerate of what we think?

We must be careful at this point. We will not and cannot take on the role of pagan priests and magicians who attempt to control the gods. We do not,

God's purpose and promise to bless the whole earth through Abraham's legacy do not change.

cannot, and will not try to control God. We cannot name it and then claim it as if God is obligated to do our bidding. God is free to do as He chooses. He chooses to invite us[9] into conversation with Him.

God has a plan for the salvation of the world in His mind, and He wants to hear from His partners. So it is that He invites Abraham to talk with Him. God shares His plans for destroying the cities of the plain. Abraham asks God tough questions that we can identify with:

Question #1: Will You harm good people? "*God,* would You really sweep away the people who do what is right along with those who are wicked?" (Gen. 18:23). When Abraham learns of God's plans, he is shocked. Is God so vehemently committed to retribution that He destroys good people along with bad? Is God so bent on setting things right through death and destruction that He will destroy kindness with cruelty?

Abraham poses another possibility to the Lord. Abraham opens the bargaining with fifty righteous people. "What if there were 50 upright people within the city? Would You still wipe the place out and not spare it on behalf of the 50 upright people who live there?" (Gen. 18:24).

The issue for Abraham is the same concern for us: How much righteousness is enough for salvation? Abraham bargains for smaller and smaller numbers of righteous people—forty-five, forty, thirty, twenty, or ten righteous people (Gen. 18:24–32). The exact numbers are not the issue. Abraham is pressing a point: How much righteousness does it take to save a wicked city?

Saving a wicked city is a contemporary issue. Recently, I met with nine student teachers in a group study room on the first floor of the library of the university where I teach. Each of the students has testified to a specific call to be a Christian teacher in public schools situated within urban centers of poverty.

For months they researched the question, "What is life like for an urban child of poverty?" They studied food deserts,[10] lack of medical facilities, parental opposition to education, crime, gangs, and destructive forces in the lives of children of poverty.

At one of our early morning meetings in the quiet sanctuary of our group study room at the library, we looked at the story of God and Abraham discussing the wicked cities of Sodom and Gomorrah. The students instantly understood the application to their calling.

I asked them what they could tell me about these wicked cities based on what they were learning about wickedness in modern cities. They noted that for every vicious crime there were broken victims. They imagined seedy back alleys and dark passageways where abused women and molested children huddled in dreadful expectation of every kind of evil. My students also knew that most people who grow up with injustice and crime become criminals.[11]

Our discussion reached the point where Abraham, in the fashion of a Middle Eastern bazaar, bargained with God to spare the city for the sake of fifty, forty, thirty, twenty, or even ten good people. The students envisioned the faces of children they knew in the inner city. How much is each child worth? It is a question we must ask. We can pray and ask God for the salvation of one child from poverty and evil. Our discussion slipped into silence for a moment.

In the quiet, I looked into the faces of each of my nine Christian student teachers sitting at the table. I was moved by their dedication and calling. Taking a deep breath, I put my heart's question to them, "Is it possible, in the calculus of grace, that nine good people could save a wicked city?"

After a moment of reflection, one student spoke up, "It only took one righteous person to save the whole world." "If we were in the heat of combat with God when His Son reconciled us by laying down His life, then how much more will we be saved by Jesus' *resurrection* life? In fact, we stand now reconciled *and at peace* with God. That's why we celebrate in God through our Lord Jesus, the Anointed" (Rom. 5:10–11).

Jesus is the one righteous person who saves the world. Jesus announces the presence of God's kingdom of reconciliation.[12] The way of retaliation has passed away. Christ's confidence in the power of God's kingdom to change the world is so great that He shocks us by saying of Sodom, "Had I gone to Sodom and worked miracles there, *the people would have repented, and* Sodom would still be standing, *thriving, bustling*" (Matt. 11:23).

Imagine that! Jesus believes that the miracles of the kingdom, the reign of God's righteousness on earth, are enough for the forgiveness, cleansing, and new creation of Sodom and Gomorrah. Do we have such faith?

Question #2: What kind of God are You? Abraham calls God's character into account. Abraham demands that God must act like God. "Surely it can't be Your nature to do something like that—to kill the right-living along with those who act wickedly, to consign the innocent to the same fate as the guilty. It is inconceivable to me that You, *my God,* would do anything like that! Will not the *'Merciful and Loving* Judge' of all the earth do what is just?" (Gen. 18:25).

Abraham's boldness is startling. Dare we call God on the carpet? Dare we question God? Yet, Abraham treats this questioning—expecting and demanding God to act like God—like a duty of faith. We are not only allowed to question God, but we are encouraged to voice our complaints to Him. The Psalms teach us to take our complaints to God.[13]

We are not only allowed to question God, but we are encouraged to voice our complaints to Him.

To be sure, God is God. He will do as He chooses. Abraham's daring question, followed by hard bargaining, brings the story to an unsatisfactory ending: "At this point the Eternal ended the conversation with Abraham and went on His way, and Abraham returned to his home" (Gen. 18:33). God keeps His thoughts to Himself. We are left wondering if the conversation, the intercessory prayer, made a difference in God's decision or simply dissolves into empty words. God does not say.

We know what it is like to pray and feel that the heavens are silent. Indeed, Christians across the generations have devised methods and means of coping with unanswered prayer. Nonetheless, the silence of God is confusing and often painful.

God ends up destroying the cities. Yet, in utter destruction, there is a note of grace, just a note in a crescendo of destruction. We see the gracious concern of Abraham as he returns to the place where he questioned God. We also see the mercy of God in the salvation of Lot:

> Abraham rose early in the morning and went out to the place where he had stood at *the feet of* the Eternal One. He looked down toward where Sodom and Gomorrah *had been.* He looked up and down the valley, and *everywhere he looked* clouds of smoke were billowing up—*black,* like smoke from a giant furnace. Now *you know the story of* how God destroyed the cities of the valley, but remembered Abraham *and His covenant with him.* So He sent Lot out of the destruction—out of the cities where he had been living. (Gen. 19:27–29)

When Abraham questions God, a small flame of the gospel leaps out of the dark story of

When Abraham questions God, a small flame of the gospel leaps out of the dark story of destruction.

destruction. In a small way, a first step, righteousness overcomes some bit of evil in the world. A human being, God's partner Abraham, grasps the inner nature of God and demands that God act accordingly.

Yet, the small flicker of grace is hardly enough of an answer for us. The story twists our hearts and minds; we cannot put our hearts into it nor get our minds around it. In the struggle to grasp the meaning, we are confronted with a reality expressed by A. W. Tozer: "The freest bird is, along with every other created thing, held in constant check by a net of necessity. Only God is free. God is said to be absolutely free because no one and no thing can hinder Him or compel Him or stop Him. He is able to do as He pleases always, everywhere, forever."[14]

We are left with our question: Will God do what is right? In the story of Sodom and Gomorrah, an ultimate and satisfying answer is simply not there. To find the good work, to know that God does what is right, we must turn to Jesus and see the story through the heart of Christ.

JESUS, THE CHOICE IS YOURS

The small kernel of the good news of love is almost lost under the fire and brimstone of the story. Yet, this small seed bursts on the scene in Jesus Christ. What began in Abraham is fulfilled through the Son of God. Let the love of Jesus guide your vision.

Let the love of Jesus model your vision of God. Do you think you see God's true colors as fire and brimstone fall on Sodom and Gomorrah? Or do you find God's authenticity in the crucified Christ pouring out His love for the world, for you?

Let the love of Jesus guide your view of the Scriptures. In faith, you may choose to read, struggle, understand, and apply the Scriptures in the Spirit of Jesus Christ. Jesus understood that all of Scripture concerned Him (Luke 24:27) and should be interpreted in view of His love and His Spirit (Luke 24:32).

Let the love of Jesus determine how you face wickedness. Jesus turned vengeance on its head: "You know that *Hebrew Scripture* sets this standard *of justice and punishment*: take an eye for an eye and a tooth for a tooth. But I say this, don't fight against the one who is working evil against you" (Matt. 5:38–39).

Let the love of Jesus control the way you see life. The evidence sides with a view of the universe that is cruel, unjust, vengeful, and ruled by bad karma. There is another way to see life. On the throne of the universe stands "a Lamb who appeared to have been slaughtered" (Rev. 5:6). The center of life is love.

SUMMARY: Will God Do What's Right?

The question presses toward a deeper issue: What is the best way to do what is right—the way of retribution or the way of reconciliation? Your answer to this question colors the way you see God. A second question involves you: Does God make the world right through His partners or without His partners? Your answer determines your relationship with God.

God's purpose is to make the world right again. With His first human partner, Abraham, He drew out the lesson that even a small number of righteous people can save a wicked city. In Jesus, we are reminded that the world is headlong for destruction, but God sent Jesus, the righteous one, to reconcile the world. As the Father sent Jesus, Jesus sends you. The better question is, will God make things right? The answer is yes.

THINK: Reflection and Conversation

1. What has been your acquaintance and understanding of the story of the destruction of Sodom and Gomorrah? Have you learned about it in sermons, Bible teaching, television specials, or some other source? How did you align the story of fire and brimstone with your understanding of God?

2. What has been your experience with people who believe that it is God's task to bring about retribution, to settle the score, or balance the account? What has been your experience with people who believe that God seeks to make the world right by making wicked people good? What do you think about these two different views: 1) destroy the wicked, and 2) make wicked people good?

3. How would you help someone work through the difficult question, how can God really be God if He lets bad things happen to good people?

4. Practical matters for partners of God:
    - How has God used you to make the world a better place, set things right, or reconcile the world to God?
    - What could you be doing that God could use to make the world a better place, to set things right, and to reconcile the world to God?
    - How can we help each other remain confident and trusting so that even if our efforts appear to fail, God is still moving, working, and setting things right?

Looking Ahead: In the final chapter of the story of Abraham, we see Abraham's old and disgraceful ways mature into deep and wondrous faith as a true partner of God.

TEST THE RELATIONSHIP

Can I Know for Sure?

O Eternal One, my heart is not occupied with proud
thoughts;
my eyes do not look down *on others*;
I don't *even begin to* get involved in matters too big,
matters of faith, state, business,
or the many things that defy my ability *to understand them*;
Of one thing I am certain: my soul has become calm,
quiet, *and contented in You.*
Like a weaned child resting upon his mother, *I am quiet.*
My soul is like this weaned child.
O Israel, stake your trust *completely* in the Eternal—
from this very moment and into the vast future.

—Psalm 131

The following story is an excerpt from *The Desert Wings*, a publication of Edwards Air Force Base, California.

Murphy's Law ("If anything can go wrong, it will") was born at Edwards Air Force Base in 1949 at North Base. It was named after Capt. Edward A. Murphy, an engineer working on Air Force Project MX981, a project designed to see how much sudden deceleration a person can stand in a crash. One day, after finding that a transducer was wired wrong, he cursed the technician responsible and said, "If there is any way to do it wrong, he'll find it."[1]

Murphy's Law may have an appropriate application in the world of technology. However, for most of us in our daily life, Murphy's Law describes our perception and emotions more than it does the actual situation. It is a rare moment indeed when everything goes wrong. It is more common when we feel like everything goes wrong.

Upon closer examination we discover that not everything has gone wrong, but we ascertain that the one thing that must go right has fallen apart. This was Abraham's experience. The one thing that had to go right was the birth of a son, Isaac. Now, at God's bidding, all was about to go wrong.

There are moments, events, and situations that hinge on a solitary decision, one toss of the dice, or a lone, disastrous outcome. For example:

- The judge makes one dubious decision against your lawsuit and your case falls apart.
- The admissions officer misplaces your documents only to discover them after the deadline for acceptance.
- Your most significant client goes bankrupt and puts your business on the verge of bankruptcy.
- At the moment of your significant presentation, you come down with the flu.
- Your house that has been on the market for months is about to close when the buyers back out.
- You plan to buy a surge protector tomorrow, but the electrical storm comes tonight and destroys your computer.

THE STORY IN SUMMARY
Genesis 20:1–22:19

Following Abraham's bargain with God over the city of Sodom, and God's subsequent destruction of the city, Abraham moves off the mountain overlooking the valley and into the region of the Negev. Old weaknesses reappear: Abraham once again asks Sarah to pretend she is his sister (she is a half sister) in order to deceive King Abimelech. If we take the story in chronological order, this must have happened during Sarah's pregnancy. God intervenes on behalf of Sarah and the king.

Following this incident, Sarah gives birth to Isaac. Soon after the birth, the old rivalry between Sarah and Hagar erupts again. Sarah sends Hagar and Ishmael into the desert to die, but God intervenes and rescues them.

The years roll on as Abraham and Sarah settle into life with young Isaac. When Isaac is a teenager or young adult, God comes to Abraham with a terrifying test. God asks Abraham to take Isaac to a specific mountaintop and sacrifice him to the Lord. Abraham obeys. Just as the father is about to kill his son, the heavens open, the angel of the Lord appears, and he provides a lamb for the sacrifice.

When the one thing goes wrong. When this one thing goes wrong, everything collapses. To make the situation more difficult, more often than not, this one thing lies beyond our control. When the one thing goes wrong, we are brutal at second-guessing ourselves, taking on guilt and shame, passing out blame, and stoking the fires of resentment.

I remember the devastation that came to a friend when the one thing that had to go right went wrong. In this case it was a business venture. Designed to meet the needs of thousands of families who were losing their homes during the housing crisis, the new business venture combined refinancing with practical financial counseling. Everything was in place—marketing, finances, financial counselors, and a cadre of people with high integrity in the business as well as compassion for people in need. All that was needed was one more signature from one bureaucrat in one office. It was then that the one thing that had to go right went wrong. The bureaucrat would not sign. The business failed, sinking the fortunes and good intentions of several families.

For Abraham, one thing must go right. In the life of Abraham, many things have gone wrong: deception in Egypt, Lot's refusal to participate in the promise, rivalry between Sarah and Hagar, and skeptical laughter in the face of God's promise. All these setbacks were overcome by the graceful intervention of God. Yet, there was one thing that had to go right: Abraham and Sarah must give birth to a son.

God had promised again, "I will return here to you when life emerges from her womb. *I'm telling you,* Sarah will give birth to a son" (Gen. 18:14). God kept His word. Baby Isaac was born to Abraham and Sarah. All was right.

The years roll on. Suddenly, intrusively, and inexplicably God intervenes with the darkest and most frightening test of His relationship with Abraham: "Take your son, your only son Isaac whom *I know* you love *deeply,* and go to the land of Moriah. *When you get there,* I want you to offer Isaac to Me as a burnt offering on one of the mountains. I will show you which one" (Gen. 22:2).

This cannot be. Without Isaac there is no legacy, no descendants like the sands of the sea or the stars of the heavens,

Dare we trust God with the one thing that has to go right?

no generations to follow, and no multitude of nations to be blessed through Abraham. Dare we trust God with the one thing that has to go right? This is the ultimate test of Abraham's partnership with the Lord. Will Abraham sacrifice his love—his legacy, his only son—for his Lord? Will the Lord sacrifice His plan and His purpose in order to test Abraham?

For God, a test was needed. Thus far, we have seen the development of the relationship between God and His partner, Abraham. Abraham has embraced the call, faced the disappointment, and challenged his Creator, but now comes the greatest test of all. Why the test? We catch a hint of the need for a final test for Abraham in the events surrounding the birth of Isaac. At the moment when the promise is, at long last, fulfilled, Abraham and Sarah both recoil into their disgraceful behavior pattern of fear and duplicity, jealousy and cruelty, when they choose to deceive King Abimelech.

The disgraceful behavior of our faith's founders also tests God's grace. Will God abandon Abraham and Sarah? Will God abandon His plan to bless all people? God's grace shines through the stories of shame and scandal. Somehow, Abraham's faith matures. But can Abraham be fully loyal to God no matter the price or the task? God wants to know. In this chapter we explore God's amazing grace and Abraham's mature faith. The test reveals the qualities of mature faith. Abraham, at last, comes home to God.

GOD'S AMAZING GRACE

The birth of the long-awaited baby is reported in the space of a few verses: "The Eternal One kept His promise, and Sarah conceived and gave birth to Abraham's son (in their advanced age) exactly as the Eternal had indicated. Abraham named his child, who was born to Sarah, Isaac" (Gen. 21:1–3).

The point is clear and singular: this birth is the gracious gift of God. Sarah recognizes the amazing grace of God. To this old couple, almost at death's door, God fulfilled His promise. The God who spoke the world out of nothing, who raised Jesus Christ from the dead, graciously kept His promise and gave a baby when it was humanly impossible.

In the New Testament, the gracious promise in the birth of Isaac becomes the image of our gracious promise of salvation, "So you *see now,* brothers and sisters, you are children of the promise like Isaac" (Gal. 4:28).

The gracious gift of the baby ignites the faith of Sarah. The name Isaac means laughter. A year earlier, Sarah had laughed in skepticism at the thought of bearing a child (Gen. 18:11–12). Now she laughs in joyous and uncontainable faith. She believes the child is from God. "God has graced me with the gift of laughter! *To be sure,* everyone who hears *my story* will laugh with me. Who would ever have said to Abraham that Sarah would *one day* nurse children? Yet I have given birth to his son at this late stage in his life!" (Gen. 21:6–7).

This is such a happy, sweet story of God's gift of grace. However, grace is not designed for only happy, sweet places. Grace descends on places of disgrace, scandal, and shame. The Scripture hems in the birth of Isaac (Gen. 21:1–7) with stories of disgraceful shame on each side, before and after. Before the birth, we see a display of Abraham's nagging fears and tendency to deceive (Gen. 20:1–18). After the birth, Sarah's old jealousy and cruelty come back into play (Gen. 21:8–21). In their failings, their human frailty, we see the wideness of God's grace for the whole world.

The disgrace of fear and deceit. In the year between the final promise of the child and the birth of Isaac, Abraham and Sarah moved into the land of Gerar. King Abimelech wanted Sarah as his wife after Abraham deceived the king by telling him that Sarah was his sister.

How pitiful. God has already made the birth announcement. Sarah is probably pregnant by this time. How could Abraham fall into his old ways at a moment like this? There is nothing helpful in the story. Abraham is up to his old tricks. Abraham is neck deep in his old fears.

A lifetime of lies comes to light. We know of two times when Abraham asked Sarah to lie for him. But by his admission, we learn that fear and deceit was a lifetime pattern for him. He confesses, "Ever since God called me away from my father's house *years ago,* I told [Sarah], 'I need you to do this favor for me—whenever we visit or stay in some *strange or foreign* place *you need to* tell people I am your brother'" (Gen. 20:13).

So much for Abraham's virtuous example of courage and integrity. Under stress, we all resort to our best-known behaviors. I did not say our best behavior, but the behavior patterns[2] we know the best. Fear and deceit were Abraham's fallback position. Here is an uncomfortable question: Under great stress, what is your best-known behavior?

The disgrace of jealousy and cruelty. Sarah's example is no better. After baby Isaac is born, after her faith-filled laughter, her old rivalry with her servant, Hagar, flares into a feud. The jealousy turns vicious.

> *Time went on,* and Isaac grew and was weaned *from his mother.* Abraham prepared a special feast *in Isaac's honor,* to celebrate the day he was weaned. But *a damper was put on the day when* Sarah saw the son Hagar (the Egyptian girl) bore for Abraham laughing and teasing *her son.* She *became jealous and* demanded of Abraham:

SARAH: Throw this slave woman and her son out *right now*! The son of this slave is not going to share the inheritance along with my son, Isaac, *if I have anything to do with it*! (Gen. 21:8–10)

Sarah, a strong-willed woman,[3] demands that Abraham drive Ishmael and Hagar into the desert to die. It is a pitiful picture painted in Scripture. The water is gone, and the boy is dying of thirst. His mother cannot watch, but turns away and begins to sob.

So much for the nurturing compassion of mother Sarah, the "*princess* of nations to come" (Gen. 17:16). The story of Sarah sending her servant and the servant's child (Abraham's child also) is a horrifying tale. It is an account of disgrace, scandal, and shame.

God's grace and intervention. If I were writing the Bible I would never include these disgraceful stories of Abraham and Sarah. My temptation would be to include only stories of courage and integrity, kindness and compassion.[4] Why would the Bible reveal such awful stories about the man and woman who are the foundation of faith? Because the disgraceful stories are not so much about Abraham and Sarah's scandal and shame but about God's grace in the face of our failures. Note three things about God's grace falling on our disgrace:

First, stories of disgrace demonstrate that grace pours into places of shame, failure, and cruelty. We imagine that the lovely things of God must be found in pleasant, sanitized, and honorable places. Not so! We find God, and God sends us to places and people who desperately need His grace. If our churches are filled with only good people, we are not fulfilling our calling:

When the Pharisees saw this, they asked Jesus' disciples,

PHARISEES: Why does your Teacher eat with tax collectors and sinners?

> **JESUS** *(overhearing this)*: Look, who needs a doctor—healthy people or sick people? I am not here to attend to people who are already right with God; I am here to attend to sinners. *In the book of the prophet Hosea, we read,* "It is not sacrifice I want, but mercy." Go and meditate on that for a while—*maybe you'll come to understand it.* (Matt. 9:11–13)

When you read the stories of Abraham's deceit and Sarah's cruelty, it is clear that they are not the heroes. In these stories, God champions the day and comes to the rescue. God salvages the deceived king from falling victim to Abraham's lie. God rescues Hagar and Ishmael in the desert.

Second, stories of disgrace demonstrate that God's plan is always bigger than you and me. Abraham was fearful, and Sarah was jealous of a younger woman. That is all they could see.

When the world closes in on us, when life is unfair, when pain is uppermost in our minds, our life perspective collapses like a black hole in the heart. We retreat to Murphy's Law—everything has gone wrong. The light of heaven is gone. Nevertheless, God's perspective and plans continue to reach wide and long. He promised He would bless Abraham when He said, "You will become a blessing *and example to others*" (Gen. 12:2).

In moments of disgrace, God reaches out beyond Abraham and Sarah to bless other people. In the place of Abraham's deceit, God speaks directly to a non-Israelite king (Gen. 20:3–7). To an Egyptian woman and her half-Israelite son, God provides a well of water and

The disgraceful stories are not so much about Abraham and Sarah's scandal and shame but about God's grace in the face of our failures.

the promise that this young man will become a great nation (Gen. 21:16–21). God's love and plan are intact.

Third, stories of disgrace are followed by time to reflect, repent, and mature. Abraham needs to live with the promise, Isaac. As Isaac grows, Abraham matures into deep faith. God needs to know if Abraham (or any human being) can truly partner with Him in blessing all peoples on earth.

The test is coming. It will be another fifteen or twenty years later. In the meantime, Abraham lives with the promise fulfilled. Isaac grows from an infant into a young man. This is Abraham's time to reflect and mature. This time of solitude is also a gift of grace for Abraham.

"After a period of time, God decided to put Abraham to the test" (Gen. 22:1).

ABRAHAM'S MATURE FAITH

At this point in Abraham's story, it has been a long time since he left his traditions, his place of belonging, and his identity within his father's house to follow God.

Through it all, he continues to be the man who became homeless with God. There have been failures, alternate routes, doubts, and many years of disappointment. Abraham's great moments of faith also shine. He graciously supported Lot in spite of the fact that Lot abandoned him. In his disappointment, God showed him the stars and Abraham believed that God would keep His promise, and "God counted it to his favor as righteousness" (Gen. 15:6).

Abraham remembers all of it—the wonderful years when Ishmael was a child, the unbearable rivalry between Sarah and Hagar, and the cynicism and doubt when it seemed that this promise was too hard for God to keep. He thinks about his debate with God over Sodom and how the righteous might save a wicked city. And he remembers the baby Isaac in his arms for the first time.

At this point in the story, all those memories are from years ago. Abraham's faith has matured. God is ready for the final test. God needs to test and know the depth and commitment of Abraham's faith.

God's test. God calls Abraham to a most wretched and horrible assignment—to take his son Isaac and sacrifice him. How did such a thought come to Abraham? How did his mind fix upon it? How did he know it was truly the voice of God and not a different, evil voice whispering in his soul? These questions are unanswered in the Scripture. We simply know that Abraham heard the command and obeyed. Through mature faith, he knows God's voice and responds in obedience.

Abraham's obedience. The structure of the story revolves around three short conversations. The first includes the Lord God and Abraham. God gives an inexplicable command that sends Abraham into a crisis. God tests Abraham. The Lord wants to learn something about Abraham.

> **ETERNAL ONE:** Abraham!
>
> **ABRAHAM:** I am right here.
>
> **ETERNAL ONE:** Take your son, your only son Isaac whom *I know* you love *deeply,* and go to the land of Moriah. *When you get there,* I want you to offer Isaac to Me as a burnt offering on one of the mountains. I will show you which one. (Gen. 22:1–2)

Abraham responds to the command with complete obedience, "Abraham did *as he was told*" (Gen. 22:3). Obedience is the first mark of mature faith. Abraham has come home to the obedience he displayed at the beginning of his journey (Gen. 12:4). Yet, Abraham does not walk in the innocence of young faith but with a measured respect for the mysterious ways of God.

Through obedience to God's Word, Abraham is a changed person. The relationship between God and Abraham has changed. Obeying a great command from God shatters your world and transforms you. Whatever might happen on the mountain where Abraham takes Isaac, life will be different. Abraham will come down the mountain a changed man.

> Mighty transformations are wrought by the coming of the word of the Lord to human hearts! They can never be the same as before. It will either exalt them to the place of partners and coworkers with God, and give them a seat with Jesus on his throne, or it will banish them from His presence and doom them to hell. If obedient to the word, they will be saved, empowered, brought into closest fellowship with God, into confidential relations with Him, and they will be transformed into the likeness of His Son.[5]

Abraham puts everything on the line. God does the same. Their relationship is bound in mutual purpose, a legacy and a destiny for Abraham and his descendants. Without Isaac, all is lost. To sacrifice Isaac is an incomprehensible and audacious act of obedience. Abraham demonstrates that his shared relationship with God is more important than his shared purpose with God.

Abraham's confidence. The second conversation takes place between Abraham and Isaac. Isaac wants to know something: Where is the lamb for the sacrifice?

ISAAC *(to Abraham)*: Father!

ABRAHAM: I am right here, Son.

ISAAC: Look, we have the fire and the wood, but where is the lamb for the burnt offering?

ABRAHAM: God will provide the lamb for the burnt offering, my son. (Gen. 22:7–8)

It is one thing to obediently commit to action. It is another thing to exude confidence that God will provide. Abraham does not tell Isaac all Isaac wants to know. He gives no details concerning a possible location of a lamb or how a lamb might have come to be there in the first place. Abraham does not tell Isaac these things because Abraham does not know. He does not know how God will provide. Could it be that Isaac serves as the lamb God provides? Or could it be that God might rescue Isaac? Abraham does not know. He trusts God unconditionally whatever the outcome might be.

The Scripture does not open the inner world of Abraham as he walks up the mountain with the son he loves. We can only imagine the emotions running through his heart and the thoughts pounding in his brain. With each step, Abraham demonstrates his confidence in God.

> Commit your path to the Eternal; *let Him direct you.*
> Put your confidence in Him, and He will follow
> through *with you.*
> He will spread out righteousness for you
> as a sunrise *spreads radiance over the land*;
> He will deliver justice for you into the light of the
> high sun.
> Be still. Be patient. Expect the Eternal to arrive *and*
> *set things right.* (Ps. 37:5–7)

Each step up the mountain of uncertainty is a step of faith. Confidence in God when faced with uncertainty is a second sign of mature faith. You may choose to put confidence in a specific outcome, or you may put confidence in the One who holds the future regardless of the outcome. Confident faith, regardless of outcome, is found at the high moments of faith in the Bible.

Job did not understand the reasons for his trials; nevertheless, he stood before God with confidence and said, "He may well kill me, but I will hope in Him" (Job 13:15).

Three Hebrew men faced a furnace of fire without a reasonable chance of rescue. Their conviction and obedience inspires us: "If you throw us into the blazing furnace, then the God we serve is able to rescue us from a furnace of blazing fire and release us from your power, Your Majesty. But even if He does not, O king, you can be sure that we *still* will not serve your gods and we will not worship the golden statue you erected" (Dan. 3:17–18).

At a moment when the enemy pounded the gate, the nation was in peril, and doom was certain, a choir member from the temple in Jerusalem sang words of confident faith.

> Even if the fig tree does not blossom
>   and there are no grapes on the vines,
> If the olive trees fail to give fruit
>   and the fields produce no food,
> If the flocks die *far* from the fold
>   and there are no cattle in the stalls;
> Then I will *still* rejoice in the Eternal!
>   I will rejoice in the God who saves me! (Hab. 3:17–18)

In the great hall of faith recorded in the New Testament, we read of heroes and victories. Their stories are thrilling:

> I could speak more *of faith*; I could talk until time itself ran out. If I continued, I could speak *of the examples* of Gideon, Barak, Samson, and Jephthah, of David and Samuel and all the prophets. *I could give accounts of* people alive with faith who conquered kingdoms, brought justice, obtained promises, and closed the mouths of hungry lions. *I could tell you how people of faith* doused raging fires, escaped the edge of the sword, made the weak strong, and—stoking great valor among the champions of God—sent opposing armies into panicked flight. (Heb. 11:32–34)

Nevertheless, the validity of faith can also be found when the outcome is tragic. In the hall of faith, there are others listed whose experience was dreadful. These people also placed their confidence in God: "Others suffered mockery and whippings; they were placed in chains and in prisons. The faithful were stoned, sawn in two, killed by the sword, clothed only in sheepskins and goatskins; they were penniless, afflicted, and tormented. The world was not worthy of these saints. They wandered across deserts, crossed mountains, and lived in the caves, cracks, and crevasses of the earth" (Heb. 11:36–38).

Mature faith places confidence in God, not in the outcome.

God provides and God tests. The third conversation on the mountain takes place between the angel of the Lord and Abraham. The angel speaks for God, as God.

The drama of the scene takes your breath away. Abraham builds the altar and arranges the wood. Will God rescue, or is Isaac the lamb to be slain?

Mature faith places confidence in God, not in the outcome.

Abraham binds his son with rope and lays him on top of the wood. At this point, the relationship between Abraham and Isaac has forever changed, whatever the outcome. Is it too late for rescue?

Abraham slips the knife out of his belt. How much of this does God need in order to know the heart of Abraham? He draws the knife above his head. Then, and only then, does the angel of the Lord come out of heaven:

> **SPECIAL MESSENGER:** Abraham! Abraham!
>
> **ABRAHAM:** I am right here!
>
> **SPECIAL MESSENGER:** Don't lay your hand on the boy or do anything to *harm* him. I know now that you respect *the one True* God *and will be loyal to Him and follow His commands,* because you were willing to give up your son, your only son, to Me. (Gen. 22:11–12)

There it is, what God wanted to know: "I know now that you respect *the one True* God *and will be loyal to Him and follow His commands*" (v. 12). What God did not know, He now knows with certitude: Abraham reverences God and loyally obeys His commands.

Abraham looks up and sees a ram caught in the thicket. He takes the ram and sacrifices it in place of his son. This is a moment and a place to be remembered, "*From that day forward,* Abraham called that place, 'The Eternal One will provide.' Because of this, people still today say, 'On the Mount of the Eternal, all will be provided'" (Gen. 22:14, also 2 Chron. 3:1).

Again, Abraham's mature faith shines. He accepts God as God, the One who provides as well as tests. At times, the God of love advances His purpose by providing blessings. The God of love will also advance His purpose by testing.

We celebrate the God who provides blessings. Perhaps we are prone to ignore the fact that the same God may bring trials, tests, struggles, and burdens. One indication that we have ignored the God who tests is this: When a test or struggle comes, in bitterness, we ignore all His blessings and act as if God only brings us trouble. To trust and obey when there are provisions or when there are only trials is the third mark of mature faith.

Some time ago I taught a philosophy class. This is not a popular subject among nineteen and twenty-year-olds. I taught the course through arts integration. Students presented various philosophers using drama, poster art, music, and so forth.

Sara signed up to present *Fear and Trembling*, a most challenging book about the story of Abraham and the sacrifice of Isaac. The night before her presentation, I received this email. I share it with her permission:

> **From:** Davis, Sara
> **Date:** April 7, 9:39:57 PM CDT
> **To:** "Parrott, Richard"
> **Subject: Existentialism Project**
>
> Dr. Parrott,
> I've been trying to figure out Kierkegaard's "Fear and Trembling" philosophy. The main point I can come up with is that he believed we need to trust God no matter what, and life without God and His love would be completely pointless. I think that is all there is. Can you help clarify for me?
> Thank you,
> Sara Davis

My response to Sara was clear and concise: "Sara, you've got it!"

Abraham's mature faith places his relationship in God over his purpose with God. His mature faith places confidence in God rather than in the outcome. Finally, mature faith receives both blessing and testing from the Lord. Abraham, the one who became homeless for God, has now found his true home in God.

SUMMARY: Can I Know for Sure?

This last question in our study of Abraham is not Abraham's question for God, but God's question for Abraham. God wants to know Abraham's heart. This is the reason for the test. The result is that God now knows. "I know now that you respect *the one True* God *and will be loyal to Him and follow His commands,* because you were willing to give up your son, your only son, to Me" (Gen. 22:12). God says, "I know now." This implies that He did not know before.

God needed to see that Abraham knows what it means to be God's partner.[6] Through Abraham's trust and obedience, God now knows Abraham's heart, a heart of respect and loyalty. God knows that Abraham knows.

It is impossible for us to know all that transpired on the mountain between God and Abraham. It was more than words. It was a knowledge of one another that bound them together as partners for eternity. In total surrender, the heart of Abraham and the heart of God were locked together in love and purpose.

THINK: Reflection and Conversation

1. God pours His grace into places of disgrace, scandal, and shame. How have you experienced grace in the place of disgrace? How are we to share grace in places of disgrace, scandal, and shame?

2. The first mark of mature faith is obedience. How has the idea of obedience and the life of obedience changed and matured in you?

3. The second mark of mature faith is confidence in God, even when you are uncertain of the outcome. In what ways have you matured in this mark of faith?

4. The third mark of faith is trusting God when He brings provision or trial, blessing or challenge. Do you see maturity in your life in regards to this mark of faith?

5. God knows all things; yet there was something in His relationship with Abraham He did not know. Relationship knowledge is shared knowledge. God did not know if Abraham knew what it means to be God's partner. What does it mean to you to be God's partner?

PART TWO

TROUBLED BY GOD

The Path of Wounds

"Manifest Your will here on earth,
as it is manifest in heaven."

—Matthew 6:10

This petition from our Lord's Prayer opens a door to trouble. The will of heaven conflicts with the will of earth. When you pray for heaven's will, you enter God's struggle, the struggle between earth and heaven. Jacob made a reluctant journey of conflict, struggle, and trouble that left him wounded yet blessed.

Jacob's troubles did not begin with him, but with God. In Jacob, the Lord imbedded the value system of God's kingdom, a system in direct conflict with the value system of the world: "Many of those who are first *in this world* shall be last *in the world to come*, and the last, first" (Mark 10:31), and "the older will serve the younger" (Gen. 25:23).

Jacob beheld the door between heaven and earth, a stairway of angels ascending and descending, the place where the conflict ensues. In John's gospel, this same image introduces our Lord and Savior, Jesus Christ. In Jesus we will "see the heavens standing open while heavenly messengers ascend and descend, *swirling* around the Son of Man" (John 1:51, also Gen. 28:12).

Jacob struggled with the conflict between the will of heaven and the will of earth; Jesus also bore the conflict between God's will and His own: "Yet not My will, but Your will, be done" (Luke 22:42). Jacob wrestled with God until the Lord placed heaven's name on an earthly man: "*Your name will be* Israel because you have wrestled with God and humanity, and you have prevailed" (Gen. 32:28). The name of Jesus receives honor from all creation: "When His name is called, every knee will bow, in heaven, on earth, and below (Phil. 2:10).

THE TROUBLE WITH GOD

Did You Do This to Me?

> We are cracked and chipped from our afflictions on all sides, but we are not crushed by them. We are bewildered at times, but we do not give in to despair. We are persecuted, but we have not been abandoned. We have been knocked down, but we are not destroyed. We always carry around in our bodies the reality of the brutal death *and suffering* of Jesus. As a result, His *resurrection* life *rises and* reveals its wondrous power in our bodies as well.
>
> —2 Corinthians 4:8–10

God has a solution for the world's brokenness. However, God's solution comes with a lot of trouble and conflict. Jacob, grandson of Abraham, became a repository of God's trouble. He was a man who lived in conflict—conflict with his parents, his two wives, his father-in-law, and especially his older twin, Esau. Jacob, God's chosen partner, lived in a whirlpool of family rivalry and resentment.

Perhaps one reason the story of Jacob's family is so intriguing to us is that it is so human. We also have families in trouble and conflict, full of family squabbles and family politics. Jacob's story is one of trouble, scandal, and conflict. This chapter examines three sources of trouble in Jacob's life and God's greater purpose in Jacob's trouble.

THE STORY IN SUMMARY
Genesis 25:19–34; 27:1–46

Rebekah cannot get pregnant. Her husband, Isaac, prays to the Lord, and they are granted twins. Esau becomes a hunter, and Jacob stays at home around the tents. Isaac loves Esau, but Rebekah loves Jacob. Jacob trades a bowl of stew for his brother's birthright. Rebekah helps Jacob fool Isaac into giving him the blessing. Isaac trembles. Esau is bitter and vengeful. Rebekah helps her favored son escape the camp. Jacob becomes a fugitive from his own family.

A DYSFUNCTIONAL FAMILY: A HOUSEHOLD FULL OF TROUBLE

Jacob's life is what I term a psychological "midden." The word *midden* is properly used by archeologists to describe the pile of the generational debris of daily life.[1] Each individual contributes to the mix. The pile grows with each succeeding generation. Rain and decay pack down the refuse until we forget what is buried underneath. Yet the rubbish pile attracts the next generation's trash.

Apply the metaphor to the life of a family. Each family, Abraham's family and your family, has a psychological midden—deposits of resentment, deceit, fear, pain, cruelty, rage, betrayal, gossip, and rivalry.

- Grandfather Abraham's deception, repeated by his son Isaac, lives again in his grandson Jacob.[2]
- The rivalry between Grandmother Sarah and her handmaid, Hagar, returns in the jealousy between Jacob's wives, Leah and Rachel.[3]

- Abraham's nephew, Lot, chose self-interest as did his cousin of two generations later, Esau.[4]

The family midden is the pile of stuff we want to hide. The heap carries a stench of shame and embarrassment. We are desperate to keep some secrets buried. We are quick to cover our own midden and just as quick to confess someone else's dirt and debris. Scripture outlines a healing strategy: "So own up to your sins to one another and pray for one another. In the end, you may be healed. Your prayers are powerful when they are rooted in a righteous life" (James 5:16). This plan creates panic if it comes too close to home.

To use the common understanding of a psychological term, Jacob lived in a dysfunctional family.[5] His parents took sides when the twins were born: "Esau was Isaac's favorite because he was fond of good meat, but Jacob was Rebekah's favorite" (Gen. 25:28). Mother Sarah sided with Isaac to the expulsion of Ishmael from the family (Gen. 21:8–10). In the next generation, Jacob is evicted from his family (Gen. 27:43–44).

What a mess! Nevertheless, waist deep in the muddle, we find a word of hope: God loved this dysfunctional family and forged a partnership with them. If God partnered with Jacob's dysfunctional family, then God loves your family, dysfunctions and all. God desires to forge a partnership with you.

Jacob's story, like our story, mixes blessing and deception without enough explanation to satisfy our need for answers. It is simply family. The answer we are giving is that God has a purpose, and He has chosen Jacob as His partner. We do not understand it. We are left to simply marvel at the grace of God at work where we would never expect God to be found.

BAD CHARACTER: A SCANDALOUS MAN

The trouble with Jacob was embedded in his character. He emerged from the womb "with his hand clutching Esau's heel, so they named him Jacob" (Gen. 25:26). His name means "grasping the heel." Figuratively, it means to deceive. However, in modern parlance we say, Jacob was a heel! He bargained away his brother's birthright and deceived his father into granting him the blessing. Then, he turned heel and ran.

Jacob learned to make his way in this world of conflict with two skills. He became a hard negotiator and a deceptive impostor.

The hard negotiator. Jacob knows how to take advantage of a situation. He knows how to take advantage of a person. Esau is in need; he is hungry. Jacob is clever, and Esau, not so much. What begins with hunger ends with anger. Jacob demonstrates skill at negotiation. Immediately he shifts the conversation from Esau's hunger to Esau's birthright. Esau is an easy mark. He lives in the immediate while Jacob takes the long view. Jacob works with the skills of a con artist pulling a scam (Gen. 25:29–34).

The deceptive impostor. With the bargain in hand, the father's blessing is the next order of business. Mother Rebekah plays the spy and overhears that the blessing will be transferred soon. She takes Jacob aside and teaches him a bit of tradecraft—disguises, deception, and tending to details. A favorite dish and fresh baked bread complete the ruse. Jacob appears before his father pretending to be Esau. Isaac is old and almost blind. The trick works! Father Isaac gives the blessing to Jacob, thinking he is Esau. In a culture in which words matter, the deed was done and could not be undone (Gen. 27:1–29).

Psychiatry has discerned the family dynamics of people who become impostors—parents are at odds with each other, the mother treats the child with extreme possessiveness, and the child is forced into an adult role prematurely.[6] These patterns parallel Jacob's story.

To some extent, we are all imposters and negotiators. We all are on a stage.[7] We play our role and act as we do in the public setting of our organizations, our families, and our churches.

It is arguable that learning to negotiate and learning to play your role are life skills, but they are skills that come at a price. Beware of becoming like those who "*in their greed* . . . rob widows of their houses and *cover up their greed* with long pretentious prayers" (Luke 20:47, also Matt. 6:1).

The stumbling block. Jacob's actions are scandalous. How could God possibly choose Jacob? It is a scandal of the grace of God.

Some time ago, I taught a lesson about Jacob that was well received. However, a woman I greatly appreciate came up after class and unloaded her disgust and anger. She is capable of expressing her feelings with strength and clarity. This day, she was in fine form.

Now, you may think she was upset with me. Not at all! She was upset with Jacob. "I hate this story. Jacob is a terrible man, a scoundrel. I can't even read these chapters in the Bible because his behavior makes me so angry. Look what he did to his brother and his father. It's awful."

Jacob is a scoundrel, no argument. God chose a scandal. Like it or not, approve or disapprove, understand or find yourself confused, God called Jacob to be His partner. God gave this rascal the same promise given to his grandfather, Abraham: "I am the Eternal One, the God of Abraham your father and the God of Isaac. The land on which you are now lying is the land I *have promised to* give to you

If God selected a partner like Jacob, I believe there is hope for us.

and your descendants. Your descendants will be as many as there are specks of dust on the earth. You will spread out to the west, east, north, and south. Through your descendants, all the families of the earth will find true blessing" (Gen. 28:13–14; compare with Gen. 13:14–17).

From our vantage point, Jacob is simply not the right man for the job! He is ethically challenged and morally unmoored. My friend from class could not comprehend how God could choose such a reprobate as a partner.

Right here Jacob and Jesus meet. The Greek word for scandal is *skandalon.* The word is most often translated "stumbling block" or "scandalous." Paul, a partner in the gospel, used the term as well: "*But we tell a different story.* We proclaim a crucified Jesus, God's Anointed. For Jews this is scandalous, for outsiders this is moronic, but for those of us living out God's call—regardless of our Jewish or Greek heritage—we know the Anointed embodies God's *dynamic* power and God's *deep* wisdom" (1 Cor. 1:23–24).

Is the cross a scandalous stumbling block of foolishness? First-century people saw it this way. From their perspective, God could never use a cross of suffering to change the world. Yet in faith, we know—indeed we are passionate about—the truth that Christ crucified is the power and wisdom of God. And this is how God works.

Jacob looks like God's foolish choice, a stumbling block, and a scoundrel. Not Jacob. It cannot be. Yet it is. And "*we are* the pride of Jacob, the ones He loves" (Ps. 47:4). The will of heaven sees purpose in God's choice of Jacob, while on earth the choice appears irrational and indignant. We cannot understand God's choices and God's ways. "My thoughts and My ways are above and beyond you, just as heaven is far from your reach here on earth" (Isa. 55:9).

Here we find a second word of hope: If God selected a partner like Jacob, I believe there is hope for us.

THE TROUBLE MAKER: A GOD OF CONFLICT

We cannot put the entire burden and blame for the scandal on either the dysfunctional family heritage or Jacob's bad character. God is at work. He works against the dysfunctional values and systems of the world. In the eyes of the world, God's work is scandalous. To achieve His goal, God's work with Jacob brings trouble. However, God's trouble and scandals carry heavenly vision and salvation. All the trouble in Jacob's life began with God, and began before Jacob was born. God set the conflict in motion.

> Isaac prayed to the Eternal One on behalf of his wife because she wasn't becoming pregnant. The Eternal granted his prayer, and Rebekah conceived *after 20 years*. But the children she carried struggled *and fought* with each other until, *in great pain,* she exclaimed, "What is going on? Why is this happening to me?" *In frustration* she inquired of the Eternal One *why this civil war was occurring inside of her.*
>
> **Eternal One** *(to Rebekah)*: Two nations are *growing*
> inside of your womb,
> and the two peoples will be divided *in the future.*
> One will be stronger than the other,
> and the older will serve the younger. (Gen. 25:21–23,
> also Rom. 9:10–12)

In the last line of God's promise, the trouble begins in six words: "the older will serve the younger." God assaults tradition. In the culture of Isaac, the older son receives the father's blessing. The younger always serves the older. That is how it works. That is the way it is. That is the way it should be.

In six words, God assaults the broken value system and flawed wisdom of the world. By reversing the traditional order of the family, elder and younger, God sets in motion a troubling scandal.[8] God breaks convention, counters the values, and drives a stake of conflict into the family: the older will serve the younger. While still in his mother's womb, Jacob's troubles are born.

A conflict of purpose. Why would God do this? Why would God bring trouble on His chosen ones, on His human partners? God does not dump troubles on life for His personal entertainment. God has a purpose. In this case, God was setting up the conflict between the selfish purpose of a fallen world and the saving purpose of His kingdom. God's partners are called to engage the troubling conflict between the world system and the kingdom of Christ. That's the deal! To partner with God creates conflict with the system of the world.

- The world system promotes corruption and prejudice, self-interest and vengeance, injustice and death. In contrast, "*When God reigns, the order of the day is* redeeming justice, true peace, and joy made possible by the Holy Spirit" (Rom. 14:17).[9]
- When we sign on with God, we are "now representatives of the Anointed One, *the Liberating King;* God has given us a charge to carry through our lives—urging all people on behalf of the Anointed to become reconciled to *the Creator* God" (2 Cor. 5:20).
- To the world system of greed, vengeance, and duplicity, we look dangerous. Jesus was a realist: "In this world, you will be plagued with times of trouble, but you need not fear; I have triumphed over this corrupt world order" (John 16:33).

- Jesus also promised, "Blessed are those who are persecuted because of righteousness—the kingdom of heaven is theirs" (Matt. 5:10).

A conflict of values. The life of Jesus echoes the story of Jacob. Jesus also had a scandalous birth (Matt. 1:18–19) that created conflict from the beginning of His life (Matt. 2:1–3). The Beatitudes oppose and redress the values of the world (Matt. 5:3–11). On the cross, Jesus engaged in the decisive battle with the world system, the system controlled by sin, death, and the Devil. Jesus won the day and defeated the value system of the world (Col. 1:19–20).

The world system insures that the first remain first and the last do not stand a chance. The world's system of values determines:

- Who is a winner and who is a loser;
- Who takes control and who is under control;
- Who gives the orders and who takes orders;
- Who is privileged and who is ordinary;
- Whom we accept and whom we hate;
- Who takes care of us and who had better beware of us;
- Who is worth knowing and who is not worth our time;
- Who is on top and who gets trampled;
- Who advances and who is eliminated;
- Who calls the shots and who does the dirty work;
- Who is number one and who does not even count.

Jacob and Esau's struggle in the womb marks a milestone in God's battle against the values of the world system. God turns the system on its head: the older shall serve the younger (Gen. 25:23).

Jesus repeats the same inverted value system: "The last will be first and the first will be last" (Matt. 20:16).[10] What God begins with Jacob, He fulfills in Jesus. God reverses the values of the world system:

> **JESUS:** You know that among the nations of the world the great ones lord it over the little people and act like tyrants. But that is not the way it will be among you. Whoever would be great among you must serve and minister. Whoever wants to be great among you must be slave of all. Even the Son of Man came not to be served but to be a servant—to offer His life as a ransom for others. (Mark 10:42–45)

I have a class in which I write on the board the statement, "You can't keep a good man down." I ask my class of young Americans, mostly middle class, if the statement is true. (They want to exchange the term *man* with *person*, and I agree.) But is the statement true? They agree that it is. I then explain, "But you must understand that five thousand years of human history have been devoted to keeping good people down and in their place."

Most of human history has been designed to keep people in their place according to their birth. If your father was a servant, you became a servant. If your father was royalty, you received royal treatment. Your birth certificate determined your destiny.

In Jacob, for the first time, God tears up the birth certificate and declares that His purpose takes precedence over convention, tradition, or human decision.[11] God takes the side of the young, the widow, the orphan, and the stranger.[12] In Jesus, we see the completion of God's purpose in siding with the outcasts, tax collectors, and sinners.[13] Our physical birth does not determine destiny. In Christ we experience "birth for a second time" (John 3:3).

A conflict of kingdoms. The struggle of conflicting values is embedded in a greater conflict, the conflict of two kingdoms—the kingdom of God and the system of the world, which is ruled by the Prince of Darkness.[14] The battle rumbled in Herod's attempt to kill the infant Jesus (Matt. 2:13) and stormed in Christ's temptations in the desert (Matt. 4:1–11). The crucial battle was on the cross. "He disarmed those who once ruled over us—those who had overpowered us. *Like captives of war,* He put them on display to the world to show His victory over them *by means of the cross*" (Col. 2:15).

The battle cry in the conflict is the prayer of our Lord: "May Your will be accomplished on earth as it is in heaven" (Luke 11:2). This is a bold prayer. It is a prayer that requires courage. When you pray this prayer, you step into the conflict of kingdoms, a conflict full of trouble and scandal.

"May Your will be accomplished on earth as it is in heaven" is the prayer of our Lord, and the prayer He taught God's partners to pray. It is a troublesome prayer. Jesus knew persecution would come (Matt. 5:8–11). The disciples were warned of the trouble (John 16:33). Early Christians experienced disgrace and distress (1 Peter 4:12–14).

A conflict that's personal. When you, as a follower of Christ, stand for and live with compassion, you look dangerous to people of self-interest. When you pray and live for God's will to be done on earth as in heaven, you are in conflict with the world, and the world will strike back. Even the comfortable world of church traditions and conventions defends itself against the revolutionary aims of the kingdom of God.

When you, as a follower of Christ, stand for and live with compassion, you look dangerous to people of self-interest.

In chapter four, I shared a story of a group of students working in the inner city. The story of Sodom and Gomorrah challenged them to believe that only a few good people can make a difference in an evil place. Let me share with you another story about a different group of students who were preparing to teach in the inner city. In this story, the students learned that being a blessing comes at a price.

Our guest in class led an independent faith-based ministry for inner city children. The discussion began with how, where, and when—questions of tactics rather than vision and purpose. In time, both students and our guest felt ready to venture into the more demanding and personal questions. Within an hour, a fellowship was forged in this group of people dedicated to bringing the will of heaven to children in the inner city.

I closed the conversation with a request for our guest: "List words that describe life for a child in the inner city." Our guest turned her eyes upward as if she was reviewing situations and experiences. Her list emerged slowly and thoughtfully: "Fear, abuse, hunger, pain, rage, frustration, loneliness, rape." She stopped and told the story of a child. Then she continued, "Violence, injustice, deceit, evil." Tears filled the eyes of each person in the room.

Pressing forward in this tender and Spirit-filled moment, I probed our guest: "Your organization partners with a church. I suspect that not everyone in the church embraced the idea of allowing these poor children into the church building and into the classrooms with the children of church families."

A careful nod indicated her answer. I continued, "I further suspect that in the process of bringing this ministry to life, you have encountered your own fear, abuse, anger, and loneliness."

God brings purpose into life. With purpose comes trouble.

Again, a single nod affirmed her experience. This was a teachable moment. I turned to my class of students: "As you seek to minister to those in need, you will also experience tears, anxiety, loneliness, and discouragement. These troubles will be God's gift of helping you identify with those you serve. The blessing of ministry always comes with the burden of empathy."

Jesus prayed, "May Your will be accomplished on earth as it is in heaven" (Luke 11:2). This bold prayer brings trouble, scandal, and conflict into our lives. Do not pray lightly or without thought and commitment. When you align your life with God's plans for the world, you will, at some point, be in conflict with the world.

The seed of our Lord's Prayer is found in Jacob, the man who "saw a ladder set up on the earth, and its top reached to the heavens. He saw some messengers of God ascending and descending on it" (Gen. 28:12). We pray for the will of heaven to be done on earth. Jacob saw the portal between heaven and earth and the messages of God and His people moving back and forth. God works in the world. We choose to align with His work, knowing there will be a price to pay for the blessing of partnering with God.

It is Jacob, the younger, weaker, and lesser, who receives the promise. In the story of Jacob, the grace of God becomes a scandal. God's grace upsets the way we expect life to be organized. In the conflict, God's grace offers another promise: "Whatever you did to the least of these, so you did to me" (Matt. 25:40).

SUMMARY: Did You Do This to Me?

The answer depends on what *this* is. God does not bring trouble into a life in the way we think of a trickster or bully. God does not bring trouble into a life in the way we bring trouble on ourselves. God brings purpose into life. With purpose comes trouble. When you question the values that order your life and the values accepted in the tradition of the world, you look dangerous. You are stepping into trouble when you side with God's values and God's kingdom. You join the conflict when you pray, *Your will be done on earth as it is in heaven.*

THINK: Conversation and Reflection

1. This chapter outlines three sources of trouble in life: family dysfunction, personal character, and partnering with God. How do these three ways of looking at trouble help you understand the troubles you face?

2. God's choices may appear foolish, weak, and scandalous to us. Yet, this is how God often works. Read the scripture below. Where do you see yourself in this outrageous promise?

   > But *celebrate this*: God selected the world's foolish to bring shame upon *those who think they are* wise; likewise, He selected the world's weak to bring disgrace upon *those who think they are* strong. God selected the common and the castoff, whatever lacks status, so He could invalidate the claims of those who think those things are significant. (I Cor. 1:27–28)

3. Jesus had three things to say about the trouble that comes into our lives because God chooses us to be His partners. First, He tells us that He experienced trouble in spirit and soul (John 11:33; 12:27, 13:21). Second, He encourages us to trust in Him when we face trouble (John 14:1; 14:27). Third, He reminds us that even in our trouble, we may know victory in Christ:

> I have told you these things so that you will be *whole and* at peace. In this world, you will be plagued with times of trouble, but you need not fear; I have triumphed over this corrupt world order. (John 16:33)

What troubles have you experienced from committing yourself to God's purpose? How do you handle these difficulties?

4. There are practical matters about being a blessing in a world of trouble.

- What do you think of the idea that the blessing of following Christ is living free of trouble?
- How do you respond to the thought that praying for God's will on earth may bring trouble to your life?
- How do your values differ from or align with the values of God's kingdom?
- Where are you involved in the conflict between the kingdom of this world and the kingdom of God?

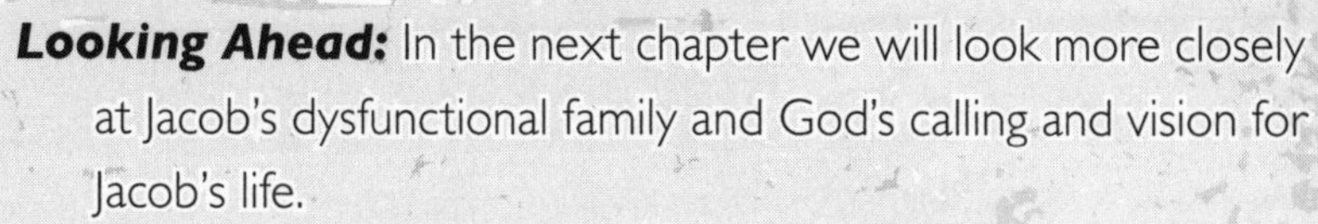

Looking Ahead: In the next chapter we will look more closely at Jacob's dysfunctional family and God's calling and vision for Jacob's life.

THE PROMISE OF GOD

Why Did You Choose Me?

> Do not allow this world to mold you in its own image. Instead, be transformed *from the inside out* by renewing your mind. As a result, you will be able to discern what God wills and whatever God finds good, pleasing, and complete.
>
> —Romans 12:2

Your first mirror is your mother's face. In your mother's look, you form your first understanding of yourself and the world.[1] The emotions that consistently radiate from your mother's face—love, fear, disgust, joy—influence the foundation of your emotional development. The you viewed in the mirror of your mother reflects a degree of realism as well as distortion. And winning the gleam of approval in your mother's eye becomes a prize to grasp.[2]

When you were a child, your mother and family set the perspective and expectations for you. You learned and lived within your family's beliefs, limits, and dysfunctions. Each member of your family played a part. The family system weaved patterns of self-image and relationship into life. To survive in a family, you learned early on to conform to patterns of your family. At a deep, personal, and soulful level, you are converted, born again, when you turn away from the mirror of family and find your true self in God.

THE STORY IN SUMMARY
Genesis 27:1–28:21

Isaac loves Rebekah and prays for their children. After the children are born, however, he turns his attention to the family business. Using the tricks of his father, Abraham, he deceives a neighboring king, secures the water rights in a dry land, and becomes so wealthy he intimidates the kings and wealthy families around him.

Rebekah, mother of Jacob, overhears her husband, Isaac, promising the family blessing to Esau. Rebekah intends to secure the blessing for her favorite son, Jacob. With cunning, stealth, and deception, she schemes to secure the blessing by teaching Jacob to disguise himself as his brother, Esau. The plan works, as Jacob negotiates the blessing away from his brother and plays the imposter with his father, Isaac.

Following the ruse, Rebekah overhears Esau's pledge to kill Jacob. Again, she schemes, this time to get her son to safety by sending him to her brother, Laban.

On the journey to his uncle's home, Jacob receives one of the most dramatic and significant revelations of God in the Bible. While sleeping, Jacob sees a stairway between heaven and earth with angels ascending and descending. God sits at the top of the stairway.

Jacob also hears the voice of God bless him with the blessing of Abraham. Jacob names the place the house of God (Bethel) and commits his life to the Lord.

DYSFUNCTIONAL FAMILY/DYSFUNCTIONAL WORLD

Family life can be difficult, but, for the most part, we keep our family troubles at bay or in secret. I live in the South where, perhaps more than other parts in the country, family is esteemed idealistically. In the South, Thanksgiving meals may include scores of people, all part of an extended family. Church baby baptisms and dedications often sport several pews filled with family members as they honor another entry into the family system. If there is trouble in the family, the rule is to hide it if possible. There may be resentment and rivalry, backbiting and betrayal, and all the weapons of family politics, but conventional wisdom keeps dirty laundry in the laundry room.

All families struggle, and all families struggle with what to do with the struggle. Perhaps this is one reason the story of Isaac, his wife Rebekah, and their twin boys, Jacob and Esau, both intrigues and disturbs us. The dirt is displayed; the hidden closet opens, and the secrets are revealed.

God removed Jacob from Isaac's family in order to give Jacob a vision, a calling, and a promise. To accomplish His goal, God broke the tradition, the conventional wisdom of the day, and determined that "the older will serve the younger" (Gen. 25:23). God's plan tossed the family system into chaos. The dysfunction buried under a surface of harmony reared its head:

- Each parent favors a different son.
- One brother tricks the other out of the family legacy.
- The mother teaches her son to deceive his father.
- The older brother threatens to murder the younger one.

How do we understand such behavior in Isaac's family as well as our own families? First, do not think of family as a collection of individuals living under the same roof. Think of your family as a system that, at times, functions effectively while, at other times, dysfunctions. The dynamics of a family system,[3] your family system, are laid bare in Isaac's family.

1. Every family creates, maintains, and draws its life from a family system. As real as the air you breathe and just as difficult to see, the system of a family[4] influences what happens in the family. The action of one person affects everyone else.

For example, few of us would give all the credit to the football player who ran the ball across the goal line. We know it takes team effort. The same can be said of a family that functions or dysfunctions.

The same system dynamic describes a tornado. Temperature plus humidity plus barometric pressure equal the conditions for a tornado. A twister is the result of a system, not a single event in itself.

Another example is the system of the human body. The color of the skin may indicate a problem in the liver. If your jaw hurts, it could be referred from angina. If your kidneys have trouble reducing salt, the result may increase stress on the heart. Stress on the kidneys leads to a failure in the production of insulin. A failing pancreas may stress the kidneys. All the parts are related to one another.

Paul, the missionary leader of the early Christian movement, described systems theory as an explanation of dysfunctional behavior in the family of the church:

> *Here's what I mean:* the body is not made of one large part but of many *different parts*. Would it seem right for the foot to cry, "I am not a hand, so I couldn't be part of this body"? Even if it did, it wouldn't be any less joined to the body. And what about an ear? If an ear started to whine, "I am not an eye; I shouldn't be attached to this body," in all its pouting, it is still part of the body. Imagine the entire body as an eye. How would a giant eye be able to hear? And if the entire body were an ear, how would an ear be able to smell? (1 Cor. 12:14–17)

In a family, everyone has a part to play. Even the most dysfunctional family (or church) carries on if its members play their expected dysfunctional role. When someone steps outside the family's conventional expectations, the dysfunction is exposed. God had an unconventional plan for Jacob.

2. The relationship between mother and child forms the foundation of the family. The mother/infant relationship creates a garden of relational and emotional patterns. Look at the relationship between Rebekah and her twins. Esau took to the open country while Jacob stayed among the tents, and the mother preferred Jacob (Gen. 25:27–28). Mother Rebekah was a bit of a drama queen; she demanded her way with a false threat of suicide (Gen. 27:46) concerning whom Jacob would marry. Rebekah used a ploy to secure the safety of her beloved Jacob (Gen. 27:41–46). Step by step, Rebekah created a plausible reason for Jacob to leave the family and escape the murderous threats of his brother, Esau.

Children respond in sync with mother. Jacob wishes to please his mother, seeking her advice, taking her instruction, and fulfilling her wishes. Esau, the other son, grows distant under her spell. Esau marries two local women, which creates pain and division in the family (Gen. 27:46). Esau learns of his mother's disgust with the local Canaanite women. In response, he goes to uncle Ishmael and marries one of his uncle Ishmael's daughters in addition to his Hittite wives (Gen. 28:6–9). This is the stuff of soap operas, the melodrama of a dysfunctional life.

3. The father also shapes the family. Fathers play a dynamic or changing role in the family. As fathers change, the family transmutes.

When someone steps outside the family's conventional expectations, the dysfunction is exposed.

Isaac changed from a spiritual fountain of love into an emotionally distant father.

At first, Isaac loved his wife, Rebekah, and she brought comfort to him (Gen. 24:67). The story of Rebekah's selection for marriage to Isaac reads like a debutant's rise to prestige and prominence. Prayer, praise, and family politics combine to produce the union of Isaac and Rebekah, each from powerful families (Gen. 24).

Isaac's involvement in the family from the beginning is through prayer, a beautiful and significant task for every father. He prays for Rebekah that she might have children. His prayers are answered, and she gives birth to twins (Gen. 25:21–26). However, Isaac's role as the fountain of spirituality in the family disappears in the years that follow.

Fathers relate to families in one of three ways: calming, reactionary, or distant.[5] The quality of a father's calming presence brings health to a family. Reactionary fathers are easily spotted by their outbursts, demands, anger, and control. It appears that Isaac became an emotionally distant father.

Like some fathers today, Isaac focused on his business and his personal pleasures and preferences. Concerning the business, immediately after receiving the promise of God's blessing (Gen. 26:2–5), Isaac mimicked the trickery of his father, Abraham. He deceived another King Abimelech,[6] using the ruse of telling the king that Rebekah was his sister (vv. 7–10). Despite his duplicity, he amassed a fortune by controlling water rights (wells) in a dry land (vv. 12–27).

Concerning Isaac's pleasures and preferences, he enjoyed his meals; references to tasty food appear five times in the story in Genesis 27 alone.[7] But, of his relationship with his family, we are told only "his eyes were so bad he could see only shadows"

We need a good Parent, our Father in heaven.

(v. 1). What a sad image of a father who has grown distant from his family.

As you think of your own family, I pray your parents are more functional and relationally healthy than Isaac and Rebekah. However, many grown children know the scars and open wounds of growing up in excessive dysfunction. For all children, however, parents look like demi-gods—all-powerful, doing whatever they like. At some point, each child discovers that parents are not demi-gods; they are flawed. For all people—you, me, everyone—we need a good Parent, our Father in heaven.

God is preparing to remove Jacob from his dysfunctional family. The Lord Himself will become a calming presence of assurance and promise to him (Gen. 28:13–15).

4. The family's dynamics come to light in times of crisis. How does the family respond to crisis? When Isaac discovered he blessed the wrong son, he "began trembling violently" (Gen. 27:33). On hearing the plot to steal his birthright and blessing, Esau blames his brother: "'Jacob' is certainly the right name for him! *He has once again grabbed me by the heels!* He has deceived me now two times. He took away my birthright, and now he has taken away my blessing!" (v. 36). Esau conveniently forgets that he bargained away his own birthright. From that time on, "Esau hated Jacob *with a fury*" and vowed, "The days of mourning for my father are approaching. When he has died, I will kill my brother, Jacob" (v. 41).

In spite of their flaws, our hearts go out to Isaac and Esau. Rebekah and Jacob deceived them. Nevertheless, God chooses the deceiver as His partner. He removes him from the family; "So Isaac sent Jacob away" (Gen. 28:5).

A VISION OF HEAVEN/LIFE'S PURPOSE ON EARTH

Isaac's family provides a microcosm of a dysfunctional world. God created the world to function as His temple: "Holy, holy, holy is the Eternal, the Commander of *heavenly* armies! The earth is filled with His glorious presence!" (Isa. 6:3). In the creation of the world, God builds His temple, a temple of worship and praise.

In ancient temples of the Middle East, the most sacred place held the image of the god. When God created the world as His temple, He displayed His image in human beings. This is how the world was meant to be—the temple of God with each human as an image-bearer, bearing the image of God. This is how the world was to function!

Like a snake in the grass, dysfunction slithered into the world, the temple of God. Sin, death, and the Devil crept into the garden of paradise with deception and false promises. This was the result: all people have sinned and cannot reach the glory of God (Rom. 3:23). God is determined to win back His temple and rid the world of the dysfunctional effect of that most unholy trinity—sin, death, and the Devil. The final and decisive battle Christ won on the cross. This is God's ultimate purpose in partnering with Jacob.

God's next move involves Jacob, a victim as well as a propagator of the world's dysfunction. You break the system, the dysfunctional system of the family and the world, when you differentiate yourself.[8] You differentiate when you step outside the system, when you disengage your identity from the system. The Devil and his world system tempts you to be a chameleon, needing everyone to agree with you, or a bully, forcing everyone to agree with you, or a rebel, proving that nobody agrees with you.[9]

Connect your identity to God rather than the system of this world. Once free from the system, partner with God in bringing healing and salvation to the broken sin-filled world system. "Do not allow this world to mold you in its own image. Instead, be transformed *from the inside out* by renewing your mind. As a result, you will be able to discern what God wills and whatever God finds good, pleasing, and complete" (Rom. 12:2).

You do not have to think like the world thinks. As a Christian, God differentiates or transforms you by renewing your mind so that you may follow God's path, calling, and purpose rather than conform to the dysfunctional patterns of family and the dysfunctional patterns of the world. Each of the founders of faith left family before they could fulfill God's calling.

- Jacob's grandfather, Abraham, heard and responded to the call to "Leave your relatives and your father's home, and travel to the land I will show you" (Gen. 12:1).
- In the next section of this book, you will see that Joseph was abused by his brothers, tossed in a dry well, and sold into Egyptian slavery. He experienced a harsh way to leave home.
- In this chapter, Abraham's grandson, Jacob, leaves his father's house. Indeed, Jacob is exiled from his family. Nevertheless, banishment concealed God's call. God called Jacob out of the promised family so that one day he might lead the promised family.

Jacob felt the isolation, banishment, and exile. Alone in the wilderness, his experience anticipates the experience of Israel many years yet to come and the experience of broken and dysfunctional families:

> Do not trust your neighbor or rely on a friend.
> Do not tell your secrets even to the spouse who shares your bed,
> For the son insults the father, the daughter rebels against the mother,

> and the daughter-in-law *rises up* against the
> mother-in-law.
> Your enemies can be found within your own
> household.
> But as for me, I will look to the Eternal One, and my
> hope is in the True God
> who will save me. My God will hear me. (Mic. 7:5–7)

The journey away from home. Jacob faced his banishment alone. Exile is a frightening thing. Even if home promises resentment, fears, and cunning calculations, still, home is familiar. This new place on Jacob's journey has no name. It is nowhere, off the grid of ancient Canaan. Here, in this desolate and neglected place, Jacob will begin the process of untangling his identity from his family. He will secure his inner self in partnership with God.

Most of us will not mirror Jacob's precise experience of exile, but we all require a moment and a process of separation from family in order to align our lives in full commitment with God. In a dysfunctional and codependent family, to differentiate, to step outside the system, means banishment. In a dysfunctional and codependent world, to differentiate and join the kingdom of God is to face exile, to be an outsider.

In this lonesome place (Gen. 28:11), God comes to Jacob. What a shock! We do not expect a vision of grace in this place or to this man. God is so utterly unconventional. And, what about you and me? Could it be that even in our questionable morality, our self-centered bargaining, and our deceptive actions, God prepares us to face Him?

I know the experience of exile and banishment. My experience happened more than twenty years ago. Troubles I had brought on myself and troubles from within a family system expelled me from home. I stole away for two days to hide from my family and my friends. In this story, I was not the hero but the one hiding in exile.

The two days were up. It was Thanksgiving morning and time to go home for a family gathering. Multiple generations of my family were assembling at the house. Before heading home, I needed a cup of coffee.

There are not many restaurants open early on Thanksgiving day. I found one place, slid into a booth, ordered my coffee, and sat there. Looking around I could see other lonely people like myself. At first I thought, What are they doing here on Thanksgiving day? The question ricocheted and struck my heart.

A waitress delivered the coffee, and I held the warm mug with both hands. I stared at the coffee waiting for it to cool enough to take a sip. That is when it happened. It came so suddenly that it startled me. The silent voice within me called my name. I knew at once it was God. It was so real I looked up from the coffee almost expecting to see God sitting there with me. Without thinking, I blurted out my question, "Lord, what are You doing here?"

The answer from God's silent voice within was definite: *Waiting for you to notice.*

An encounter with God. Imagine Jacob's troubling thoughts as he tries to sleep. God comes to him in a dream, which is an image of a new and different life. Jacob could not envision God in his day-to-day life. When awake, Jacob's world is crowded with terror, loneliness, and unresolved guilt.[10]

Could it be that even in our questionable morality, our self-centered bargaining, and our deceptive actions, God prepares us to face Him?

In Jacob's dream, his guard is down. He sees reality in a different way, a new way. God gives Jacob a vision of the portal between heaven and earth: "*During the night, God gave* him a dream. He saw a ladder set up on the earth, and its top reached to the heavens. He saw some messengers of God ascending and descending on it. At the very top stood the Eternal One" (Gen. 28:12–13).

This encounter presents the foundation of biblical spirituality. This is the moment when heaven and earth meet. To understand the significance of this event for us, we need a biblical worldview.

The Bible views God as the Lord of creation, maker of heaven and earth.[11] Heaven is half of God's creation with the earth being the other half. The earth is our home, and heaven is God's home. In Jacob's vision, heaven and earth are not eternally separated but joined. The angels, God's messengers, travel between heaven and earth. The messengers carry the will of heaven to earth and the prayers of earth to heaven.

The will of heaven comes to Jacob in a word from God who stands at the top of the stairway: "I am the Eternal One, the God of Abraham your father and the God of Isaac. The land on which you are now lying is the land I *have promised to* give to you and your descendants. Your descendants will be as many as there are specks of dust on the earth. You will spread out to the west, east, north, and south. Through your descendants, all the families of the earth will find true blessing" (vv. 13–14).

The promise God gave to Abraham and Isaac now falls on Jacob. God includes a unique promise for Jacob: "Know I am with you, and I will watch over you no matter where you go. *One day* I will bring you back to this land. I will not leave you until I have done all I have promised you" (v. 15).

The soul's response. How does Jacob respond to God's revelation? Jacob, for the first time in his life, becomes aware of God's presence and purpose. He knows of God, the God of his father and grandfather, but at this moment, Jacob's spiritual awareness forms the foundation for his life and for all who follow after: "There is no doubt in my mind that the Eternal One is in this place—and I didn't even know it!" (v. 16).

God "is in this place—and I didn't even know it!" Biblical spirituality, indeed, biblical faith, is based on "the absolute conviction that there are realities you've never seen" (Heb. 11:1).

Jacob finds the world of the unseen more convincing than the world of fear and guilt. He sees the kingdom at hand.[12] He is ready to repent and believe, to abandon his old ways of dread for the new reality of loyalty to God.

Such a transcendent moment bursts into worship. Jacob vows to remember the place and this moment. He makes a decision to commit all of his life to God. Here we see the primary response to God's presence—to remember and to decide. He remembers the moment and place with an altar. It is a place and moment to which he will return again and again in his mind and on his journey. He makes the life-orienting decisions to trust God and live a life of worship: "Then Jacob made a vow. If God is going to be with me, keeping me *safe* on this journey and giving me bread to eat and clothing to wear so that I return to my father's house in peace, then the Eternal will be my God. And this stone I have made into a pillar will be *the first stone laid in* God's house. And *Lord,* of everything You give me, I will give one-tenth always back to You!" (Gen. 28:20–22).

Jacob has left his father's house and encountered his Father in heaven. The blessing Isaac had spoken over Jacob is never mentioned again. The blessing he receives from God sets the pattern and

As Jacob came out of a dysfunctional family, Jesus entered a dysfunctional world.

purpose of his life. The heel of the family is now in the hands of God. (Yet, Jacob is still Jacob, the negotiator: he adds an "if.")

A BROKEN WORLD/A HEALING SAVIOR

As Jacob came out of a dysfunctional family, Jesus entered a dysfunctional world. Jacob witnessed the doorway between heaven and earth. Jesus embodies the doorway (John 10:9) between heaven and earth. In Jesus, God was incarnate, fully human and fully divine. Jesus introduces Himself with reference to the story of Jacob's vision: "I tell you the truth: *before our journey is complete*, you will see the heavens standing open while heavenly messengers ascend and descend, *swirling* around the Son of Man" (John 1:51).

Our life in Jesus. As followers of Jesus Christ, our relationship with God forms our core identity, guides our decisions, and affords God's calm presence in life.

God, in essence, removed Jacob from his family so that Jacob might learn God "is in this place—and I didn't even know it!" (Gen. 28:16). God determined to free Jacob from his family; God determined to take priority over Jacob's family. The result, as we shall see in the next chapter, is that Jacob became his own man, a man in God.

Here is a truth that sounds odd upon modern ears: Commitment to God takes priority over commitment to family. A modern term for this kind of commitment is differentiation, finding your own identity. We might use the term *spiritual differentiation* for finding our own identity in God. Think of it this way:

- If we believe God is Lord, we have no other lords before Him.
- If we believe God is our Father, we have no other fathers before Him.

The first and full commitment to God is the ground of the life and teaching of Jesus Christ. One of the most controversial and unconventional sayings of Jesus describes differentiation from family in stark terms:

> I have come to turn men against their fathers, daughters against their mothers, and daughters-in-law against their mothers-in-law. You will find you have enemies even in your own household. If you love your father or mother more than you love Me, then you are not worthy of Me. If you love your son or daughter more than you love Me, then you are not worthy of Me. If you refuse to take up your cross and follow Me *on the narrow road*, then you are not worthy of Me. To find your life, you must lose your life—and whoever loses his life for My sake will find it. (Matt. 10:35–39, also Luke 14:26–27)

Jesus uses the common method of hyperbole[13] or exaggeration in order to make His point vivid and memorable. To turn against means we turn toward God fully. This was the experience of Jacob and message of Jesus, and is the challenge for us.

Our partnership with Jesus. Jacob saw the door between heaven and earth; Jesus is the door between heaven and earth. The prayer of our Lord is, "May Your will be accomplished on earth as it is in heaven" (Luke 11:2). The prayer is bold and daring. The prayer demands a change of heart. When your identity is firmly rooted in God, God's purpose becomes your purpose. In whatever God wants to accomplish on earth, you are His partner. This is different from asking for your will on earth to be blessed by heaven. Your treasure is no longer on earth; your treasure is God, His purpose, and the will of heaven:

> Some people store up treasures *in their homes* here on earth. *This is a shortsighted practice*—don't undertake it. Moths and

> rust will eat up any treasure you may store here. Thieves may break into *your homes* and steal *your precious trinkets*. Instead, put up your treasures in heaven where moths do not attack, where rust does not corrode, and where thieves are barred at the door. For where your treasure is, there your heart will be also. (Matt. 6:19–21)

Your small purposes and fragile will are vulnerable to the world's tyranny and thievery. They will steal your soul if you are not alert and vigilant. Anchor your purpose and your personhood in God. God is your fortune.

SUMMARY: Why Did You Choose Me?

God is unconventional. He does the unexpected. Jacob was an unconventional and unexpected choice. "God selected the world's foolish to bring shame upon *those who think they are* wise; likewise, He selected the world's weak to bring disgrace upon *those who think they are* strong. God selected the common and the castoff, whatever lacks status, so He could invalidate the claims of those who think those things are significant" (1 Cor. 1:27–28).

May I speak so boldly as to assert that God, in His audacity, chose you? However, and note this, unconventional and unexpected choices are difficult. Lifting a person out of a dysfunctional world and giving them a new function, to fulfill the will of heaven on earth, is a task only God can accomplish. And He does it again and again. Praise Him!

THINK: Conversation and Reflection

1. Think about your spiritual journey toward and in God. How would you describe your journey? Abraham left home to follow God. Jacob left home and found God. What about you? What is your story?

2. Now for a difficult topic for conversation—dysfunctional families. This is an "undiscussable"[14] in some circles. To the degree you are comfortable and courageous, think and talk about the dysfunction in Jacob's family. Now, consider your own family. How has God and/or how is God lifting you out of your dysfunction?

3. This chapter introduced the term *spiritual differentiation*. Think of Paul's phrase "When I was a child, I spoke, thought, and reasoned in childlike ways *as we all do*. But when I became a man, I left my childish ways behind" (1 Cor. 13:11). What has been your experience of putting away the things of your childhood, your home and family, in order to become your own person in Christ Jesus?

4. There are practical concerns about praying for God's will to be done on earth.
   - When have you caught yourself praying for God to bless your will (your treasure on earth) rather than bringing about His will on earth?
   - If we pray for God's will on earth, to what extent does the prayer require action on our part?
   - To the best of your knowledge and insight, how does God want to partner with you specifically to bring about His will on earth?

Looking Ahead: In the next chapter, Jacob's new identity in God is tested as he moves in with a new family and starts a family of his own. Jacob learns difficult and practical lessons about what it means to follow God in a pagan world.

THE MATURING WORK OF GOD

Are You Still with Me?

"So no matter what your task is, work hard. *Always do your best* as the Lord's servant, not as man's, because you know your reward is the Lord's inheritance. You serve the Lord, the Anointed One."

—Colossians 3:23–24

Everybody has a story, and God has a story too. When God's story embraces your story, the story changes. And so it was with Jacob. He had encountered God. He had seen the doorway between heaven and earth. He had received the promise of his grandfather Abraham with an added promise just for him. Jacob vowed to follow God (Gen. 28:11–22).

For the next two decades, through the vagaries of life—the ups and downs, joys and betrayals, the breakthroughs and fallouts—God shaped the story of Jacob's life. Maturity grew as Jacob faced and handled life's frustration through dependence on God. Maturity develops as one learns to postpone the immediate for the lasting, accept the daily stress with calm, handle the injustices with dignity, and face the ambiguities with faith. For twenty years, Jacob matures in life and in faith.

- At the beginning, he is an empty-handed fugitive; at the end, he is a wealthy man of prominence and power.

- At the beginning, he is a lonely outcast from his family; at the end, he is the head of a family with multiple wives and a dozen children.
- At the beginning, he is the banished son of Isaac; at the end, he is prepared to return home, to the home of his birth, upon the word of God.

THE STORY IN SUMMARY
Genesis 29:1–31:55

Jacob arrives in the land of his mother's brother, Laban. He spies a beautiful shepherdess, Rachel. His interest is piqued. (Jacob's mother, Rebekah, has sent Jacob to her brother for two reasons: to save him from the anger of Esau and to find a bride.) Jacob learns that Rachel was his uncle Laban's youngest daughter. Uncle Laban arrives, and hugs and kisses are shared all around.

The two men strike a deal: for seven years labor, Jacob receives Rachel as his bride. However, on the night of the wedding, Laban secretly switches his younger daughter for the older, Leah (the Bible describes her as the one with weak eyes). A week later Laban allows Jacob to marry Rachel as his second wife. Laban also demands another seven years labor as the bride price for Rachel, Jacob's true love.

For the next dozen years, the sisters (Leah and Rachel) compete for Jacob's attention by producing children. Leah produces four children while Rachel is childless. Rachel, like Jacob's grandmother, Sarah, is barren. And, like Sarah, Rachel commissions her servant to bear children with Jacob for her. After two children are born to Rachel's servant, Leah sends her own servant to Jacob and two more children are born. Leah herself conceives again and

Life happens! It happens with hugs and kisses as well as betrayal and deception. This chapter in Jacob's life is filled with common and real issues as well as practical wisdom for daily life as it unfolds across the years. The central themes of Jacob's years of maturing are conflict and trouble. Conflict embeds itself in Jacob's life. Whether in his birth home of Isaac and Rebekah or his second home with Laban,

again, and two more boys are born. Leah conceives once more and gives birth to the only daughter in the family. At last, Rachel bears her first child, the favored son, Joseph.

During this time of sister-rivalry and multiple babies, Jacob works for his father-in-law, Laban. The men strike a deal concerning the sheep and goats. Jacob receives the spotted and speckled animals. Jacob uses striped sticks at mating time, and the herd produces an exceptional number of spotted and speckled young. In this way, Jacob grows in wealth while Laban's prosperity diminishes.

With the birth of Jacob's favored son, Joseph, and the shift of wealth from Laban to Jacob, Laban's attitude toward Jacob changes. At this point, the Lord instructs Jacob to gather his family and return to the home of his parents, Isaac and Rebekah. Jacob's family leaves without a word to Laban. Laban pursues them. When they meet, suspicion rules the day. Accusations fly. Laban's household gods are missing. Rachel has stolen and hidden them. Pervasive mistrust results in an unsettling treaty between Laban and Jacob. Yet, this is family. Therefore, in spite of the suspicion, there is another round of hugs and kisses before they part.

Jacob lives in struggle. Days roll into weeks, months, and years, which pile up in decades. The story of Jacob reminds us of our own stories. Consider two hard truths about life: first, not everyone likes you, and second, you do not always fit in. Jacob understood these facts.

Not everyone likes you. Some conflicts will not be resolved. "Can we all get along?" lamented Rodney King[1] in response to the national controversy over the way the police treated him. It is true that some people seem to live free of conflict; they just get along with everyone. Others go along to get along. Still others scoot under the radar or vanish when the dark mist of disagreement rolls in. This is not so with Jacob or with most of us. Perhaps you have also learned that not everybody likes you. That's life!

Jacob's life was embroiled in conflict. He battled his father-in-law, Laban. He did not choose the fight, but the fight found him. Like escalating conflict in our lives, the two meet with warm greetings but part with an uneasy truce. At first Jacob rejoiced when he found his relatives. Twenty years later Jacob and his father-in-law parted ways with angry accusations, threats, and a dubious détente. Imagine suspicion in their hearts and scowls on their faces as the father-in-law sets up the terms of the truce:

> **LABAN:** May the Eternal One watch us when we are away from one another. If you *in any way* mistreat my daughters or if you take wives in addition to my daughters, even though no one else is with us, remember that God is a witness between you and me.
>
> See this pile *of stones* and this pillar which I have set between us. This pile is a witness and this pillar is a witness that I will not pass beyond this pile *of stones* to harm you, and you will not pass beyond this pile and this pillar to harm me. May the God of Abraham and the God of Nahor (the

> God of their father *Terah*) serve as judge between us. (Gen. 31:49–53)

This is not a sweet family farewell. This is a cautionary armistice between warring parties. For Jacob and Laban, a parting of the way between them, the two tricksters, both members of the same family, is best for all concerned. They intend to never see one another again.

We do not care for stories of unresolved conflict. In beautiful churches with lovely songs and gracious words, we romanticize that all conflict can be resolved. Truth be told, some conflict will not be resolved.

One story of unresolved conflict features New Testament heroes Paul and Barnabas. Barnabas introduced Paul to the leaders of the Christian church. Together they began the missionary movement that launched the gospel of Christ into the world. God's hand moved through them, changing lives, bringing miracles, and advancing the kingdom of Christ.

Yet, they had a falling out. The issue that divided them was young John Mark, a member of the extended family of Barnabas. John Mark, who accompanied Paul and Barnabas on their missionary tour, was unable to keep up with the rigors of missionary work. Barnabas, ever the encourager, voted to give the young man another chance. Paul would not put the enterprise at risk. "Their difference of opinion was so heated that they decided not to work together anymore" (Acts 15:39).

Unresolved conflict is a burden, a strain, and a worry. It is best to resolve conflict, to "go to your brother, *repent and forgive one another,* be reconciled" (Matt. 5:24). Nevertheless, there are situations, painful situations, when resolution cannot be forged. Over the decades of your life, you will in all likelihood encounter a conflict that will not be resolved. How does one press on in faith when he cannot resolve a conflict?

We know "how good and pleasant it is when brothers *and sisters* live together in peace" (Ps. 133:1). Yet, there are times when peace fails, when our attempts to produce harmony miscarry, and when our futile efforts exacerbate the problem. As with Jacob's experience, family members choose sides, gossip, or sanctimoniously dismiss themselves from the clash.

At such a time, the pain in the heart may believe that "even my best friend, my confidant who has eaten my bread will stab me in the back" (Ps. 41:9). At such a time, hold steady and stay on the Lord's path. "O Eternal One, lead me in *the path of* Your righteousness amidst those who wish me harm; make Your way clear to me" (Ps. 5:8).

How do we live with unresolved conflict? Jesus provides the kingdom response, the perspective that matures the soul and advances God's purpose: "And when everyone speaks well of you, you are in danger for their ancestors spoke well of the false prophets too. If you're listening, here's My message: Keep loving your enemies no matter what they do. Keep doing good to those who hate you" (Luke 6:26–27).

We are in the world, but not of the world. In simple terms, as followers of Christ, we do not always fit in. We are out of place. The world has a system, and we are not part of it. The world knows it. We build our lives among people who do not think like we think, who do not believe as we believe, and who do not live as we live.[2] And we have to deal with it.

Centuries after Jacob's life, Joshua gathered God's people in the valley of Shechem. The valley contains Jacob's well on land given to his favored son, Joseph (John 4:4–6). In this valley, Joshua assembled all the tribes of Israel, and they presented themselves to the Lord.

In Joshua's speech, he called on the memory of Abraham, Isaac, and Jacob as he challenged God's people:

> So remember: fear the Eternal and serve Him sincerely and faithfully. Put away from you any gods your ancestors served across the *Euphrates* River or in Egypt, and serve only Him. If you decide that you're not willing to serve Him, then today is the day for you to choose whom you will serve, whether the gods your ancestors bowed to in the land beyond the great River, or the gods of the Amorites whose country you possess. But as for me and my family, we will serve the Eternal. (Josh. 24:14–15)

In the country of his uncle Laban, Jacob lives among "the gods your ancestors bowed to in the land beyond the great River." Jacob, like Joshua, dedicated his life to the God of Abraham and Isaac when the Lord spoke to him through the door of heaven (Gen. 28:10–22). Uncle Laban, however, worships the gods of his forefathers. Laban's family deals in magic; Leah and Rachel bargain for mandrakes to aid conception (Gen. 30:14–18). Rachel steals Laban's household gods, perhaps to assure her inheritance or, perhaps, for the security of old ways (Gen. 31:19).

Uncle Laban uses a magic spell and divination. These are the old ways of the ancient gods. Much to Laban's surprise, he discovers that the prosperity Jacob brings to the family is a blessing from the Lord God (Gen. 30:27). Jacob lives among people of the old ways. And even Jacob employs specially crafted sticks to influence the genetics of the sheep and goats. "In this way, Jacob grew extremely rich, and he ended up with very large flocks, male and female slaves, and camels and donkeys too" (Gen. 30:43).

In a land of paganism, living with a family

We should be pained and concerned with the mingling of secularism in our New Testament faith.

who still clings to ancient gods, magic spells, and incantations, Jacob faces the challenges of declaring that his household will serve the God of Abraham and Isaac.

We do not live in a land of ancient gods, but a land with no god, a land of secularism. For us, we learn to follow our Lord Jesus Christ in a conventional world of secularism. Secularism creeps up and attaches itself to the true faith of the New Testament.

- It is one thing to believe there is a God as many secularists believe. It is something quite different to believe God for all of life.
- It is quite conventional to have faith in faith, to believe it and achieve it.[3] For New Testament believers, we place faith in Christ, the promise and purpose of God.
- It is a secular spirituality to follow a path of helping yourself.[4] This is quite different from trusting the Spirit of God in all things.

Jacob's admixture of the old gods and the Lord of heaven stirs a bit of discomfort in us. Perhaps we should be just as pained and concerned with the mingling of secularism in our New Testament faith. George Holyoake coined the term *secularism* and defined it in 1896. This definition exposes the faith of many people in our nation and even in our churches:

> Secularism is a code of duty pertaining to this life, founded on considerations purely human, and intended mainly for those who find theology indefinite or inadequate, unreliable or unbelievable. Its essential principles are three: (1) The improvement of this life by material means. (2) That science is the available Providence of man. (3) That it is good to do good. Whether there be other good or not, the good of the present life is good, and it is good to seek that good.[5]

We are not secularists! We live under the guidance of the Holy Spirit in a secular world; we are, in effect, aliens on earth (Eph. 2:19; Heb. 11:13; 1 Peter 2:11). Jesus prays for us, for our protection from the evil one, and for our mission in partnership with Him. He prays for us because we live in the world where we do not fit in, indeed, cannot fit in:

> **JESUS:** I have given them Your word; and the world has despised them because they are not products of the world, in the same way that I am not a product of the corrupt world order. Do not take them out of this world; protect them from the evil one.
>
> Like Me, they are not products of the corrupt world order. Immerse them in the truth, the truth Your voice speaks. In the same way You sent Me into this world, I am sending them. (John 17:14–18)

How do we live with fidelity to God when life presses us into conflict with people and with the culture? Further, in the conflict, how do we mature in faith as we press on with life in God? (Phil. 3:12–14). Let me draw out four practical lessons from Jacob's sojourn in the country with Uncle Laban that apply to our lives today:

1. We overcome injustice with God's wisdom.
2. We handle life's stress through faith in God.
3. We deal with money by honoring the Lord.
4. We live each day with our eyes on God.

INJUSTICE IN LIFE AND WISDOM IN GOD

Jacob's relatives welcomed him. The Bible pictures a reunion of family members who have never met, complete with vows of family fidelity: "You are surely my flesh and bone!" (Gen. 29:14).

Passion kindled between Jacob and Rachel. Within a month, Laban spied the blush of their tender glances. He stealthily sold Jacob on a wage for his work. Jacob, as Laban anticipated, requested his work be counted as a bride price for Rachel. The future father-in-law agrees with a twinkle of treachery in his eye.

The seven years pass of laboring for the bride price. You can imagine growing expectancy between Jacob and Rachel. The wedding arrives. And Laban, the old con artist and gifted flimflam man, pulls the ultimate bait and switch. On the night of the wedding, he slips the wrong sister into the tent and under the camel skin blanket (Gen. 29:15–29).

The crafty old man marries off his older daughter with the weak eyes (v. 17). If Jacob wants to marry Rachel, it will cost him another seven years labor. In fairness, arrangements are made for the passionate couple to be united. Seven days after the first wedding, there is another wedding for Jacob and Rachel. Thus, Rachel receives the dubious honor of being the second wife. No doubt, Laban's fraud creates tension in Jacob's home. Consider the complicated relationships hinted at in verse 30: "Then Jacob also slept with Rachel, and he clearly loved Rachel more than Leah. *As agreed,* he served Laban for another seven years."

When Jacob discovered he had been tricked, emotions of disappointment, betrayal, and anger exploded: "What have you done to me? Did we not have a deal—*seven years of* labor in exchange for *your daughter* Rachel? Why have you deceived me?" (v. 25).

Jacob's emotions are understandable, but could there be more to it than the deception of his father-in-law? Perhaps Jacob felt a tinge of guilt, a sense of the tables being turned, and a moment of getting his comeuppance. Jacob's mother, Rebekah, and his uncle, now father-in-law, Laban, rival one another in the skills of duplicity and betrayal. Is Jacob wise enough to realize he is inheriting a legacy of deception as well as marrying into a family of trickery? Both his wives use their own tricks and deception.[6]

In MBA (master of business administration) programs and leadership classes, there is a classic essay students read and discuss: "How Come Every Time I Get Stabbed in the Back, My Fingerprints Are on the Knife?"[7] The endpoint of the class discussion of the essay is not complaints about injustice. Injustice happens to all people. The point to take home is what to learn from the injustice.

God's fingerprints are not found on the design of Laban's deception, but God's wisdom speaks through Jacob's troubles. God's wisdom speaks through your troubles if your spiritual ears are open. Stand on God's wisdom when you face difficulties and injustice, and you grow through the storm, the wind, and the floods. Leaning on God's wisdom in difficulty expands your soul. Jesus concluded His Sermon on the Mount with these words: "Those people who are listening to Me, those people who *hear what I say and* live according to My teachings—you are like a wise man who built his house on a rock, *on a firm foundation. When storms hit,* rain pounded down and waters rose, *levies broke* and winds beat all the walls of that house. But the house did not fall because it was built upon rock" (Matt. 7:24–25).

God's fingerprints are not found on the design of Laban's deception, but God's wisdom speaks through Jacob's troubles.

During a time of pain and distress in my own life, a lovely, wise, and gracious Southern woman reminded me, "You need a little suffering to season you." Jacob had just that, a season of suffering. Torrents fall, rivers flood, and hurricane season passes through. You have had and will have again a season of suffering. What have you learned from suffering and injustice about life, yourself, and God? How has your heart grown? To mature through life's conflicts, seek God's wisdom in the tempest.

STRESS IN LIFE AND FAITH IN GOD

The next phase of Jacob's life is as stressful as you might imagine. He has two wives, which has to be a stressful arrangement. Each wife has a servant girl. The wives compete to be the favorite wife. The women believe the contest will be decided by the propagation of children. In order, the births come as follows:

- Leah bears the first four children.
- Rachel's servant births two children.
- Leah's servant produces two children.
- Leah herself has three more, including the only girl, Dinah.
- At last, Rachel gives birth to Joseph, the favored son.

You can't make this up.

We all deal with stress. What is stress? I remember a story my father told in a sermon of a significant meeting of scientists who determined to define stress. At an international meeting, scientists from a host of disciplines, including psychiatry, psychology, physiology, anatomy, and medicine, invested their first full day of meeting filling blackboards, debating, considering, and dealing with complex information and theories. On the morning of the second day, the arguing continued. Halfway through the second day, almost in exhaustion, the scientists put down their charts, their reams of data, and their complex theories. At last, they came to agreement: stress is life, and so you had better learn how to live with it.

When I was in college a new book on stress was released from a Harvard professor and became quite the rage: *The Relaxation Response*.[8] In the book, Dr. Herbert Benson described how in moments of stress we turn to fight or flight,[9] an accepted theory from forty years earlier. Dr. Benson's book updated the accepted theory. He proposed that in addition to fight or flight, there is a third response to stress: relax! His theory, the relaxation response, became the basis for a secular form of meditation.

I remember thinking about this idea as it turned over and over in my head. I knew there was something here, but I also knew there was more to it than talking ourselves into a relaxed state. I also knew there was a deep and biblical practice of meditation,[10] quieting the mind and focusing on God.

- God's world: "I gaze to the skies and meditate on Your creation" (Ps. 8:3).
- God's Word: "I *study and* meditate on Your testimonies" (Ps. 119:99).
- God's wonders: "I will meditate on Your wonders, *sing songs of Your worth*" (Ps. 145:5).

In a stress-filled world, there is something calming, reassuring, and maturing about thinking about God's world, God's Word, and God's wonders. In one of my earliest sermons, I shared this discovery in Scripture: under stress you can fight, or you can flee, or you can put your faith in God. Unfortunately, through the decades, the term *meditation* has become a conflicted term filled with a jumbled assortment of contradictory meanings.

Nevertheless, the Scriptures teach the ideal of meditating on the wisdom, the decrees, the creation, and the way of the Lord.[11] For Christians, to meditate is to focus, contemplate, and think deeply on God's words, works, and wisdom. Christians meditate when they reflect, ruminate, and remember the presence, power, and purpose of God.

Focusing on God changes our perspective and attitude in the midst of stress. Filling our thoughts with faithful beliefs and memories of God's presence creates calm. Prayerful meditation releases inner strength. Conflict creates stress. We can fall prey to stress, or we can mature through stress. The psalmist describes stress and the faith-filled relaxation response:

> How long will you attack a man?
> How long will all of you strive to crush your prey
> when he's like a leaning fence or a wall on the
> verge of collapse?
> Their only purpose *in life* is to knock him down from
> his prominent position;
> they love deceit.
> *When others are around,* they speak a blessing *on*
> *someone,*
> but inwardly they are mumbling a curse.
>
> My soul quietly waits for the True God alone
> because I hope only in Him.
> He alone is my rock and deliverance,
> my citadel *high on a hill*;
> I will not be shaken. (Ps. 62:3–6)

THE POWER OF MONEY AND THE CHOICE OF MASTERS

A third source of conflict in our lives is money. The meaning we give to money also carries the potential of increasing spiritual maturity. When money changes hands, personalities change. Jacob found it so. His cousins become jealous as they saw their wealth transferred into Jacob's account. The tension grows between Jacob and his father-in-law. Accusations fly as twenty years of working together erupt in rage. The tension is so aggressive that God steps in and tells Jacob it is time to leave.

> *As time went on,* Jacob overheard what Laban's sons were saying *about him.*
>
> **LABAN'S SONS:** Jacob has taken everything that belonged to our father; he gained all his wealth from *taking advantage of* him.
>
> And Jacob also noticed a change in how Laban looked at him and treated him. He seemed colder toward him than before.
>
> **ETERNAL ONE** *(to Jacob)*: *You must now* return to the land of your ancestors and to your own family. I will be with you *always.* (Gen. 31:1–3)

A common misquotation of a verse of Scripture goes, "Money is the root of evil." The misquotation certainly feels true when your family is in the midst of a contentious settlement of an estate or bickering over the family business. However, the Bible never says that money is evil. It does say that our perspective, our attitude, and our motivation concerning money can cause evil:

> But those who chase riches are constantly falling into temptation and snares. They are regularly caught by their own stupid and

harmful desires, dragged down and pulled under into ruin and destruction. For the love of money—*and what it can buy*—is the root of all sorts of evil. Some already have wandered away from the true faith because they craved what it had to offer; *but when reaching for the prize,* they found their *hands and* hearts pierced with many sorrows. (1 Tim. 6:9–10)

The love of money and all money can buy is the cause of much suffering and cruelty. For those who have not found a way to tether their money to the guidance of their faith, money will always be trouble. It is not the money itself that is the problem; it is the meaning attached to the money, the love of the power, possessions, and prestige that the money affords.

The controlling power of money is expressed in a story reported in Jacob Needleman's book *Money and the Meaning of Life.* Dr. Needleman, a professor of philosophy at San Francisco State University, finds a profound message in an old third-rate western titled, *Waterhole #3.*[12]

The comedy is loosely based on the classic film, *The Good, The Bad, The Ugly.* It is not a great film but did bring together a collection of well-known actors including James Coburn as an exuberant card shark and Carroll O'Conner as the greedy sheriff.

The plot builds on comic twists and tangled relationships. Three men in the Arizona desert steal a shipment of gold and bury it near Waterhole #3. Coburn discovers their map to the treasure scrawled on a twenty-dollar bill.

What follows are the bungling efforts of the pair of thieves, the local sheriff's department, an Armenian shoemaker, a gun-toting madam, the U.S. Cavalry, and, of course, the

It is never "only money," unless it is someone else's money.

Sheriff's vivacious daughter. Everyone is greedy and conniving. The gold changes hands several times.

As Professor Needleman points out, it is the last scene of the film that is worthy of our attention:

> All their absurd gambits and conspiracies have failed, and only James Coburn has come out ahead. They have all been greedy, but only Coburn never really forgets his aim of getting all the money for himself. All the others are at one point or another deflected from their greed by fears, emotions, fantasies, and wishful thinking. At the same time, Coburn is the only one who is able to separate himself enough from his desire for the money to allow himself some moments of tenderness for the girl and compassion for her comically beleaguered father.
>
> As he is about to cross the border to safety, Coburn turns around in his saddle to face the viewer. "Maybe we take gold too seriously," he says to us with a smile. Then, amid the hoofbeats, shrieks, and gunshots coming from the horde of people chasing him, he calmly turns around again as the camera closes in on him. He is now quite serious, almost stern. His final words to us are: "We don't take gold seriously enough,"
>
> He rides off and the film ends.[13]

Dr. Needleman's point is one we should underline: we must take money seriously. Money has enormous impact on our lives. It is part and parcel of everything we do. I will occasionally see people shrug their shoulders and say, "Well, it's only money."

It is never "only money," unless it is someone else's money. Money is merely the exchange of effort for something you want or need. Sometimes the need is simply to keep the wolf from the door. Sometimes the want is a winter vacation. Money makes possible a college degree for a child and security for the future. Sometimes we want or need a better car. But always, there is something more than just money.

It goes deeper than this. Because money is the exchange of effort for wants and needs, it touches us at a deep personal level. Our wants and needs express our hopes and fears, our identity and purpose. When your money is on the table, your heart is on the table. Money has a unique way of revealing your inner person. "No one can serve two masters. *If you try,* you will wind up loving the first master and hating the second, or vice versa. People try to serve both God and money—but you can't. *You must choose one or the other*" (Matt. 6:24).

TRUST IN GOD FOR ALL OF LIFE

An early Christian father, Irenaeus of Lyons, is credited with a saying that has become popular in the last several years: "The glory of God is a human being who is fully alive." Actually, the translation is not accurate. What the ancient Christian leader was saying is far more profound than God's desire for human fulfillment. The church leader was teaching that God's vision is the purpose of our lives. Here is a better translation of the church father's saying:

> *Gloria Dei est vivens homo*
> (The glory of God is a living human being.)
> *Vita hominis visio Dei*
> (The life of a human being is the vision of God.)[14]

God's vision is the fulfillment of His intention for the world and all people. And, we are His partners in this great endeavor. Life in this fallen world comes with conflict, pressures, stress, tragedy, fear, and pain. In the midst of all these things, the source of life, God Himself, is bigger than our difficulties, our stress, and our money.

There was one final lesson from Jacob's twenty years of maturing: he came to see God in all things. In these years of conflict and stress, Jacob and his family called upon the Lord again and again. God is referred to more than two dozen times in these chapters.[15] Here is a lesson in learning to see God in our lives. Jesus instructs us to look for the light of God and to share the light of God: "The eye is the lamp of the body. *You draw light into your body through your eyes, and light shines out to the world through your eyes.* So if your eye is well *and shows you what is true*, then your whole body will be filled with light" (Matt. 6:22).

SUMMARY: Are You Still with Me?

Maturing is hard. How many times must a baby fall before her legs and balance are mature enough to walk? Further, it is the falling that strengthens her legs and balance. There is no easy street to Christian maturity. The journey is laced with troubles, conflict, worries, and stress. The tempter would like us to believe that God has abandoned us. The truth is that God is leading us. He is still with us: "The Spirit led Him from place to place in the desert, and while there, the devil tempted Jesus" (Luke 4:2). Life happens! We can complain and grumble our way through it or look for God in it. If you look, you find that He is with you.

THINK: Conversation and Reflection

1. Jacob struggled in conflict with people and the culture. What are the conflicts with people and culture you have faced in the past? Did God use the difficulties to help you grow as a Christian?

What conflicts are you facing today? How do you think God will use your current struggles?

2. This chapter speaks of trouble with injustice, stress, and money. What struggles have you had with these issues in the past? What did you learn from your struggles? Are you currently struggling with injustice, stress, or money? What would you like to ask God about your struggle?

3. This chapter outlines three spiritual disciplines for dealing with life:

   - When wronged, look for God's wisdom.
   - When stressed, meditate on God's words and works.
   - When dealing with money, put God first.

   In what ways have you found these disciplines helpful in your life? What other spiritual disciplines help you with your daily life?

4. Think about and discuss practical issues concerning the light of God in daily life (Matt. 6:22).

   - When is it easy and natural for your inner eye to spot the light of God?
   - When is it difficult for your inner eye to find the light of God?
   - What can we do to help each other improve our spiritual eyesight so that our whole lives "will be filled with light" (Matt. 6:22)?

Looking Ahead: On the return home, overwhelmed by the fear of meeting his estranged and dangerous brother, Jacob experiences the greatest encounter with God in the book of Genesis.

THE WOUND OF GOD

Is This the Price of Blessing?

Yet it was our suffering he carried,
 our pain and distress, our sick-to-the-soul-ness.
We just figured that God had rejected him,
 that God was the reason he hurt so badly.
But he was hurt because of us; *he suffered so.*
 Our wrongdoing *wounded and* crushed him.
He endured the breaking that made us whole.
 The injuries he suffered became our healing.
 —Isaiah 53:4–5

Many years ago, I had the opportunity to participate in the executive program of the Ross School of Business on the campus of the University of Michigan, Ann Arbor. The topic of the six-day seminar was leading deep change.[1] The presenters were professors Robert Quinn and Jeff DeGraff. The essence of the seminar was this: one person can change the entire organization.

Although he did not realize it, Jacob was about to become the one person who would bring deep and permanent change to his family. Jacob was about to become Israel. Abraham's family of nomads would soon move off the hill country of Canaan and on to the world stage as they journeyed from the promised land into Egypt. Out of Egypt they would emerge as a nation, the nation of Israel. However, before they could become the nation of Israel, Jacob had to become the man Israel.

THE STORY IN SUMMARY
Genesis 32:1–32

Jacob, with his two wives (Rachel and Leah) and his twelve children, leaves his home of twenty years. Jacob had arrived as a fugitive with nothing. He was received into the family of Laban with hugs and kisses. Now, two decades later, the two men part company with a vow to never deal with one another again.

On the journey, word comes to Jacob that his brother Esau is traveling toward him. Jacob had stolen his brother's birthright and his brother threatened to kill him. The report arrives in Jacob's camp that Esau is traveling with an army of four hundred men.

Jacob makes preparations by dividing his camp into two parts, believing that if his brother attacked one, the other could escape. He also sends word to Esau, hoping to make peace. Indeed, he arranges for a series of peace offerings to be presented to his brother in the morning.

Finally, Jacob sends all of his family and belongings across the brook where he is camped, leaving himself as an easy target for a late-night assassin. In fact, someone slips into the camp of Jacob and wrestles with him all night. In the morning, we learn that the stranger was God Himself. God gives Jacob a new name, Israel, because he has struggled with God and man.

The classroom at the Ross School of Business was filled with C-level executives[2] from multinational companies representing oil, finance, trade, and entrepreneurship. Then, there I was, a seminary professor feeling somewhat out of place but honored to be part of the program. We discussed, debated, and dealt with the issue of deep and profound change in our organizations and in ourselves. We looked at the causes, ethics, and models of change. We explored why people resist and respond to the need for change.

On the last morning Dr. DeGraff summarized the dynamics of change in a simple sentence that I will always remember. He said, "People only change for two reasons: they are in love or they are in trouble."

The two dynamics of change filled Jacob's life; Jacob loved Rachel and baby Joseph, and Jacob lived with troubles all his life. He had troubles with his parents, his brother, his father-in-law, his wives, and his cousins.

At the point in his life where we pick up the story in this chapter, Jacob is on a journey (Gen. 32:1). On the journey, he is surrounded by trouble behind him and before him. Behind him was a line in the sand, a marker on the road that signified the continuing conflict with his father-in-law (Gen. 31:45–50) and his cousins. Before him was his brother Esau (Gen. 32:3) carrying a quarter-century-old grudge and death threat. J. R. R. Tolkien put well in *The Hobbit*: "Escaping goblins to be caught by wolves!"[3]

Can you find your story in Jacob's story? Do you know what it is to be between the rock on one side and a hard place on the other?[4] Do you know the choice between frying pan and fire? The place reeks of fear and insecurity. Nevertheless, the place is filled with spiritual potential for Jacob and for us. For Jacob, this place between angry brother and angry father-in-law was: 1) a spiritual journey, 2) spiritual maturity, and 3) a spiritual struggle.

THE SPIRITUAL JOURNEY

I like road trips. They are a time to have conversations that seem to be reserved for a long journey in the car. On a long journey, you have time to remember and reflect. And so, "Jacob went on his way . . ." (Gen. 32:1).

Imagine Jacob's reflections and memories on this journey away from the land of his father-in-law and back to the land of his birth. A journey offers time to think deeply. Jacob has a lot of thinking to do.

Maturity does not result from experience, but comes from reflecting on experience in order to learn from experience. Because of this dynamic, all acquired wisdom is painful. All practical wisdom comes at a price. The painful wisdom extracted from Jacob's experience reveals a clear lesson for your life and mine: pain and blessing are cronies. Blessing and pain are buddies. They hang out together, confer with one another, and are seldom separated. Notice how this bit of practical wisdom comes through in the life of Jacob:

- He escaped the murderous plan of his brother to be captivated by the beauty of Rachel.
- He was exiled from the home of his parents to be lovingly received into his uncle's family.
- His mother, Rebekah, used deception to win his father's blessing while his mother's brother, Laban, deceived him on his wedding night.
- He lived with the continuous rivalry of his two wives for two decades, which resulted in the blessing of a large family.
- He received a large amount of wealth as well as false accusations from his cousins.

By reflecting on his experience, Jacob learned that pain and blessing are comrades. In addition to reflecting, Jacob also remembered his encounter with God. On this journey Jacob was retracing his steps into exile from many years before. He remembered the lonely night when he was a fugitive, a refugee, and God came to him. The heavens were opened, and he saw the angels ascending and descending. The memory was from long ago. Yet, the memory comes back to life with new vigor and consecration at this place on his journey.

Jacob remembers and rehearses the night from long ago, the night God made a promise to bless Jacob, and the night Jacob made a promise to be faithful to God. The old memory of a stone of covenant with God comforts Jacob in the wake of the turmoil over the newly raised stone of discontent with his father-in-law. "If God is going to be with me, keeping me *safe* on this journey and giving me bread to eat and clothing to wear so that I return to my father's house in peace, then the Eternal will be my God. And this stone I have made into a pillar will be *the first stone laid in* God's house" (Gen. 28:20–22).

The journey of the soul requires reflecting and remembering, and also renewing vows of consecration. God honors Jacob's journey toward his birth home by again sending angels to Jacob: "As he went, messengers of God met him *along the way*. When Jacob saw them, he acknowledged that this was God's camp, so he named that place Mahanaim, *which means 'two camps*'" (Gen. 32:1–2). What a gracious image: God and Jacob travel together, side by side. This is the way of the spiritual journey.

SPIRITUAL MATURITY

When the wrong in your past catches up with you, it is awkward at best, deadly at worst. Jacob's past was just over the horizon. Brother Esau was near. The situation was worse than awkward.

Step into the situation with your own story. God's forgiveness of your sin is complete and eternal. However, in this fallen world, the consequences of your wrong may dog you for decades. This is

Jacob's experience. He has a choice: run or face it. To run, he would have to abandon all he held dear: his family and fortune. To face it meant he put everything at risk. Now was the time to face the past. He learned the truth of William Faulkner's most famous line, "The past is never dead. It's not even past."[5]

Here we pick up the story. Jacob prepares to meet Esau. This meeting has no guarantees and no assurances. Jacob frets and fears because he is vulnerable. The gap between resentment and reconciliation swirls in a bubbling cauldron of ambivalence and anxiety. At this moment, Jacob is headed home to a place he has never been, a place of reunion with Esau.

To grasp the picture, you need an understanding of Esau. Think warlord in the mountains of Afghanistan with four hundred armed men riding camels and horses. Esau's ancient storm troopers thunder their way toward Jacob and his wives and children and servants and herds. Facing the gathering clouds of fear and death, this moment would test anyone's mettle.

Yet, at this moment we see it, the burgeoning maturity of Jacob. The twenty years in exile from his birth home have nurtured painful lessons in wisdom and experience. His maturity serves as an example for us.

Maturity when dealing with an enemy. Not everyone has enemies, but most folks do. How we deal with enemies both shapes and tests our maturity. We see new maturity in the way Jacob makes first contact with Esau.

> **JACOB** *(to his messengers)*: This is what I want you to say to my master Esau: "Your servant Jacob says this: 'I have lived with Laban as a foreigner and stayed *there working for him* until now. I have oxen, donkeys, flocks, and male and female slaves. I have sent my messengers to inform you, my master,

of all this so that I might regain your trust and favor.'" (Gen. 32:4–5)

Meeting an old enemy, especially an estranged family member, is like making first contact with an alien from another world or traveling back in H. G. Wells's time machine.[6] What do you say to someone whose heart is angry and closed? Much to our surprise, Jacob does not follow conventional counsel. There are plenty of people who might tell Jacob to vilify yourself and beg for pity. Jacob surprises us; he does not follow established advice. Instead, he makes no amends, he does not grovel, and we see no evidence of remorse at all.

Take the challenge to heart. If you were Jacob, what message would you send to Esau? How would you make first contact with an old enemy? If you have been in this spot, you know that the conventional prescription of confession, groveling, and demeaning yourself is not always a good, wise, or best choice. Before you fall on the ground, you must measure the ground upon which you fall.

It is difficult to step into a place where there is no promise of grace. When we come before God, we rest in His promise that He will forgive and restore. Before God, it is right, wise, and good to confess all, fall on the mercy seat (Eph. 1:7), and commit our eternal being into the Lord's hands (Rom. 10:9). God's promise is trustworthy. His grace is sufficient. The ground is solid. We come to Him in utter faith that He will receive us. Scripture says, "Everyone who calls on the name of the Lord will be saved" (Rom. 10:13, also Joel 2:32).

A telling and difficult demonstration of spiritual maturity is in how we deal with our enemies.

When you attempt to reconcile with an enemy, the ground is unstable and uncertain; there may be no promise of grace on which to trust. So, how do you first approach an old enemy? Do you lead with contrition, sorrow, some act of penitence, and blurt out your intention to do anything it takes to make it right? This is the way to approach God, but what about a human enemy?

Jesus instructs us to make things right with an enemy and to do so quickly: "Therefore, if you are bringing an offering to God and you remember that your brother is angry at you or holds a grudge against you, then leave your gift before the altar, go to your brother, *repent and forgive one another,* be reconciled, and then return to the altar to offer your gift to God" (Matt. 5:23–24).

Reconciliation is the purpose and priority. Jacob seeks reconciliation with his brother. Eventually, Jacob bows before his brother. In response, his brother embraces him (Gen. 33:3–4). But at this point, the first contact, the situation is delicate.

Jacob, as a first approach, chooses deference over contrition. He chooses courteous respect and gracious submission as his opening request for peace. This is vastly different from the Jacob who relied on deception and denial so many years ago.

A telling and difficult demonstration of spiritual maturity is in how we deal with our enemies. Jesus did not envision life without enemies, but He did live and teach that our enemies are an opportunity to live true to our best. "I'm challenging that. I'm telling you to love your enemies. Let them bring out the best in you, not the worst" (Matt. 5:44 The Message).

Maturity in prayer. Jacob's new maturity shines through in his prayer. The messengers return from Esau, and the news is not good. Jacob's sincere gesture of respect and submission opens the ground to reveal Esau's intentions. Esau marches toward him in full force. In a desperate measure, Jacob divides his family and his belongings into two camps, hoping that if one is attacked and destroyed the other will have an opportunity to escape. What else can he do?

Jacob prays.

His prayer is the longest prayer in the book of Genesis. It is the prayer of God's desperate partner at the end of his rope with nowhere to turn except to call on the God who has called him, blessed him, and promised him a future. There is maturity in this prayer unseen in Jacob's younger years.

The wisdom of the long view. Jacob places the crisis of the moment in the context of God's presence in the past and God's promise for the future: "O God of my father Abraham and God of my father Isaac, O Eternal One who said to me, '*You must now* return to the land of your ancestors and to your own family. I will make good things happen for you'" (Gen. 32:9).

Jacob's prayer is about more than just himself. When faced with overwhelming crisis, it is a common Christian cliché to declare, "It's not about me." This is a fine sentiment, and I appreciate it. However, it is possible that the phrase may become a subtle excuse to abdicate, dismiss ourselves, and shun our responsibility in the crisis. Jacob's approach is different: "It is not about me; it is about more than me." He knows he carries the seed of Abraham back to the land of promise. When facing our most difficult moment, we cannot abandon our responsibility. We carry the seed of Christ (Gal. 3:29).

The comfort of God's goodness. Jacob places the crisis in the hands of God's faithfulness and goodness: "*I know* I am not worthy *of even a little* of all of the loyal love and faithfulness You have shown to me, Your servant. *You have already blessed me* because I *left home and*

When facing our greatest fears, we need the comfort of God's love.

crossed the Jordan with nothing except my staff. Now I have grown into two large camps" (Gen. 32:10).

Jacob recognizes that he is the least, the younger son, yet he has received abundance. God, in loyalty and kindness, embraces Jacob. In the counseling center at the seminary where I taught some years ago, a local sculptor crafted a larger-than-life size image of Jesus in a seated position. It was large enough and strong enough for children and even adults to curl up in the lap of Jesus.

The location of the statue became somewhat of a sacred place. If faculty or students passed through and someone was sitting in the lap of Jesus, everyone treated the moment with reverence and respect. We all knew that a broken heart and a fractured life were trusting Christ for healing. When facing our greatest fears, we need the comfort of God's love.

The cry of the heart. In the context of God's plan, and in the arms of God's love, Jacob now speaks the cry of his heart: "Rescue me now, please, from the hand of my brother, from the grip of Esau. I am afraid that he may come and crush us all, the children alongside their mothers. *Remember* You told me, 'I will make good things happen for you and make your descendants as many as the *grains of* sand on the shores, which are too numerous to count'" (vv. 11–12).

Jacob displays an attitude in prayer that I want to emulate; he is at one and the same time submissive and bold! He lays bare his fear. He grips tight God's promise. He prays as a partner with God.

THE SPIRITUAL STRUGGLE

All has been leading up to one moment, the night Jacob will struggle with God. The memories and reflections on the journey, the fears and confidence in prayer—all this prepares the heart and mind of Jacob for what is about to happen next.

Jacob sends an emissary to make first contact with his old rival, brother Esau. Jacob renews his covenant with God in prayer. Now, he prepares the practical gesture of a peace offering for his brother. He sends gifts, more gifts, lavish gifts, indeed, a caravan of gifts. He thought, "I might be able to appease Esau with these gifts. He will see them before he sees me. When I see his face, I'll know whether he'll accept *and forgive* me (Gen. 32:20).

Picture the scene in your mind. Jacob has divided his possessions and flocks into two large camps in the hope that one may escape while the other is destroyed. In addition, he has sent out three additional emissaries, each with lavish gifts for his brother. He sends them one after the other into the setting sun so that they will meet his brother in the morning. Now, he tries to settle down in the camp that includes his own wives and children.

He cannot sleep. He paces back and forth. He has done everything that he knows to do.

Again, he tries to settle down and sleep. But sleep escapes the camp this night.

Ah! Jacob leaps on one more strategy that may give an added opportunity of escape for his own family: "Jacob got up and took his two wives, his two female servants, and his 11 children; and he crossed the Jabbok River. He sent them all *ahead* across the stream along with everything he had; but Jacob *stayed behind,* left alone *in his distress and doubt*" (vv. 22–24).

In this final move, Jacob leaves himself utterly vulnerable and alone. Put yourself in his place: He shudders when he hears the click-clack of stones turned in the stream. Suddenly the snap of a dry branch reverberates through the night. Jacob holds his breath. Long moments pass. Then comes the sound he has feared—soft footfalls in the darkness. The sound paces Jacob's every move.

Jacob is scared, exceptionally scared. His mind imagines assassins Esau has sent to kill him. Then, he wonders if perhaps it is Esau himself who comes for his revenge. Will Esau take his vengeance with a single and merciful plunge of the sword? No, Jacob thinks it will not be quick and with mercy. Esau has been planning for decades. He wants to waken the night with tortured screams and lingering death. At least the screams will warn the family to flee. This is Jacob's last thought before it happens!

The flicker of firelight tricks the eyes. Jacob pulls on the last ounce of courage in his heart and shouts into the blackness:

Is someone there?

Come out from hiding.

Face me, you coward.

Then, he appears, a stranger in the glow of the flames. The Bible understates the drama in a single sentence: "*In the twilight of his anguish,* an *unknown* man wrestled with him until daybreak" (v. 24).

The Bible withholds the identity of the stranger. Only after the battle is done, the sun has risen, and words are exchanged do we learn that the stranger is God Himself: "you have wrestled with God" (v. 28). Jacob anticipated the arrival of his enemy, but it was God who showed up. Jacob was not attacked by an enemy; God mugged Jacob. That experience changed his life.

Jacob and God, partners in heaven's plan to save the world, tussled and grappled through the night. Grandfather Abraham was tested for trust when he obeyed the Lord and took Isaac to the mountain of sacrifice. God stepped in and provided the lamb. Now, Jacob faces his test, the test of his tenacity. Will Jacob go the distance? Can he struggle with God? Can he struggle

God is heaven-bent on saving the world. God has entered into the struggle.

with humanity? Can Jacob join God's struggle to save the world? This is Israel's call; this is our call.

God is heaven-bent on saving the world. God has entered into the struggle.

- The struggle will lead to slavery in Egypt and freedom in the Exodus.
- The struggle winds its way through the successes and eventual failure of the nation of Israel to carry out God's plan.
- The struggle is nailed squarely on the cross of Jesus in one decisive battle with sin, death, and the Devil.

The test of Jacob carries God's question for us: Will you join Him in the struggle? Will you go the distance? Will you partner with God in the battle to save the world? Are you willing to struggle with God?

As daylight breaks across the horizon, God ends the contest by wounding His partner, Jacob. At this point, God remains incognito: "When the man saw he was not winning the battle with Jacob, he struck him on the hip socket, and Jacob's hip was thrown out of joint as he continued to wrestle with him" (Gen. 32:25).

The injury God inflicted was real. The pain Jacob felt was real. The wound foreshadows the partnership between Jacob (Israel) and God and, in the New Testament, between Christians and our Lord. God's people will receive many wounds in the centuries and generations that follow Jacob. In this moment, in this battle, God prepares His wounded healer. Centuries later, Jesus became the wounded one who brings God's deepest desire to the world:

> Yet the Eternal One planned to crush him *all along,*
> to bring him to grief, *this innocent servant of God.*

> When he puts his life in sin's *dark* place, *in the pit of wrongdoing,*
> this servant of God will see his children and have his days prolonged.
> For in His servant's hand, the Eternal's deepest desire will *come to pass and* flourish.
> (Isa. 53:10)

What began in Jacob is completed in Jesus Christ: "He endured the breaking that made us whole. The injuries he suffered became our healing" (v. 5). For Grandfather Abraham, the promise of God rang true: "I am going to put a *special* blessing on you . . . so that you will become a blessing" (Gen. 12:2). For Grandson Jacob, his experience with God speaks loud and clear: I will wound you, and you will be a blessing.

And, Jacob demands the blessing.

We are told very little about the wrestling match between God and Jacob, only the wounded outcome. What follows the night of brawling are three exchanges that hint at the transformation taking place in Jacob.

From bargain to blessing. Jacob possesses his negotiation skills. He knows the moment to voice his demands.

MAN: Let me go; the dawn is breaking.

JACOB: I will not let you go unless you bless me. (Gen. 32:26)

He demands a blessing. Years earlier he stole a blessing from his father, Isaac. The blessing from God is a much weightier matter.

Immature Jacob used a deceptive bargain to acquire the blessing of his father. In our immaturity, we are tempted to make blessings the product of bargains: "I will believe if . . ." and "I will behave when . . ." or "If you bless, then I will . . ." Beneath the immaturity of bargaining for blessings lies a crypt containing a creature more sinister than we realize. Satan bargained with Jesus, "If you are the Son of God, tell these stones to become bread" (Matt. 4:3).

The past with its deceptive bargaining is behind Jacob. At this moment, for Jacob, the longing for blessing came out of his struggle with God. Even after receiving his wound, he would not let go. He would not turn loose of God or the battle with God until he received the blessing.

Jacob has changed, and Jacob's concept of blessing has changed. God had already blessed Jacob when he first saw the angels ascending and descending between heaven and earth.

> I am the Eternal One, the God of Abraham your father and the God of Isaac. The land on which you are now lying is the land I *have promised to* give to you and your descendants. Your descendants will be as many as there are specks of dust on the earth. You will spread out to the west, east, north, and south. Through your descendants, all the families of the earth will find true blessing. Know I am with you, and I will watch over you no matter where you go. *One day* I will bring you back to this land. I will not leave you until I have done all I have promised you. (Gen. 28:13–15)

Jacob's deep need for God's blessing has changed. He is not asking for a new blessing for the old Jacob, but a new blessing for a new man. This blessing is not up for bargain or barter. This is the treasure in heaven "where moths do not attack, where rust does not corrode, and where thieves are barred at the door. For where your treasure is, there your heart will be also" (Matt. 6:20–21).

A new name, a new identity. God does not grant the blessing, at least not yet. Delay is not denial, though it may feel like that sometimes. More work is to be done with Jacob.

MAN: What's your name?

JACOB: Jacob.

MAN: You will no longer go by the name Jacob. From now on, *your name will be* Israel because you have wrestled with God and humanity, and you have prevailed. (Gen. 32:27–28)

Jacob is not the only one with the skill of turning a conversation in a new direction. God is not ready to talk about blessing. He wants to talk about a new name.

We use names as labels, markers for easy reference. A name appointed by God points to the soul's identity. The wrestling match was a prelude to the name. God crept into the camp and picked a fight with Jacob. Out of the struggle, Jacob is ready for a new identity, the identity God has designed for him.

Before receiving the new identity, God requires Jacob to rehearse his old identity: "What's your name?" The old name, Jacob, means "heel," "trickster," "overreacher," or "supplanter."[7] How well Jacob knows the meaning of his name. But things are different now; Jacob is different now. The name must reflect the new man.

He has struggled with God and not given up. He has entered God's struggle and wants a blessing out of it. The scripture reports that the new name is the result of struggling with God and struggling with humanity (Gen. 32:28). The name is almost poetic:

You have striven with God
And with men you have prevailed.[8]

The name describes a partnership with God in the struggle to transform the world. And, so, Jacob becomes Israel. Wrestle with this thought for a moment. Like his grandfather, Abraham, Jacob is God's partner. In this moment, Jacob becomes Israel, the name of

God's people. In the name given to Jacob, God prepares for the next stage in the history of salvation. God will partner with a group of people. In a profound sense, we are included in this moment of new identity, the new name: "But you are a chosen people, *set aside to be* a royal order of priests, a holy nation, God's own; so that you may proclaim the wondrous acts of the One who called you out of *inky* darkness into shimmering light. Once you were not a people, but now you are God's people; once you had not received mercy, but now you have received it" (1 Peter 2:9–10).

We are transformed into God's partners when we cease to struggle against God and choose to enter into God's struggle. Jacob's story of wrestling with God is not a model for each individual's personal spiritual encounter. However, it is the story of how the nation of Israel was born out of Jacob's struggle with God. Again, it is our story as God's people who choose to struggle with God for the salvation of the world.

In addition to the macro meaning of Jacob's story, we find personal and intimate meaning and identification with the struggle. As individuals, we find hints, echoes, questions, and struggles in our own stories.

- The battle with enemies that gives way to a battle with God
- Fear that overcomes us until God overcomes us
- A new perspective of self and of God
- A transformation in the life of faith from self-focused to mature

God embraces our struggles and makes them His own just as God stepped into Jacob's struggle with Esau. When our struggle against God becomes a struggle with God, we are transformed just as Jacob became Israel.

The wounded blessing. Jacob is not a shy man. Indeed he is so bold as to ask for the name of God: "And what's your name?" God is not ready to reveal His name; He saves it for His encounter with Moses.

God does ask why Jacob wants to know His name. It is a good question. Knowing a name produces intimacy. But there is a hiddenness in God, a mystery yet unrevealed. The exchange between God and Jacob ends with a blessing. The delay is over. God blesses.

JACOB: Please, tell me your name.

MAN: Why do you ask what my name is?

> *Right then and right* there the man blessed Jacob. So Jacob called the place Peniel because as he said, "I have come face to face with God, and yet my life was spared." The sun began to rise as Jacob passed by Penuel, limping because of his *dislocated* hip. (Gen. 32:29–31)

The sun rises on a new day and Jacob carries a wound and a blessing. He has become the first in a long line of wounded blessings. The nation itself, Jacob's namesake, Israel, will become a wounded blessing.

Jesus is our wounded blessing. He chose the will of God over His own: "Yet not My will, but Your will, be done" (Luke 22:42). In choosing God's will, God's struggle to save the world, "He took on our sins in His body *when He died* on the cross so that we, being dead to sin, can live for righteousness. *As the Scripture says,* 'Through His wounds, you were healed'" (1 Peter 2:24).

We are called to follow Jesus. "But if you suffer for doing good and you endure it, this is commendable before God. To this you were called, because Christ suffered for you, leaving you an example, that you should follow in his steps" (1 Peter 2:20–21 NIV).

SUMMARY: Is This the Price of Blessing?

In a single word, yes, God brings blessing to the world through the wounds, the suffering, and the pain of His followers. The practical book of James also makes the same point: "Don't run from tests and hardships, brothers and sisters. *As difficult as they are, you will ultimately* find joy in them; if you embrace them, your faith will blossom under pressure *and teach you true patience* as you endure. *And true patience brought on by* endurance will equip you to complete the long journey *and cross the finish line*—mature, complete, and wanting nothing" (James 1:2–4).

The wounding and blessing of Jacob (who became Israel) foreshadows the call of God's people (Israel). Israel's call is fulfilled in Jesus Christ, the ultimate wounded blessing. As followers of Jesus, we take up our cross (Mark 8:34), follow in His steps (1 Peter 2:20–21), count it all joy (James 1:2–4), and believe that God works in all things (Rom. 8:28), including our wounds, to bring about His purpose and plan.

THINK: Conversation and Reflection

1. Describe your spiritual journey. Where and when did your journey begin? What are the most significant moments along the journey?

2. A faithful journey in Christ leads to maturity in Christ. Jacob's maturity was demonstrated in how he dealt with enemies and how he prayed.

   - What have you learned about dealing with enemies?
   - What have you learned about facing fear?
   - What have you learned about prayer?

3. Do you remember a time in your spiritual journey (or more than one time) when there was a shift between struggling against God to joining God's struggle (God's purpose, plan, resolve)?

4. There are practical matters concerning the call to be a wounded blessing.

- How has God used your wounds, pain, or hurt to bring a blessing to others? In other words, how has God used you as a wounded blessing?
- How would you explain to a new Christian that God will use wounds, pain, and hurt to bring hope and love to others?
- Consider this verse as a call to be a wounded blessing: "We are confident that God is able to orchestrate everything to work toward something good *and beautiful* when we love Him and accept His invitation to live according to His plan" (Rom. 8:28). What needs to be our attitude toward our suffering if God is to use our wounds to bless others?
- Think about your personal wounds and suffering as you read the following verse:

He gathered the crowd and His disciples alike.

JESUS: If any one of you wants to follow Me, you will have to give yourself up to God's plan, take up your cross, and do as I do. (Mark 8:34)

Is God using you as a wounded blessing right now? How? Why?

PART THREE

HIDDEN FROM GOD

The Path of Wisdom

"Give us each day that day's bread—*no more, no less*—And forgive us our debts as we forgive those who owe us something."

—Matthew 6:11–12

With grandiose concerns crowding our life in God, we may miss God in the daily struggles for bread and belonging. Joseph's unwilling journey took him through famine, forgiveness of enemies, and faithfulness when God's hand is hidden.

The third path on the reluctant journey is the way of wisdom. We are not talking about wisdom from books or learned professors, but hard earned wisdom from the cruelties of life. God set the path in motion with a hint in a dream—a dream of Joseph, the younger brother, ruling the family, indeed ruling the cosmos as sun, moon, and stars bow to him. The fulfillment of the dream took decades. Joseph never understood God's plan until all was fulfilled.

Joseph's struggles on the path of wisdom took him through slavery, false accusation, imprisonment, and abandonment. Yet, God weaves human decision, cruel action, selfish ambition, and Pharaoh's nightmares into a plan to place Joseph as second in command of the greatest empire on earth, Egypt.

While in Pharaoh's palace, famine strikes and Joseph is in a position to provide daily bread. When his cruel brothers stand before him, Joseph learns to forgive their wrong. At that moment, the hidden hand of God is revealed. Joseph understood, "Even though you intended to harm me, God intended it only for good, and through me, He preserved the lives of countless people" (Gen. 50:20). In Jesus, "What was hidden for ages, generations and generations, is now being revealed to His holy ones" (Col. 1:26).

A COMPLACENT AND SMUG FAITH

Why Do I Ignore God?

When the light shines, it exposes *even the dark and shadowy* things and turns them into *pure reflections of* light. This is why they sing,

Awake, you sleeper!
Rise from your grave,
And the Anointed One will shine on you.

> So be careful how you live; *be mindful of your steps.* Don't run around like idiots *as the rest of the world does.* Instead, walk as the wise! Make the most of every *living and breathing* moment because these are evil times. So understand *and be confident in* God's will, and don't live thoughtlessly.
>
> —Ephesians 5:13–17

Change! Two emotions accompany change: hope and fear. With excitement we proclaim, "Things are going to be different." With anxiety we mutter, "Things are going to be different." Change born of stress, pain, and crisis generates the loudest and longest grumbles.

How do you deal with unwelcomed and unexpected change? Here is a list of several reactions you may have experienced:[1]

- I don't understand the reason for change.

- I am connected to my old ways.
- I am afraid of the unknown.
- I know one change always leads to another.
- I have learned that change means work.
- I don't like to learn new things.
- I get embarrassed when I try things a different way.
- I don't know how to handle the change.
- I feel out of control when I have to change.
- I harbor resentments about previous changes.
- I can't imagine the change will improve things.
- I am not even thinking about change.

The last one, not even thinking about change, describes Jacob's family. They prefer life the way it is. Jacob's older sons own the status quo. Life is good for them. Change? Not even on the radar.

Nevertheless, God has change on His mind.

God is a change agent.[2] Or you might say a change artist. God plans to move Jacob's family to Egypt. God plans to place Abraham's legacy on the world stage, a place where Jacob's family will grow into the people of Israel, a place where they will be set free through God's exodus, and a place where they begin the journey toward becoming the nation of Israel. God's change is the next step in advancing His mission toward the day when all people on earth will be blessed through His people and through His person, Jesus Christ.

God chose Abraham as His partner, promising to bless him so that he might be a blessing. Abraham left his home in Mesopotamia to go to the land God promised.

Abraham's grandson, Jacob, was an unlikely choice, but God's choice nonetheless. God selected a scoundrel, the younger twin, to

THE STORY IN SUMMARY
Genesis 37–44

Abraham's family is now in the fourth generation. Grandson Jacob has two wives with respective families. The first family, with wife Leah, is strong and large, boasting eight grown sons, six from Leah's womb and two from her maidservant. The second family, with wife Rachel, is small. Rachel's maidservant bore two older sons for Jacob. Rachel's direct children were the youngest, Joseph and Benjamin.

In his teen years, Joseph has a dream that threatens the older brothers, the sons of Leah. They, in turn, plot to kill Joseph, but when cooler heads prevail, they settle on selling Joseph into Egyptian slavery. To cover the deed, the brothers lie to their father, telling him a wild animal killed Joseph. Jacob is heartbroken and continues to grieve for years to come.

In Egypt, Joseph rises to power, first in the home of Potiphar (Pharaoh's captain of the guard), then in Pharaoh's prison, and finally in Pharaoh's palace.

Because Joseph has predicted God's plans for years of plenty and years of famine, Pharaoh places Joseph in charge of the national granary. When famine strikes the promised land of Jacob, Jacob through Joseph enriches Pharaoh.

Among those who are suffering in the famine are Joseph's family, his father Jacob and his eleven brothers. Jacob sends the brothers to Egypt to acquire grain. There, they face the brother they sold into slavery many years before.

be His colleague in the clash between heaven and earth; Jacob wrestled with God and received the blessing of heaven and the burden of the name that would mark the family legacy, God's people, and the nation—Israel.

Now, in the fourth generation, God moves again. God brings change to the family. The change is big; the change is irrational. God moves the family off the promised land and into the markets, granaries, construction sites, and administrative halls of the empire of Egypt.[3]

We don't like change. Jacob's family is not ready or willing to change. Indeed, moving to Egypt is not even an imaginable possibility. For the older brothers especially, all is as it should be. Life is good. They do not want any changes. For them, Robert Browning's poem reveals their world:

> The year's at the spring,
> And day's at the morn;
> Morning's at seven;
> The hill-side's dew-pearled;
> The lark's on the wing;
> The snail's on the thorn;
> God's in His heaven—
> All's right with the world![4]

From the perspective of the ten older brothers, the world is all right! It certainly looks like God's promise to Abraham, Isaac, and Jacob is now a reality. The brothers possess the land. For all self-centered intents and purposes, the ten oldest sons of the fourth generation own the highlands of Canaan. These ten men are masters of their own kingdom, moving flocks from one place to another without rivalry or opposition (Gen. 37:12–17). They take wives and concubines, engage prostitutes, and follow the customs of the day (Gen. 38:1–5, 8, 15).

Life is good. For all personal intents and selfish purposes, their great-grandfather's dusty old vision of a promised land is a reality under the control of the brothers. Change? Move? Not a chance.

These older sons of Jacob will do whatever it takes to protect their positions of power and wealth.

God had also promised Abraham, Isaac, and Jacob that their prodigy would be numbered like the stars of the heavens or the dust of the earth (Gen. 13:16; 15:5). Imagine these ten grown men, each with a family, moving through Canaan. They kick up plenty of dust. They are the stars of the hill country. Again, it appears that the old great-grandfather's vision of the family holdings has come to pass.

Will they consider a change for the sake of God's purpose? Are they caught up in whatever it takes to follow God's mission? Will they risk what they own on a promise from God? No way. For the brothers, the world-transforming purpose of heaven must be hemmed in, buckled down, and limited to the present generation.

You and I experience the same temptation to truncate God's grand schemes in order to make heaven's will serve our agenda:

- The church that cannot see purpose or possibility of ministry in a changing neighborhood;
- The retired and tired Christians who let others do the work now;
- The young and self-serving who limit God to helping them get their lives in order;
- The followers of Christ who commit enough to be respectable but not enough to be useful;
- The believers who believe God's primary assignment is to protect their personal lifestyle.

Partnering with God is risky and costly. It is not convenient and easy. That is the deal with partnerships: "Partnerships assume that profits, liability, and management duties are divided equally among partners. If you opt for an unequal distribution, the percentages assigned to each partner must be documented in the partnership agreement."[5] In our partnering with God, we are attracted to assigning God His part and keeping the profits and management duties we prefer for ourselves.

Let me paraphrase the definition of partnership given in the previous paragraph: Partnering with God assumes that blessings, burdens, and mission are shared in deep and personal relationship between you and God. And here is the kicker: God is free to assign and reassign the blessings, burdens, and mission as He chooses. Yet, however and whatever God assigns, God assumes full and loving commitment to you and His purpose.

The older sons of Jacob had their blessings and wanted no part of burdens or mission. These troublesome concerns belong to former generations. Leave it there. (I think I recognize a few congregations I know.)

God chooses the unexpected. God has other and grander plans. God's plans, again, envision the last becoming first (Gen. 25:23; Mark 10:31). Jacob has a second family, a lesser family. How frightening when God chooses the lesser ones to partner in greater plans. For a long time, Rachel prayed for a child. At last God moved within her, and she gave birth to baby Joseph.

As this infant grows into adolescence, he becomes the instrument of God in waking up the family, moving them to Egypt, and providing them with well-being so they might increase like the stars of the heavens and the dust of the earth.

A SLEEPING FAITH: SECURITY AND SMUGNESS

Through Joseph, God prepares for change. The family, with the ten brothers in charge, settles for comfort.[6] Mission requires movement and risk. Comfort makes us complacent and protective. God was moving forward with a mission; the brothers were putting down roots. It is not that the family ceases to believe in God; they just ignore Him because they do not really need Him. Theirs is a smug faith, the kind of faith that needs Scripture's reminder "not to think of yourselves as being more important than you are" (Rom. 12:3).

Smug faith makes a travesty of genuine faith. Smug faith slips in without notice. It wears the disguise of piety, proper religion, and stalwart commitment. However, smug faith's focus subtly shifts from God's mission to personal comfort and security. Smug faith may hide under a banner—we are humble and proud of it, or blessings are meant for our enjoyment, or we deserve God's gracious gifts.

Let me outline two characteristics of a secure and smug faith. The first characteristic is a shift in passion, and the second is a shift in perspective. A secure and smug faith has little in common with the wounded blessing bestowed on father Jacob (Gen. 32:29–31).

1. Shifting passions. In a secure and smug faith, passion shifts from "Your will be done" to "what I need to get done." For the sons of Jacob, passion energized retaliation, sibling rivalry, family feuds, and the use of prostitutes.[7] When security replaces mission and commitment, passions change.

A friend of mine who works in Little Rock, Arkansas, told me a most wonderful story. He is an outgoing gentleman and often finds a new diner or restaurant in which he can pick up a conversation with strangers. In this way he gets to know the culture of a new city. In one conversation, he spoke with a woman who asked him point-blank, "You are not from Little Rock, are you?"

He admitted that he was new to the city. She went on to advise him. "There are two things you need

Smug faith's focus subtly shifts from God's mission to personal comfort and security.

to know about Little Rock. It's only these two things. But if ya don't know these two things, you'll never make it in Little Rock. So I'm gonna tell ya what the two things are. First, Elvis is King. And second, Jesus is Lord."

It is a wonderful story, and I understand it completely. After all, I live in Nashville. But aside from the smile the story brings to our faces, I want you to catch the subtle change in passion. It is not that Jesus is discarded but that other priorities, other passions, take precedence. The value of faith continues, but the meaning of the value depreciates in both the individual and the culture.[8]

That subtle shift in the passion that drives the soul's motivation modifies our attention. Rather than being motivated by praying and working for God's will to be done on earth, we focus on personal security and accomplishments. Our actions may not change, but the motive for our actions alters. We continue to build our churches, our ministries, and our lives, but the passion and energy that move us comes from our personal interest or the project itself rather than our partnership with God.

Jesus has harsh words for people of smug faith: "You are like a grave that has been whitewashed. You look beautiful on the outside, but on the inside you are full of moldering bones and decaying rot. You appear, at first blush, to be righteous, *selfless, and pure*; but on the inside you are *polluted*, sunk in hypocrisy *and confusion* and lawlessness" (Matt. 23:27–28).

This type of faith is like Dr. Frankenstein's monster.[9] All the body (church) parts are assembled, but the result is monstrous rather than missional.[10] Remember, in Mary Shelley's tale of horror, the monster turned

This type of faith is like Dr. Frankenstein's monster. All the body (church) parts are assembled, but the result is monstrous rather than missional.

against Dr. Frankenstein and took his deepest love, the passion of his life, his bride.

There are spiritual symptoms that indicate that the passion of your partnership with God needs your renewed spiritual attention:

- Heaping burdens on others without lifting a finger to help them (Luke 11:46).
- Applying the rules and tradition with such strictness that you endanger Christian community.
- Persisting in a project, routine, or ritual so tenaciously that the movement of God's Spirit is missed.
- Becoming so dry, dogmatic, and unbending that your faith becomes a set of propositions rather than a personal experience.
- Clinging to perfectionism in your thinking and actions.

In the New Testament letter of Revelation, we see a shift in spiritual passion for the church of Ephesus. After listing all their accomplishments and accolades, the Lord brings an indictment against them: "However, I have this against you: you have abandoned your first love. Do you remember what it was like before you fell? *It's time to* rethink and change your ways; go back to how you first acted" (Rev. 2:4–5).

It is not easy to admit that spiritual passion has lost its way. However, in the stressful routine of life, we become spiritually distracted from the first love, our love for Jesus Christ, our desire to see heaven's will done on earth.

2. Shortsighted perspective. In a secure and smug faith, perspective shortens to what this means for me and for now rather than the long view of God's purpose on earth as it is in heaven. The sons of Jacob had so shortened their perspective that they could not imagine God was about to do something new.

Perspective is a crucial spiritual dynamic. While I was completing my schooling, I served as pastor of a church in a small college town in the Northwest. It was my first full-time position at leading a church, and I was also a full-time student pursuing a PhD. The church grew rapidly, which multiplied the challenges. Scores of new families and college students began to attend. The building was overcrowded, and we found ourselves in search of new property for a new building. At the same time, the demands of my academic program increased, and my work on my doctoral dissertation shifted into high gear.

There were many days when my perspective was so shortsighted that all I could see was the next problem. However, I had a little spiritual discipline that worked almost every time. I would get in my car and drive to the top of the highest mountain in the area, Mary's Peak. From there, I could look down on the whole valley. Way off in the distance I could see a tiny speck that was the church I pastored. Just to the right, if I looked most carefully, I could see a group of buildings that was the University of Oregon where I attended. Standing on the mountain and looking off into the distance, I would say out loud, "That little speck, that little place, that's my problem, but God's purpose is grander than this." Perspective would return.

Jesus knew that loss of spiritual perspective, a resistance to taking God's long view, results in shortsighted decisions that frustrate God's plan. A New Testament demonstration of shortsightedness that vexes God's plan is seen in the response of Jesus to Peter. After Jesus explained the need for the cross, Peter rejected the possibility of Jesus being crucified.

> And He [Jesus] went on to teach them many things *about Himself*: how the Son of Man would suffer; how He would be

rejected by the elders, chief priests, and scribes; how He would be killed; and how, after three days, *God would* raise Him from the dead.

He said all these things in front of them all, but Peter took Jesus aside to rebuke Him.

JESUS *(seeing His disciples surrounding them)*: Get behind Me, you tempter! You're thinking only of human things, not of the things God has planned. (Mark 8:31–33)

Peter's concern for Jesus is evident, but he did not share the perspective of Jesus: "You do not have in mind the concerns of God, but merely human concerns" (Mark 8:33 NIV). A partnership calls for shared perspective. Jesus invites us to be partners and share His perspective and understanding of God's purpose and our part in it: "I don't call you servants any longer; servants don't know what the master is doing, but I have told you everything the Father has said to Me. I call you friends. You did not choose Me. I chose you, and I orchestrated all of this so that you would be sent out and bear great and perpetual fruit. As you do this, anything you ask the Father in My name will be done. This is My command to you: love one another" (John 15:15–17).

However, when our perspective is shortened, God's grand purpose recedes into the background. Below are characteristics of a secure and smug faith that has lost perspective:

- Moving ahead with mission and purpose, and seeking God's blessing later;
- Being insensitive to people and God's Spirit in the pursuit to accomplish the task;
- Becoming critical in nature to the detriment of yourself and others;

- Believing that God is dependent upon you.

Peter's shortsighted perspective did him in. He claimed he would never deny Jesus (a bit of smugness), but he did (Mark 14:29, 54–72). However, Jesus did not deny him. After the resurrection, the angel in Jesus' tomb sent the word, "Go back, and tell Peter and His disciples that He goes before you into Galilee, just as He said. You will see Him there *when you arrive*" (Mark 16:7).

To regain spiritual perspective, go back to beginnings, back to your calling, back to Galilee where it all began, back to father Abraham who "*without any hesitation,* . . . did exactly as the Eternal One asked him to do" (Gen. 12:4).

A WAKE-UP CALL: BREAD AND BELONGING

"So then let's not *give in to* sleep *or wander around in a stupor* as some do, but let's stay awake and in control" (1 Thess. 5:6). Jacob's family is spiritually asleep, wandering around Canaan in a spiritual stupor. By way of famine and a family feud, God is about to bring them a wake-up call.

When our bread and belonging are in jeopardy, we come to full attention. Jesus taught us to pray, "give us each day that day's bread—*no more, no less*—and forgive us our debts as we forgive those who owe us something" (Matt. 6:11–12).

- Bread represents our livelihood, our physical resources, and the means of maintaining our lifestyle.
- Belonging is our relationships, our place in the pecking order, and our ability to influence others.

God was preparing to shake the sons of Jacob by replacing their bread with famine and their belonging with rivalry. Famine would press the family outside themselves and onto the world stage as they move into the Egyptian empire. Rivalry would reorder the structure of the family and lift them to the gospel message of forgiveness and reconciliation. God goes to startling lengths and uses unexpected means to reclaim us.

God's providence: hidden yet present. The account of Joseph is designed to wake up faith in those who are secure and smug.

When the first flush of spiritual passion fades . . .

When the mighty act of God's saving love grows distant . . .

When the great battles of faith are only a memory . . .

. . . the story of Joseph speaks challenge and renewal to the soul. Here in the saga of Joseph, God is working, but God is hidden. Catch the truth in the story: God is hidden, but not absent. God has disappeared from sight, but if you look with eyes of faith, you see Him behind coincidence, circumstance, closed doors, and open roads. God is not center stage, but He directs the action.

My grandfather on my mother's side was a hard-working minister with an entrepreneurial spirit. He saw the potential of televised ministry when most ministers in his denomination were speaking against television thoroughly. I knew him in retirement. He and Grandma purchased one of the first phones in the retirement village of Waverly, Ohio. Organizing and promoting were his gifts. He had a saying I remember. Most likely, it is a saying shared by all southern grandfathers: "It is hard to see the providence of God when you are looking forward, but you cannot miss it when you look back."

We see the providence of God in the story of Joseph. God does not appear[11] as He does in the stories of Abraham and Jacob. However, like the apostle Paul, Joseph knew:

> We are confident that God is able to orchestrate everything to work toward something good *and beautiful* when we love Him

> and accept His invitation to live according to His plan. *From the distant past, His eternal love reached into the future.* You see, He knew those who would be His one day, and He chose them beforehand to be conformed to the image of His Son so that Jesus would be the firstborn of a new family of believers, all brothers and sisters. As for those He chose beforehand, He called them to a different destiny so that they would experience what it means to be made right with God and share in His glory. (Rom. 8:28–30)

Joseph experiences the same truth firsthand. Brothers who sold him into slavery now stand before him in need of bread, for there is famine in the land. Joseph has been raised to power in Egypt so that he has control over all the food in the land. Joseph, the one sold as a slave, is now in a position to save the family. He announces with utter astonishment as he makes the discovery himself: "God sent me *here* ahead of you to make sure you *and your families* survive *this terrible ordeal* and have a remnant left on earth. So it wasn't *really* you who sent me here, but God; the same God who made me an advisor to Pharaoh, master of his household, and ruler over everyone in the land of Egypt" (Gen. 45:7–8).

Charles Spurgeon, a most famous British minister of the 1800s, captured the wonder of God's providence in the difficult and vexing trials of Joseph:

> Just look at the case of Joseph. God has it in his mind that Joseph shall be governor over all the land of Egypt: how is that to be done? The first thing to be done is that Joseph's brethren must hate him. O, say you, that is a step backward. Next, Joseph's brethren must put him in the pit. That is another step backward, say you. No, it is not: wait a little. Joseph's brethren must sell him; that is another step backward, is it not? Providence is

one, and you must not look at its separate parts. He is sold; he becomes a favorite: so far, so good. That is a step onward. Anon, he is put in a dungeon. Wait and see the end; all the different parts of the machinery are one. They appear to clash; but they never do. Put them all together. If Joseph had not been put in the pit, he never would have been the servant of Potiphar: if he never had been put in the round-house [prison], he never would have interpreted the jailor's dream; and if the king had never dreamed, he would not have been sent for. There were a thousand chances, as the world has it, working together to produce the exaltation of Joseph.[12]

Our partnership: divine and human. God is sovereign, and He carries out His plan and His will. Yet we are free to choose, and our choices make a difference. To put it bluntly and in the words of Dr. Lloyd-Jones, if "anybody is saved; it is the sovereign election of God . . . [if] anybody is lost, . . . the explanation of that is their own responsibility."[13] God's sovereignty and our freedom to choose are not a contradiction but an antinomy—"contradiction, real or apparent, between two principles or conclusions, both of which seem equally justified."[14] To illustrate the paradox of God's sovereignty and our free will, John Stott quoted the British preacher Charles Simeon of Cambridge, who lived two hundred years ago. The picture comes from the Industrial Revolution: "As wheels in a complicated machine may move in opposite directions and yet sub-serve a common end, so may truths apparently opposite be perfectly reconcilable

In a high-risk venture, God places a bit of his sovereignty in your hands so that you may choose freely.

with each other, and equally sub-serve the purposes of God in the accomplishment of man's salvation."[15]

From my college days, I remember many long, heated, and unsatisfying conversations about God's sovereignty and free will. It is a conundrum within a paradox, an inconsistency housed in an enigma, a perplexing mystery. And there the dilemma remains.

Those heady discussions are more than forty years old now. I have walked with God for a long time, a lifetime. Like Abraham and Jacob, I have known my stumbling, fumbling, and failure. I have also experienced God's resilience, tenacity, and faithfulness. After a lifetime, here is how I understand God's final control and our free choices: In a high-risk venture, God places a bit of His sovereignty in your hands so that you may choose freely.[16] Our choices make a difference. Our partnership with God is real.

The question becomes, what will we do with our choices? The ten older brothers chose cruelty and deceit. Joseph chose integrity and wisdom. Their choices were real and led to uncalculated consequences. Yet, here is the mystery and wonder of it: Through both ruthless and virtuous human decisions, the plan of God was completed. Jacob's family received a safe haven in Egypt, a place where they could grow into a nation. It is the clandestine work of God to weave our genuinely free choices into His plan and purpose. It is not that all things or all choices are good, but God works to weave all things toward the fulfillment of His purpose, the ultimate good of those who love Him (Rom. 8:28).

Joint purpose: receptive or resistant. Could God be more effective if He held tight His rightful authority to make all decisions and leave human beings with nothing but an illusion of freedom? Yes, I suppose He could be more effective with a strategy

It is the clandestine work of God to weave our genuinely free choices into His plan and purpose.

of domination rather than dominion. Yet, if that were the case, God would not be the God we know, the God of love and purpose, the God whose nature is relationship and mission. God will not give up love or purpose. Somehow, He includes our choices when accomplishing His plan.

Let me share with you the way I think of God working through our genuine choices and decisions to complete His mission of love. Think of ice on a mountaintop buried deep in a glacier. The ice begins to melt and trickle down the mountain, growing to the size of a stream, and then expanding to become a river.

The water is intent on reaching the sea. On its way, there will be frustrating obstacles as well as supportive opportunities. The opportunities come in open places that support and advance the water's movement toward the sea. These supportive places, over time, become the bed of the river, shaped and used by the water to achieve its purpose.

Obstacles are those hard places that are unwilling to give in to the water's will. The obstacles are determined to hold back the water, change its course, and frustrate its progress toward the sea.

The water faces places that enhance and obstacles that impede its advancement. Yet, here is the wonder of the water. When it is frustrated, the water gathers its strength until it goes around, flows over the top, or crashes through, continuing on its way to the sea.

There is God's great sovereignty and your free decision. There is God's will and your will, God's choices and your choices. Your choices can be like supportive places on the mountain—open, receptive, and moving in the direction of the water. Or, your choices can be an obstacle—a resistance or a frustration that attempts to hold the water back.

Here is the wisdom of God: Like water flowing to sea, God uses both receptive and resistant choices to achieve His will.

TIME TO WAKE UP THE FAMILY

Your decisions make a difference. Your choices can frustrate or advance God's plan. When you lose your spiritual perspective, your commitment to God's grand plan, you fall into spiritual slumber. God works through your rightly-placed spiritual passion for Him and His purpose. Yet, when passion is perverted, twisted into something less than God's passion, you find yourself taking a spiritual snooze. Wake up![17]

This is the case with Jacob's family. How does God invade a family who is spiritually asleep? With a dream, of course. God will leave a hint of Himself in a tantalizing dream. And the dream brings trouble to the family.

SUMMARY: Why Do I Ignore God?

Ignoring God is more often a process of falling asleep spiritually than a single decision to turn God out of your life. We fall asleep when our passion for Christ subtly becomes self-focused—what does faith in God do for me? At the same time, shortsighted perspective blinds us to the grand purpose to which God has called us. We live and act as if our partnership with God revolves around our personal lives only, rather than joining with God in His purpose to save the world. God, in a high-risk venture, grants you free will. You may use your will to align with God's will or your own will. God will ultimately weave together human choices, good and bad, to accomplish His purpose. Your choices demonstrate that you are either partnering with God or plotting against Him, or you have fallen into a sleepy spiritual stupor. Wake up!

THINK: Conversation and Reflection

1. How did this chapter affirm or challenge your previous understanding of the story of Joseph? What part of the story of Joseph is most meaningful for you?

2. The chapter provides two descriptions of smug spirituality: loss of passion and loss of perspective. Have you seen smug spirituality? Are you ever tempted to drift into smug spirituality? When and why does the temptation come? How do you handle it?

3. Spiritual sleep is described in the chapter as a shift of passion and shortsighted perspective. Look at the list of characteristics for each. Have you experienced some of these characteristics in your past? Are you struggling with any of them today? In what way is God sending you a wake-up call?

4. Practical issues of partnership with God: Discuss the following concerns:
    - In your thinking, how do you bring together God's sovereignty and your freedom of choice?
    - In what ways do your choices make or not make a difference in God's purpose?
    - Can you share a time when you saw the providence of God at work—God weaving together human choices (good and bad) to advance His purpose?
    - We all need to wake up and realize the significant role we play as God's partners. Read the following texts: Romans 13:11–13; Ephesians 5:13–15; Revelation 3:1–3. What practical instruction is found here for Christians who need a wake-up call?

Looking Ahead: God sends a dream to Jacob's family. The dream sets loose a series of shameful consequences: deception for the brothers, grief for the father, and slavery for Joseph.

LIFE IS NOT FAIR

Why Is This Happening to Me?

> But this beautiful treasure is contained in us—*cracked* pots made of earth and clay—so that the transcendent character of this power will be clearly seen as coming from God and not from us. We are cracked and chipped from our afflictions on all sides, but we are not crushed by them. We are bewildered at times, but we do not give in to despair. We are persecuted, but we have not been abandoned. We have been knocked down, but we are not destroyed.
>
> —2 Corinthians 4:7–9

Drop a pebble in a pond, and waves radiate in all directions. The ripple effect influences life. It influences economic conditions. If people have more, they spend more; others make more and spend more, and the ripple continues.[1] Happy people tend to ripple happiness while angry people induce anger.[2] Gossip has a ripple effect. One person tells several, and they each tell several more. With each telling, the story changes and increases the effect of gossip. Even computers demonstrate a ripple effect.[3] God knows how to use the ripple effect![4]

Jacob's family lived in a time of spiritual complacency. They needed a wake-up call to rekindle their passion for God and expand their perspective so that they might be able to imagine God's plans and purpose.

To wake up the family, God drops a pebble in the pond of family dynamics. The small, smooth, round stone is a dream that will launch a journey. The journey will move Jacob's family off the land of promise and onto the world stage in the great empire of Egypt. The dream has a ripple effect on God's chosen family. Eventually, the dream opens a place of safety and nurture in Egypt where Jacob's family develops into the people of Israel.

However, the first ripples on the pond of the clan psyche loose a flood of family hatred, cruelty, deceit, and grief.

THE STORY IN SUMMARY

Genesis 37:1–36; 39:1–23

Jacob has a large family—in fact, two families—representing his two wives. His second wife, Rachel, is his first love, and her son Joseph is his favorite. Jacob adorns Joseph with a beautiful robe that results in increased anger from the older brothers.

Joseph receives two dreams that seem to indicate he will one day rule the family. The brothers hate young Joseph all the more. When the brothers see him coming toward them in the fields, they plot his death. However, after negotiating the plan among themselves, they settle on the opportunity of selling him to a group of slavers heading for Egypt.

In Egypt, Joseph rises to prominence as the household manager for the captain of Pharaoh's guard, Potiphar. Joseph is a young and good-looking man. Potiphar's wife attempts repeatedly to seduce Joseph, but he rebukes her advances. She responds with false accusations against him, so her husband incarcerates Joseph in the prison of Pharaoh's guard.

LIFE IS NOT FAIR

Charles Sykes authored an essay that was printed in the *San Diego Union Tribune* titled "Some Rules Kids Won't Learn in School." He wrote:

> Unfortunately, there are some things that children should be learning in school, but don't. Not all of them have to do with academics. As a modest back-to-school offering, here are some basic rules that may not have found their way into the standard curriculum.
>
> Rule No. 1: Life is not fair. Get used to it. The average teenager uses the phrase, "It's not fair" 8.6 times a day.[5]

Injustice in life is a hard lesson to learn. Even the way we learn of injustice is unfair. Take Charles Sykes's essay for example. For more than a decade, Sykes's essay has been featured on many different Internet sites. However, these sites all identify Bill Gates as the author of the piece.[6] Life is not fair, even when you point out that life is not fair.

Families can be unfair. There was nothing fair happening in Jacob's family. I want you to notice the opening of the story of Joseph. You may have heard it in Sunday school as you used crayons to draw the coat of many colors. Today, as an adult, you will see there was much more going on in this dysfunctional family:

> Joseph, when he was a young man of 17, often shepherded the flocks along with his brothers. *One day* as he was with Bilhah's and Zilpah's sons (his half-brothers), he decided to report back to their father about things they were doing wrong. Now Israel [Jacob] loved Joseph more than any of his other children because he came along when he was an old man. So Israel presented Joseph with a special robe he had made for him—*a spectacularly colorful robe with long sleeves* in it. But when his brothers saw

> that their father loved him more than the rest, they grew to hate him and couldn't *find it in themselves to* speak to him without resentment or argument. (Gen. 37:2–4)

First, the story introduces teenage Joseph as a tattler, reporting to his father the wrong done by his older half-brothers. Did Joseph tell an exaggerated report, an unfair report, or a one-sided report designed to enhance his standing with his father? Perhaps. The terse telling of the incident seems to indicate that Jacob believed the tale of wrongdoing and rewarded Joseph.

Second, Jacob presents Joseph with a beautiful coat, a multi-colored robe that was luxurious and elegant. It was a robe fit for a king,[7] a ruler. In this family, Joseph rules his father's heart. Jacob was born in a house of favoritism and, apparently, carried on the psychological DNA of his parents.

Third, the brothers despise Joseph. They gave him the silent treatment, or perhaps they were so angry they simply could not speak. Did they hate Joseph unfairly? Did Joseph deserve such abhorrence and rejection? Or, was the seventeen-year-old Joseph merely a naive boy playing the part assigned to him in this dysfunctional family?

We all live with the awful truth—life is not fair. Injustice happens at work, in a court of law, within a house of worship, and, especially so it seems, with family. Jacob's family, like our families, is an accident waiting to happen. The family is in a dangerous situation. Tensions tighten and pressures pull the bonds of relationship to a precarious edge.

God can use injustice. At this moment, God launches a small pebble that whips up waves of confusion and fear, wafting through the soul of the family. God sends a dream—indeed, two dreams.

We all live with the awful truth—life is not fair.

God sends the first dream. The dream's context is found in fields of grain, the stuff of daily bread or destructive famine. The dream ratchets up the poisonous passions of hatred. Joseph says to his brothers, "Listen to this dream I had! There we were, binding sheaves in the field. Suddenly my sheaf rose and stood up, and then your sheaves all gathered around it and bowed down to my sheaf" (Gen. 37:6–7). Will the lesser child rule and reign over the greater ones, the younger over his elders? Joseph's naive proclamation of the dream produces a predictable consequence: "This dream and what he told them about it made them [the brothers] hate him even more" (v. 8).

We have to ask, why such hatred? It is only a dream. The brothers should brush it off the pillow and go back to sleep, back to complacency, back to the status quo, and back to selfish passions and shortsighted perspective.

However, the brothers cannot push it aside. The imagination in the collective consciousness[8] of the brothers stirs with a frightening possibility concerning their little brother. "*Are you serious?* You think you are somehow *destined* to reign over us? You think you are going to be our king?" (v. 8). Could Joseph become the head of the family?

Without time for emotions to subside, God sends the second dream. Joseph sees the result of proclaiming the first dream. Nonetheless, he blurts out the new dream, "Listen! I've had another dream: I saw the sun, the moon, and 11 stars bowing down to me" (v. 9). This dream portrays relationships between the heavenly bodies.

At this portrayal, even mom and dad shudder as the ripples of resentment gather strength and spread across the family pond:

> Even his father scolded him.

ISRAEL: What kind of dream is this? Do you actually think your mother and I and your brothers are going to bow down before you?" (v. 10)

The imagination of this spiritually complacent family is now fully awake.

God's wake-up call has done its task. The journey for God's people has begun. Yet, the family turmoil resulting from God's hint in the dream gathers speed like rapids in a river.

- Joseph, even in the best light, is naive. At worst, he is manipulative, playing on the predictable emotions of his family.
- The brothers continue circling toward the center of their whirlpool of jealousy and hatred.
- Jacob, the old man whose peace and prosperity has been interrupted, "kept this dream in *the back of his* mind" (v. 11).

Perhaps Jacob was held captive by the memory of his own mother telling him the prophecy spoken while he was still in her womb, "the older will serve the younger" (Gen. 25:23).

IT DOESN'T MAKE SENSE

The story of Jacob's family may resonate with you or amplify the turmoil of your family—manipulation, jealousy, resentment, and fear. The dynamics of family in a fallen world go back to the beginning, the early chapters of Genesis.

The account of Joseph and his brothers repeats a family plotline, the story of Cain and Abel.[9] The telling of the first pair of brothers—the injustice, the anger, and God's protective intervention—opens our understanding of Joseph. But more, it deepens our understanding of how to deal with life when it is not fair.

> Eve went on to give birth to Cain's brother, Abel. Abel *grew up to* become a shepherd, and Cain *grew up to* become a farmer. After *he had learned how to produce food from the fields,* Cain gave the Eternal One an offering—some of the crops *he had grown* from the ground. For his part *of the offering,* Abel gave God *some tender lamb meat*—the choicest cuts from the first-born of his flock. The Eternal One accepted Abel and his gift *of lamb,* while He had no regard for Cain and what he presented. Because of this, Cain became extremely angry and his face fell. (Gen. 4:2–5)

The school of injustice. In a phrase, the story does not make sense. Both boys brought their best to God. Both brought the fruit of their own labor. We feebly attempt to make sense of the story.

Perhaps the difference was in the nature of the gifts? We project forward and apply laws of sacrifice that had not been declared, laws that these boys knew nothing about. That does not make sense.

Perhaps the difference was in the nature of the givers? At the beginning of the story in the moment God accepts and rejects, the quality of character in the two boys is indistinguishable. It is only after rejection that we see the anger and murderous deed of Cain. We do not know how Abel would have responded if he had been the rejected one. It does not make sense. It is simply not fair.

The ancient story, hidden away in the days before Noah, lays out a harsh fact in a fallen world: life is not fair. And nothing in Jacob's family was fair. It was not fair that Jacob favored Joseph. It was not fair that older brothers who had worked the flocks for so many years should be expected to bow to their little brother, a Joseph-come-lately.

God's curriculum. Jacob's family in the centuries and generations to follow will face injustice time and again. Here is the point: Injustice is a twofold lesson.

God's people stand against injustice.
God's people live in the midst of injustice.

Just as the unfairness of life is a hard fact, learning to deal with unfairness is a hard lesson. It is also a lesson that God employs to prepare His people to partner with Him in His greater purpose.

I have worked with hundreds of students as they come through the doors of the university seeking advancement and academic degrees. At some point, usually early on in the process, I have a reality check for them. My short speech goes like this: "For the time you are here, the university has a curriculum. At the same time, God has a curriculum. It is God's curriculum that will change your life."

When you face injustice on the job, in your home, at your church, or in your world, God's curriculum shows up. He may teach you to stand firm, to wisely submit and wait for another day, to seek help that you desperately need, or to find an entirely new direction. God's curriculum is designed to test your perception of life, the motivation of your own soul, and the emotions that harm or help you work through it all.

God's curriculum has captured Jacob's family.

A difficult test. Let us return to Cain and Abel, the story that does not make sense. God provides no explanation for accepting Abel and rejecting Cain. What is the point of such a painful and meaningless tale?

The story demonstrates the injustice of a fallen world; it is not heaven yet. The story also demands that we learn how to live as God's people in a world that is not fair. The lesson is basic to life. We almost miss it in our desire to bring the account of Cain and Abel to a reasonable and satisfying conclusion. This fallen world does not always provide reasonable and satisfying resolutions.

In the face of injustice, God provides a warning and a lesson to all who experience the unfairness of life. He gives His lesson to Cain who is angry, and we certainly identify with Cain's anger. He has been rejected for no reason. God's lesson is a tough one: "Why are you angry? And why do you look so despondent? *Don't you know that* as long as you do what is right, then I accept you? But if you do not do what is right, *watch out, because* sin is crouching at the door, ready to pounce on you! You must master it *before it masters you*" (Gen. 4:6–7).

Here is God's demand: In the face of unfairness, do the right thing. Oh, what a difficult command. Jesus completes the requirement for God's children: "If you want to be extraordinary—love your enemies! Do good *without restraint*! Lend *with abandon*! Don't expect anything in return! Then you'll receive the truly great reward—you will be children of the Most High—for God is kind to the ungrateful and those who are wicked" (Luke 6:35).

Let us be practical. What did this mean for Cain as well as Jacob's family? What does it mean for us who profess Christ as Lord?

Dealing with injustice means learning to master or rule over your emotions. Cain was both furious and pessimistic. When injustice takes hold, it is tempting to fall into a pattern of emotion that short circuits clear thinking. When you are unable or unwilling to predict consequences, you are in a dangerous place. Wild and livid thoughts dance in your mind.

So it was in the case of Joseph and his brothers. Again, Jacob sends Joseph into the fields to check on his brothers; we know what

In the face of injustice, God provides a warning and a lesson to all who experience the unfairness of life.

happened the last time he checked on them. The report was bad. This time, the brothers see him in the distance and plot his murder, planning to cover the crime by accusing a wild animal of devouring him. Only Reuben, one of the brothers, considers the consequences of innocent blood (a memory of Abel) and their father's grief (Gen. 37:19–24).

Dealing with injustice means learning to master or rule over your actions. God told Cain to do right. In the face of injustice is it possible to rise above it and do the right thing? Cain could not: "Cain's *envy of his brother got the better of him, and he* attacked and killed Abel (Gen. 4:8).

Being treated unfairly so easily justifies indefensible behavior in our own minds. We whisper to ourselves, "Well, if they do that, I can do this! If they stole my opportunity, I can steal from them." In a matter of days or even moments, our furious thoughts turn into resentful action. The brothers of Joseph strip the beautiful coat off the teenager and throw him in a pit, a cistern that was dry (an apt image for the spiritual condition of Jacob's family).

Ever the opportunists, when traders come by headed to Egypt, the brothers sell their young sibling into slavery for a few ounces of silver. To cover the crime, they slaughter a goat and dip the beautiful robe in its blood. The robe given in love is now ruined by hatred.

Dealing with injustice means deciding what masters or rules your life. When faced with the unfairness of life, sin hunkers at the door. Sin's assault can quickly master our lives. Resentment digs in deep and will not let go. Anger clouds perception, poisons motivation, and leaks toxins into our emotions. The choice is before us. To live in this fallen world as God's people, we must trust in God as our true master.

Dealing with injustice means learning to master or rule over your actions.

In Jacob's house, the feud rages over who will be master of the clan, who will one day rule and reign. The resentful sin of the brothers comes to master the house of Jacob. Their resentment casts a spell of fear, grief, deceit, and secrets over the family for decades.

The brothers show their father the robe dipped in goat's blood and put their deceitful plan in place. The brothers will have to keep up this deceit for the next twenty years. (Do you know folks who vow to take secrets to the grave?)

Fear mastered the brothers. With each passing caravan traveling north from Egypt, the brothers fear there might be news of Joseph carried on the lips of merchants.

Grief mastered Jacob. Their old father was consigned to live with grief ruling his heart, a grief his own children put upon him.

> Then Jacob *wailed in agony and* tore his clothes *with the depth of emotional pain only a father could feel upon losing a child.* He dressed in sackcloth and mourned his son for a long time. All of his sons and daughters tried to comfort him, but he refused to be comforted.
>
> **ISRAEL** [Jacob]: No, I will go to the grave grieving for my son. (Gen. 37:34–35)

God's response to injustice. It is a gloomy thought to imagine the families, churches, schools, and places of work ruled by resentment, deceit, fear, and grief because people have not learned how to live in a fallen world where life is not fair.

Cain's response to injustice was revenge. He killed his brother Abel. The response of the brothers of Joseph was resentment. The desire to turn the tables, to collect their pound of flesh, was great. The Old Testament law puts restrictions and limitations on our vengeance, eye for an eye, tooth for a tooth, and wound for a wound.

God's response to Cain's murder of his brother Abel was similar to God's response to the sons of Jacob. Cain was sent into a strange land of famine. Jacob's sons were sent into the strange land of Egypt because of famine.

Cain cried out that he could not bear it and feared his own death: "My punishment is more than I can bear! Today You have banned me from the soil and hidden me from Your presence! I will be a fugitive and a wanderer on the earth, and anyone who meets me will *want to* kill me!" (Gen. 4:13–14). Note that regardless of all that happened to him, Cain desired and cried out for the presence of God.

God revealed His grace and protected Cain with a sign. And in a display of grace, God protects the brothers who sold Joseph into slavery. These angry men carry the seed of God's people, both the children of Abraham by flesh and the children of Abraham in faith (Gal. 3:7). All of us, all God's people are called to suffer in the injustice of the world. But the suffering has a purpose—the advancement of God's gracious purpose.

Young Joseph is leading the way. He is on his way to Egypt to prepare a place to receive his family where they might grow into a nation. Try to picture him: a seventeen-year-old, sold like a prisoner taken in battle, traveling with strangers who intend to turn their investment into a tidy profit. For Joseph, life is not fair. He struggles with a torrent of emotions: fear, anger, sadness, and disgust. How will he choose to think about his situation? What will guide his decisions in this new and strange land? What will be his driving motives? Will he give up or grow up? What would you be tempted to do?

As a slave in Egypt, Joseph takes on God's curriculum. The time has come for Joseph to grow up, to learn to live

We must learn to stand against injustice while we live in the midst of injustice.

as God's person in the perverted empire of Egypt. So we, also, must learn to stand against injustice while we live in the midst of injustice.

TIME TO GROW UP

Living in the midst of injustice is a learning process for Joseph and for us. The lessons are difficult but essential. To carry on the business of God's family, we must learn to live in an unfair world and do the right thing.

Joseph's great-grandfather, Abraham, left his country, his family, and his father's house to go to the place God showed him. God now calls his great-grandson Joseph away from the family in order to save the family.

God works incognito. The first unsuspecting Egyptian in God's plan for Joseph is Potiphar, Pharaoh's officer and captain of the guard (Gen. 39:1), who purchases the teenager as a house slave. God is preparing Joseph to be a ruler. The home of the captain of Pharaoh's guard is an excellent classroom.

God is with Joseph. "The Eternal One was with Joseph . . . and he became successful *in his own right as a slave*" (v. 2). Even Potiphar notices that God is with Joseph (v. 3). Potiphar increases the responsibility and authority of Joseph and "the Eternal One blessed the Egyptian's house for Joseph's sake" (v. 5).

The Bible tells the story so that we see the hand of God at work. However, Joseph, at this time, does not realize God is his helper. Like the disciples on the Emmaus Road who did not recognize Jesus (Luke 24:16), Joseph does not see God's working hand. Potiphar recognizes a supernatural hand at work. The Bible quickly credits the supernatural hand to God. However, an Egyptian, a captain of Pharaoh's guard, would not know of the God of Abraham, Isaac, and Jacob. The captain of Pharaoh's guard would credit an Egyptian god with Joseph's success. But the Bible wants us to know without any confusion or ambiguity that God is at work: the God of Abraham, Isaac, and Jacob. Further, the Bible wants us to understand that God is at work even when we cannot see His hand guiding the way.

Joseph is not absent of the knowledge of Abraham's God. We can be certain he received religious and spiritual training in his home. However, like many families today, the emphasis was on family tradition, not on having a living relationship with God.

Jacob's family lives in a time of spiritual complacency. Like many who grow up in spiritually complacent congregations, Joseph heard the stories and said his prayers without understanding their greater significance and meaning. In spite of a lack of understanding, God was working on behalf of Joseph.

God is at work, even if we do not fully realize it. A student shared this testimony with me:

> I grew up without God or at least any kind of understanding of God. My family didn't go to church. The idea of a relationship with God never entered my home or my mind. But I look back now and see that God was there, even when I didn't understand.
>
> It was before I went to first grade (I think I was five years old) that I asked my aunt about God. She told me he is just there. I didn't know what that meant. In my childlike imagination I saw a really bright light. The picture of the light became the foundation of my faith. I trusted the light.
>
> When I look back now, I see that God honored my simple faith and lead me out of dysfunction into health. God gave me the confidence to step out of the sin that was all around me, and He led me through the chaos and confusion of my life. I am so grateful to Jesus.

God matures us *in wisdom.* God takes charge over Joseph. The first hint of God invading the life of Joseph is in his dream of becoming a ruler. Now, in Potiphar's house, we see God's direct intervention in the life of Joseph. Yet, Joseph is not aware. Joseph's path to mature faith is different from his forefathers.

Great-grandfather Abraham heard the voice and followed. Faith was matured in Abraham through the struggle to believe the impossible—that God would give Abraham and Sarah a baby long after they were capable of producing a child. Abraham learned to trust God.

Father Jacob battled his way to mature faith through trouble and conflict. He witnessed the great conflict, the will of heaven and the will of earth. Struggling with God and humanity, he became a wounded blessing.

For Joseph, the path of faith is neither clinging to the impossible nor wrestling with God through the night. For Joseph, the path of maturing faith is the way of wisdom.[10] He learns to do the right thing in a wise way. Joseph's wisdom comes from God, and Joseph comes to realize that his wisdom is from God (Gen. 40:8; 41:16). It may be that Joseph, along with other Old Testament sages, became the inspiration for the authors of Proverbs.[11] The opening of the book of Proverbs certainly speaks to Joseph's story as well as our story:

> *I*, Solomon, David's son and Israel's king, *pass on to you* these proverbs—*a treasury of wisdom*—
>
> So that you would recognize wisdom and *value*
> discipline;
> that you would understand insightful teaching
> And receive wise guidance to live a disciplined life;
> that you would seek justice and *have the ability to*
> *choose* what is right and fair.

> *These proverbs* teach the naive how to become
> clever;
> they instruct the young in *how to grow in* knowledge and *live with* discretion.
> The wise will pay attention *to these words* and will
> grow in learning,
> and the discerning will receive *divine* guidance,
> *And they will be able* to interpret the meaning of a
> proverb and a puzzle,
> *the twists and turns in* the words of the wise and
> their riddles.
> *Let us begin.* The worship of the Eternal One, *the one True God,* is the first step toward
> knowledge. (Prov. 1:1–7)

The way of wisdom is a difficult route, as difficult as the pathways trod by Abraham and Jacob. The wisdom of God is not intellectual as much as practical. God's maturing wisdom requires we face difficult experiences and learn. As Joseph's father, Jacob, learned from his experience in a land where people did not worship the God of Abraham, Joseph will learn faithful wisdom in an empire that opposes God's purpose.

From the account in Genesis, it is clear that Joseph would not be spared difficulty, or that in the midst of difficulty he would not be rescued quickly. Joseph's troubles are long and harsh. As he finds his footing in a foreign land, Joseph faces two tests that shape the way he deals with injustice and learns to lead.

Test #1: Dealing with seduction. Jesus taught us to pray and lament "lead us not into temptation" (Matt. 6:13). Yet, temptation is precisely where Joseph is headed.

This is a sordid tale of the attempted seduction of the manager of the household by the mistress of the house. We need but a little imagination to envision the situation (Gen. 39:6–7).

Joseph is young and good-looking.

The captain of the guard is busy and away.

The mistress of the house is bored and abandoned.

Her requests and commands for Joseph's attention become more intimate, resulting in them spending more time together. The steps are all too common—the development of small talk and revealing of secrets that hint at her needs and desires.

Is Joseph naive? Perhaps. He grew up in a house of men. He was young. How would he spot a trap of feminine wiles? She reveals her true intentions: "*Come*. Sleep with me" (v. 7).

Joseph is shocked. He quickly calculates the consequences of such an action; to submit to her seduction would betray the trust of Potiphar. He rejects her. In his rejection we read the first recording of the name of God coming from his lips: "Why would I do something so *clearly* wrong and sin *so blatantly* against God?" (v. 9).

Joseph chooses a moral stand to protect loyal relationships, both human (with Potiphar) and divine (with God). It is both wisdom and faith that support Joseph in his test.

The temptation was not a moment, but an ongoing seduction. "She pursued him day after day" (v. 10). This was not an easy temptation for him to overcome. Emotions, motives, and perceptions become confused under such pressure:

- Joseph could have justified a tryst with Potiphar's wife as a means of balancing the score for all his suffering.
- He could have increased his power and influence in the household by taking his relationship with Potiphar's wife to the next level.

- He could have entered the game of sexual politics that have been part of every empire in every age.

However, "Joseph would not consent to sleep with her and refused to be *alone* with her" (v. 10).

God's deeper lesson. Joseph chose personal morality. This alone makes him the hero of the story. Yet, as significant as choosing personal morality is, God had an even greater curriculum in mind. God understood the seductive power of an evil empire, including the great nation powers of today. Resisting Potiphar's wife is a picture of resisting the seductive power of all earthly empires that would woo our loyalty away from God.

It takes only a little imagination to see that Joseph, under this pressure, remembers and reflects on the stories he was taught as a child, stories of his lineage. The empire of Egypt intimidated his great-grandfather Abraham (Gen. 12:10–20). Joseph's great-uncle Lot was seduced and carried away by thoughts of an Egyptian lifestyle (Gen. 13:10). Joseph was now in the heart of Egypt, the household of Pharaoh's captain of the guard. Joseph had to decide who would rule his life, the ways of the evil empire or the ways of the Creator God.

We also live in the tension between our loyalty to God and our livelihood in the world, which is the organization and the workplace (the empire) that does not care about God. The New Testament reveals the true and evil power we face: the prince of this world.[12]

The seductive power of the prince of this world is exposed in two phrases from the mouth of Potiphar's wife: "sleep with me" and "in her hand" (Gen. 39:12–13). The images represent desire and power. The empire works on a simple value system: I want what I want, and I want it now. This is the cold heart of evil.

Joseph, his family, the Israelites, and the followers of Christ face the tempting seduction of the empire of evil. The empire glitters with glam, promises much, and yet delivers sadness and despair. Joseph found that wisdom and faith—good sense and a committed heart—are needed to withstand the seductive powers of evil.

Test #2: Dealing with false accusations. The result of Joseph's triumph in test one leads to the second test. It is here that Joseph learns what happens when the empire, the seductress, is rejected.

> Heaven has no rage like love to hatred turned,
> Nor hell a fury like a woman scorned.[13]

Potiphar's wife cries out to the whole household: "See here! My husband brought this Hebrew into our house to take advantage of us! He came to me and wanted to sleep with me. I screamed *as loudly as I could,* and when he heard me yell, he dropped his clothes here beside me and ran outside" (Gen. 39:14–15).

You know that the other servants in the house know the real story, but no one is talking. Are they fearful of the mistress of the house? Are they jealous that Joseph has been given authority over them? Whatever the case, when Potiphar returns home, his wife sticks to her story, and none oppose her in defense of Joseph.

God's deeper lesson. Joseph learns how the evil empire works. One false accusation reminds him that he is nothing more than a Hebrew servant. Potiphar, to whom he was loyal, turns against him without so much as checking the story for its accuracy or truth. Joseph learns that the word of the angry mistress of the house becomes the truth simply because she says so.

Resisting Potiphar's wife is a picture of resisting the seductive power of all earthly empires that would woo our loyalty away from God.

It is a hard thing to bear a false accusation. Jesus suffered from false accusations (Matt. 16:21) as do His followers (Matt. 5:10–12). Why are false accusations so painful?

1. Sometimes the pain is found in the source of the accusation. The lies come from someone we trusted, someone we believed in and who we thought believed in us.

2. Sometimes the pain is found in how quickly others believe the lie. Potiphar trusted Joseph, and Joseph had been loyal in all things. Now, without due process, he was accused and convicted by his trusted master.

3. Sometimes the pain emerges because of the reasoning of others in going along with the false accusation. People may not believe the accusation, but they may gain power or prestige if they go along with the false story. They may even add to it if it serves their purpose.

4. Sometimes the pain is in the simple fact that powerful people can get away with injustice. We realize we are victims of powerful people who will not admit to an error in judgment, correct a lie they have supported, or confess to a fault of their own.

In Joseph's case, the captain of Pharaoh's guard cannot believe a slave if the captain's wife makes an accusation: "When Potiphar heard his wife's account, his face flushed with anger. So *Potiphar,* Joseph's master, put him into prison and locked him up in the place where the king's prisoners were confined. Joseph remained there *for a time*" (Gen. 39:19–20).

God isn't finished. For Joseph, it must have felt like the end of the story. However, do not count God out quite yet. Joseph is beginning to learn the lessons that God's people then and now need to know if we are to partner with God. Joseph is being shaped, formed, and transformed from a naive little brother into a man who can stand on his own with God in his heart. He is learning to live as God's man in an unjust world.

SUMMARY: Why Is This Happening to Me?

Life is hard and unfair, but perhaps becomes less so once you come to accept that fact. It is a heavy burden to live under the false expectation that life will treat you with fairness. We look forward to a day when God's plan comes to fruition: "Let justice thunder down like a waterfall; let righteousness flow like a *mighty* river that never runs dry" (Amos 5:24). However, this is not that day. Today, we can choose to be crushed by a fallen world that wants what it wants right now and does not care if we get hurt in the process. Or, we can learn to respond to injustice with righteousness and compassion, demonstrating our true and best in Christ.

THINK: Reflection and Conversation

1. How has this chapter confirmed, challenged, or changed your understanding of the story of Joseph? How has this chapter confirmed, challenged, or changed your understanding of the story of Cain and Abel?

2. This chapter suggests several dynamics of turmoil in families. To the degree that you are comfortable, share how you see the dynamics of turmoil in your family.

3. Life is not fair! What is your first and gut-level response to injustice? How do you determine the right thing to do (righteousness) when faced with injustice?

4. There are practical issues concerning standing against injustice and living in the midst of injustice by combining faith and wisdom:

- Joseph faced the temptation of sexual seduction. What other kinds of seduction are prevalent in a fallen world? Consider actions and attitudes, patterns of thought and emotion, and motivation and perception.
- Joseph also experienced false accusations. What lessons have you learned from experiencing unfairness?
- Joseph was treated cruelly by his brothers. Yet, with the help of God, he brought his best to the task given him in Potiphar's house. When being treated unfairly, how do you bring out your best?
- Jesus calls us to love our enemies. How would you explain to a new Christian how to love enemies?

Looking Ahead: The trials of Joseph continue as God's curriculum shapes him for a mighty task. Of course, Joseph, like us, does not know the assignment ahead of him. At this point, he must respond with his best when abandoned and forgotten.

THE FEAR OF ABANDONMENT

Does Any of This Make a Difference, God?

Why, then, do you, Jacob, *inheritors of God's promise,*
    you, Israel, *chosen of God*—
Why do you say, "My *troubled* path is hidden from the
        Eternal;
    God has lost all interest in My cause"?
Don't you know? Haven't you heard?
    The Eternal, the Everlasting God,
The Creator of the whole world, never gets tired or
        weary.
    His wisdom is beyond understanding.
God strengthens the weary
    and gives vitality to those worn down *by age and
        care.*
Young people will get tired;
    strapping young men will stumble and fall.
But those who trust in the Eternal One will regain their
        strength.
    They will soar on wings as eagles.
They will run—*never winded,* never weary.
    They will walk—*never tired,* never faint.

—Isaiah 40:27–31

Some years ago, I served as a lecturer for business classes at a local Christian college. I invited a Christian businessman to speak to the students. He was senior vice president of a financial services company. He was also a dynamic and strong man of God. I wanted him to speak on how to maneuver through the world of high finance while keeping your feet firmly planted in Christ Jesus.

Joseph also worked through his lessons on managing the tension between working for the empire and remaining faithful to the Creator God. For Joseph, holding to the integrity of his moral character resulted in false accusations and a jail sentence with no foreseeable parole or release date.

THE STORY IN SUMMARY

Genesis 40:1–23; 41:1–52

Potiphar, captain of the guard in Pharaoh's palace, trusts Joseph with his own home, and God blesses Joseph's management of the household. Potiphar's wife attempts to seduce Joseph, but Joseph rejects her. She responds to the rejection by falsely accusing Joseph. Potiphar places Joseph in the prison where Pharaoh's prisoners are confined, the prison of the captain of the guard. Again, Joseph's best leadership and management qualities come through. The overseer of the prison promotes Joseph to prison supervisor.

Some time later, two prisoners arrive from Pharaoh's palace, the butler and the baker. Each prisoner has a dream, and both are troubled by their dreams. Joseph interprets the dreams, giving full credit to God. The dreams indicate that the baker will die at the hand of Pharaoh, but the butler will be restored to his rank and position. Joseph asks the butler to remember him to Pharaoh. However, the butler forgets about Joseph.

Like Joseph, Christians today live and struggle in the tension between the kingdom of this world and the kingdom of God. This tension is so severe that Jesus prayed for us in His high priestly prayer in the book of John: "I have given them Your word; and the world has despised them because they are not products of the world, in the same way that I am not a product of the corrupt world order. Do not take them out of this world; protect them from the evil one" (17:14–15).

A malevolent assault often slips in under the cover of tension between the way of the world and the kingdom of God. You are set up for attack when you face a major life change, financial problems,

Two years pass. This time, Pharaoh has two dreams on the same night. He is troubled. No one understands the dreams. It is then that the butler remembers Joseph. Pharaoh sends for Joseph, who interprets the dreams: there will be seven good years and seven lean years. Joseph advises Pharaoh to take advantage of the good years, store up grain and be ready for the famine that will come. He tells Pharaoh that God has made this decision, and God will do it soon.

In response, Pharaoh appoints Joseph to be in charge of all the wealth of Egypt, the fields and storehouses, to prepare for the years of famine. Pharaoh honors Joseph with his signet ring, a beautiful robe, and a chariot ride through the nation while the people bow to him. Pharaoh also gives Joseph a wife from an important priestly family, and she bears him two children. Joseph names his two sons in memory of the suffering he has endured and the blessing God has brought.

relational difficulties, family, children, work stress, or just too much on your plate—challenges everyone confronts. The symptoms you feel in your mind, heart, and soul might include pessimism, inflexibility, unrealistic expectations, chronic worry, perfectionism, or putting yourself down.[1] At such times, Jesus prays for you, "protect them from the evil one."

Joseph learned the evil ways of the empire, ways of desire and power. False accusations and broken loyalties resided in the curriculum that prepared him for God's purpose in a fallen world. Jesus understood evil and revealed it to us: "Because the Light, *sent from God,* pierced through the world's darkness *to expose ill motives, hatred, gossip, greed, violence, and the like.* Still some people preferred the darkness over the light because their actions were dark. Some of humankind hated the light. They *scampered hurriedly* back into the darkness where vices thrive and wickedness flourishes" (John 3:19–20).

The business students who filled my classroom found my friend and church member fascinating. He regaled them with wondrous stories of business deals, ventures, and challenges. A particular favorite was when he built up the fact that he and colleagues often flew to Europe in a private jet. The thrill in the students was a setup for his next line, "Of course, the bank has a private jet to keep you working as you wing your way across the Atlantic; you don't even get to sleep on the plane."

The students laughed. They also caught on to the level of stress and pressure that exists at this level of business leadership and management. Let me broaden the application of the story: there is great pressure on all who live in the tension between the kingdoms of this world and the kingdom of God.

There is great pressure on all who live in the tension between the kingdoms of this world and the kingdom of God.

It was my privilege to set up the last question for his presentation. We arranged for the question ahead of time. The question elicits a response he shared with me over lunch, a perspective that inspired me to have him speak to each class of business students. Here is the question: "How do you maintain your integrity and consistency as a Christian when working in such high and stressful circles of business and finance?"

His answer was clear and to the point, "I begin each day with three affirmations. I believe these statements in the depth of my soul.

"First, God is good.

"Second, God is in control.

"Third, God and I are making history."

Joseph is making history with God; only Joseph does not know it yet. From his prison cell, it does not feel like making history, it does not feel like God is in control, and it certainly does not feel like God is good. It feels like his life does not make any difference at all.

Abandoned in his jail cell, Joseph has learned firsthand the cruel ways of the Empire. Now, he is about to learn that the mighty Creator God of his great-grandfather Abraham, his grandfather Isaac, and his father Jacob, continues to create history. Joseph is about to learn that God is greater than the empire. First, God prepares Joseph in Pharaoh's prison. Second, God places Joseph in Pharaoh's palace.

GOD PREPARES US

I understand God needs to prepare us, mold us, and teach us. But the classroom of a prison cell is rough duty. You know what it is to feel trapped. How can we fulfill God's purpose when we are stuck, as Joseph was stuck in a prison cell, and stuck with all those painful memories to haunt his soul?

Joseph grew up as daddy's favorite, the one who spied on his brothers, received a robe fit for a king, and had dreams of power and prestige (Gen. 37:2–10). When he was seventeen his brothers abused him and sold him into slavery (vv. 18–36). We can only speculate how long he worked at Potiphar's house to bring about prosperity as well as the unwelcomed sexual advances of Potiphar's wife. The rejected mistress of the house takes out her vengeance on Joseph and sends him to jail (Gen. 39:19–20).

It seems that the only way we learn the deep lessons of life is through personal suffering. On a terrible day of suffering in the United States, Robert Kennedy announced the death of Martin Luther King, Jr. with his own rendering of a quotation from the Greek tragedy *Agamemnon*:

> Even in our sleep, pain which cannot forget
> falls drop by drop upon the heart
> until, in our own despair, against our will,
> comes wisdom through the awful grace of God.[2]

Robert Kennedy wisely called for reflection on suffering and injustice. In a sense, it is not the suffering itself that makes the difference, but reflecting on the suffering. All people suffer to different degrees and in different ways. In the midst of awful suffering and abandonment, it feels like "nobody knows the trouble I've seen."[3] In truth, everybody knows trouble. The wisdom with which you carry the trouble makes the difference in your life and God's purpose. Michael Casey, Anglican priest and prolific writer, made the case:

> When life is very difficult, people sometimes lay hold of resources that they never knew they had. The easy-going, self-centered exterior is cast off and a person of heroic stature emerges. Under pressure, false and foolish façades slip away. A new person emerges, or rather the one who has lain dormant

> these many years, tyrannized by an outward image bearing little resemblance to what was within. Suffering causes the mirror to crack. As the pieces fall away, we see what is hidden beneath.[4]

In the prison of suffering, Joseph learned the lesson captured by John Calvin in the first sentence of his major work *The Institutes of the Christian Religion*: "Nearly all the wisdom which we possess, that is to say, true and sound wisdom, consists of two parts: the knowledge of God and of ourselves. But, while joined by many bonds, which one precedes and brings forth the other is not easy to discern."[5]

Discovering the wisdom of God. God empowered Joseph to succeed in Potiphar's house and, yet again, in Pharaoh's prison:

> But the Eternal One remained with Joseph and showed him His loyal love and granted him favored status with the chief jailor. The jailor put Joseph in charge of all of the prisoners who were confined there. Whatever needed to be done, Joseph was the one to do it. The chief jailor, *like Potiphar,* didn't need to worry about anything that was in Joseph's care because the Eternal One was with him. And whatever Joseph did worked out well because the Eternal made it so. (Gen. 39:21–23)

Joseph's skills and God's gifting opened areas of responsibility and opportunity. Rather than managing a household, Joseph now managed a prison. This was excellent preparation for managing the Egyptian Empire, the job on the horizon. However, Joseph could not

It seems that the only way we learn the deep lessons of life is through personal suffering.

see or imagine such a possibility. Freedom from prison bars was the most he could wish.

Nonetheless, he develops an inner awareness that his own competency alone is inadequate to explain his success in managing a prison. When Joseph was in Potiphar's house, he did not understand that the hand of God was at work. Yet, here, in the prison, he recognizes and credits the hand of God on his behalf.[6]

First, to reap the wisdom of God, we must become aware of God in our current situation. How did this awareness come to Joseph? Prison offers fewer distractions and more time for reflection. Prison affords time to remember the stories Joseph heard as a child. For us, it is the same as reflecting on the stories in the Bible:

- Great-grandfather Abraham went into Egypt and returned as a wealthy man (Gen. 12:16).
- Grandfather Isaac had dealings with King Abimelech, and God prospered him (Gen. 26:13).
- Father Jacob escaped into the land of Paddan Aram, and God made him affluent (Gen. 30:43).

Joseph also had time to think and reflect on his own story, the story of the dream God planted in the family, the time of abundance in Potiphar's house, and the new success in the prison. Perhaps he recalled the story his father told him, a story a father would confide in his favorite son. It was a story of a dream, a vision of heaven and earth, of angels and the Eternal One, a moment when the father realized, "The Eternal One is in this place—and I didn't even know it!" (Gen. 28:16).

Second, God's wisdom also flourishes when faith aligns our imagination with "God who can do so many *awe-inspiring things, immeasurable things*, things greater than we ever could ask or imagine"

(Eph. 3:20). Reflecting on Scripture stirs faith-filled imagination. Joseph needed faith to fire his spiritual vision. If God has done such great things in the past, what might God do through Joseph? Faith emboldens the mind with God's possibilities.

Consider the potential of a God-dedicated imagination jam-packed with faith. It requires faith to look at the world and see God at work. "Faith is the assurance of things you have hoped for, the absolute conviction that there are realities you've never seen" (Heb. 11:1).

Third, we harvest God's wisdom when we recognize God at work in our situation. In prison, Joseph comes to understand and perceive God's guidance with clarity and conviction when helping two prisoners troubled by dreams. The prisoners ask Joseph for an interpretation of the dreams. Joseph's response startles us. Perhaps it also surprised Joseph. He declares in faith, "Interpretations belong to God, don't they?" (Gen. 40:8). This statement of faith, even if embedded in the strange custom of interpreting dreams, declares that:

- God is good.
- God is in control.
- God is making history.

To be aware of God's presence, to envision His purpose, and to recognize His power at work is the wisdom of God. Joseph's priorities are altered in the prison cell. Spiritual reality took precedence over success in the empire. Joseph was successful by empire standards, but something has happened in his heart, a heart that looks for and follows the path of God.

I am reminded of two sisters, Mary and Martha. It may have been the Martha side of Joseph that blinded him in his busyness in

Potiphar's house. Now, in the prison, the more spiritually sensitive nature of Mary comes to the surface of Joseph's soul:

> Martha, a resident of that village, welcomed Jesus into her home. Her sister, Mary, went and sat at Jesus' feet, listening to Him teach. Meanwhile Martha was anxious about all the hospitality arrangements. . . .
>
> **JESUS:** Oh Martha, Martha, you are so anxious and concerned about a million details, but really, only one thing matters. Mary has chosen that one thing, and I won't take it away from her. (Luke 10:38–42)

The story of Mary and Martha teaches a lesson of priorities, not balance. Focusing on Jesus, keeping your heart in God is the first priority in life, always. Joseph's priorities are being rearranged in a prison cell. He is coming out of his complacent family and finding his own faith.

Discovering the wisdom of knowing yourself. In addition to a new awareness of God, Joseph comes to a new understanding of himself and his relationship with God. God's curriculum continues in prison.

An exciting new method in modern education holds great promise: problem-based learning.[7] I had the privilege of attending a workshop about this teaching method at McMaster's University Medical School where problem-based learning originated.[8] Here is how it works: The teacher presents students with a problem to solve. The problem must be significant and complex. In the process of solving the problem, students gather knowledge, develop skills, and sharpen their thinking. I have used this teaching method for many years.

In fact, this is not a modern educational method but a time-tested learning strategy God has used from

Focusing on Jesus, keeping your heart in God is the first priority in life, always.

the beginning. God presents Joseph with a problem. The butler[9] and the baker from the palace have angered Pharaoh. We do not know the reason for the breach with the king; it could be anything from broken trust to burnt toast. From this problem, Joseph has lessons to learn about himself and the evil empire in which he now resides as a prisoner.

First, Joseph learned he was more prepared than he realized. God prepared Joseph for a task in the palace of Pharaoh. For his teacher, God sent two servants from the palace. God also reminded Joseph of lessons from his own family history.

Joseph is put in charge of the two celebrity prisoners, the butler and the baker. He cares for them, talks with them, and learns from them how things get done in Pharaoh's palace. Imagine their conversations. Joseph learns the ways of palace politics, royal relationships, and suspicious motives. Politicos, with their intrigues and backstabbing gimmicks, carry on today. You may recognize a few of these political maneuverings in your workplace or family:

- Gossip Grandeur—telling or retelling a story to your own advancement or to harm someone else;
- Manipulative Moves—holding and sharing resources and information in exchange for favoritism;
- Head Games—for example, withholding information, divide and conquer, or sandbagging;
- Name Dropping—coercing another by suggesting that friends in high places are supporters or detractors;
- Wicked Timing—timing delivery of dishonest, false, or critical feedback to deflect, distract, or undermine another;
- No Invites—leaving people off distribution lists so they miss important meetings or information.[10]

Conversations with the palace servants echoed a familiar ring for Joseph. He grew up in a family whose father, Jacob, had two wives, two concubines, and ten sons before Joseph was born. Yes, this was all familial and familiar. Joseph knew the questions to ask: Who are the real influencers? Who is respected? Who is untrustworthy? Who is the brain of the operation? Who gets along with whom? Who is always butting heads? Whom can you trust?[11]

Joseph scoped out the politics of Pharaoh's palace, but more importantly, he learned that he knew how to make his way through the palace if the opportunity ever presented itself.

Second, Joseph learned he could understand the politics of the palace yet not be subject to them. For anyone who works or lives in a complicated organization or family, it is tempting to be seduced into gaming the system, getting ahead, and viewing the world through win-lose glasses. In fact, it is not a game you can win, for "pride precedes destruction; an arrogant spirit gives way to a *nasty* fall" (Prov. 16:18).

Joseph learns a spiritual lesson, not from conversations with palace servants, but a lesson embedded in bureaucratic politics. Let us review the list of power figures that oversee Joseph's situation: Joseph's boss, Potiphar, throws him into jail for a crime he did not commit. However, "the jailor put Joseph in charge of all of the prisoners who were confined there" (Gen. 39:22). Yet, the greater authority over the prison is the captain of the guard (Gen. 40:1–3) who we know is Potiphar (Gen. 39:1). When Pharaoh hands the butler and baker over to the captain of the guard to be placed in prison, "the captain of the guard [Potiphar] put Joseph in charge of the men, and Joseph took care of them *as he did the others*. They remained there in custody for some time" (Gen. 40:4). Potiphar, the one who put Joseph in prison, now puts Joseph in charge. Go figure! Joseph needs to sort this out in his own mind and soul.

Here is a problem freighted with learning: The man who falsely convicted Joseph and put him in prison now requires his skills and is not afraid to call on him to serve. The evil empire wants what it wants and wants it now! In the original film adaptation of *Willy Wonka and the Chocolate Factory*, Veruca Salt (played by Julie Dawn Cole) sings the anthem of spoiled brats, "I Want It Now."[12] The empire may be more sophisticated in its approach, but the desire and demand is the same.

The assignment of caring for prisoners from Pharaoh's household honored Joseph. The captain of the guard validated Joseph's skills and reputation by giving him a unique responsibility. Nevertheless, the honor presents another problem to solve. Validation from the empire is often dubious. When the empire grants recognition, it is wise to practice gracious suspicion.

In the palace of the empire, human interactions conceal hidden agendas, conscious or unconscious, positive or negative. Be wise and try to understand the varied interests of the groups and individuals you deal with. To probe the interests of others, learn and employ the art of gracious suspicion, the art of tenderly, silently, and compassionately seeking to discover the values and motives of others. You may never know their values and motives with total accuracy, but you must try to know what you can know. And you must learn to do this graciously, without judgment, superiority, or manipulation.

Jesus was clear on the subject of dealing with palace politics. "Listen: I am sending you out to be sheep among wolves. You must be as shrewd as serpents and as innocent as doves" (Matt. 10:16). Jesus practiced the art of gracious suspicion.

Never place your eternal value in the greedy hands of the evil empire, the kingdoms of this world.

- When the Pharisees "determined to trap this Jesus with His own words—*hang Him by His own rope, you might say*... Jesus knew these men were out to trap Him" (Matt. 22:15, 18).
- When a centurion approached Jesus on behalf of a paralyzed servant, Jesus graciously suspected a deeper faith. Looking past a soldier's garb, Jesus was amazed: "I have not met a single person in Israel with as much faith *as this officer*" (Matt. 8:10).
- Again, wise suspicion prompted Jesus to answer Pilate, "Are you asking Me because you believe this is true, or have others said this about Me?" (John 18:34).

Jesus would not be coerced or seduced by palace politics. Jesus taught and lived validation found in God: "As the Father knows Me, I know the Father" (John 10:15). Never place your eternal value in the greedy hands of the evil empire, the kingdoms of this world. Joseph was learning that his eternal value was not determined by Potiphar or Pharaoh.

Third, Joseph learned to align with God's plans in spite of palace politics. After some time had passed, both the butler and the baker had troubling dreams on the same night. They looked to Joseph for insight and understanding.

Joseph clearly declares that God alone holds the future, God alone can interpret the dreams, and God will interpret dreams through Joseph (Gen. 40:8). Quickly, confidently, and concisely, Joseph interprets the dreams of the two men. One will live, and the other will die (vv. 9–19).

It happens just as Joseph predicted, just as God had interpreted the dreams through Joseph. Pharaoh celebrated his own birthday with a grand feast and called together all his servants. The butler and baker were summoned from the prison. "As they were gathered together, he lifted up the head of the chief cupbearer and restored him to his former office. *That day* the cupbearer resumed placing the cup in Pharaoh's hand. But Pharaoh lifted off the head of the chief baker and impaled him *on a tree for the birds,* just as Joseph had interpreted" (vv. 20–22).

God reveals the future through Joseph; God and Joseph are making history.

When Joseph interpreted the dreams of the butler and the baker, the dream given to Joseph so many years before came back to his remembrance and reflection. It is God's dream for Joseph that requires our full attention, not the dreams of Pharaoh's servants.

Joseph sits in his cell pondering all that has taken place. God has revealed the future to him. God disclosed the future through dreams. God's dream for Joseph comes back to him with full force. Sheaves of grain bow to Joseph; sun, moon, and stars bow to Joseph (Gen. 37:6–11). What could God mean by Joseph's dream? What is God planning? Could Joseph believe that God would work on his behalf? Dare he hope that the long nightmare of slavery and prison might come to a good end?

The Bible does not promise that aligning with God's plan quickly brings a good end. The nightmare for Joseph was not over yet. Joseph does what he can to bargain for his release. He understands the way things work in the palace: do a favor and receive a favor. To Pharaoh's butler, the one whose life is saved, Joseph requests, "But *I ask one thing.* Remember me when things are going well for you. *If you have the opportunity,* do me a favor and mention me to Pharaoh. *Perhaps he will* get me out of this place. You see I was stolen from the land of *my people* the Hebrews, and I've done nothing to deserve being thrown into this pit" (Gen. 40:14–15).

The Bible does not promise that aligning with God's plan quickly brings a good end.

This is all Joseph can do. After all he has endured, all he has suffered, the tentative bargain with the butler was also a prayer to God: "Remember me" (v. 14). Surely, it is now time for God to act.

The closing sentence of this chapter on Joseph's life is filled with pathos: *Sadly* the chief cupbearer did not remember Joseph . . . instead, he forgot all about him (v. 23).

It is a terrible thing to be forgotten, looked over, ignored, and left behind. A prayer for deliverance transformed into a lament of abandonment. Had God forgotten Joseph?

> How long, O Eternal One? How long will You forget
> me? Forever?
> How long will You look the other way?
> How long must I agonize,
> grieving Your absence in my heart every day?
> How long will You let my enemies win?
> Turn back; respond to me, O Eternal, my True God!
> Put the spark of life in my eyes, or I'm dead. (Ps. 13:1–3)

GOD PLACES US

What do you do when you do not know what to do? You cannot see God working. You sit and sulk in your prison cell, the situation that traps you. How do you respond? What wisdom comes from this bit of God's curriculum?

Let me shed light on Joseph by sharing an insight I share with students. I have worked with many doctoral students as they write a dissertation. It is almost impossible for students to grasp the full extent of the practical implications of writing a dissertation. For Joseph (and for us), it is difficult to grasp all the ramifications, consequences, difficulties, and struggles when we determine to follow God.

Here is the problem: The students want to understand everything about the dissertation from the beginning of the process. They cannot. It is not a matter of me keeping secrets from them. The students do not have the experience and knowledge needed to grasp the whole. I lay out the challenge of library research, developing a design, implementing the field research, gathering data, and writing the chapters of the dissertation one by one. They hear me and take down their notes, but they are unable to embrace what this will mean in their lives.

Apply this human illustration to following God. We cannot understand it until we do it. And, then we only understand a piece at a time. Yet, piece by piece we learn, mature, and come to deeply embrace the journey with God and the challenge of fulfilling God's purpose.

At the beginning of their academic journey, my students are incapable of internalizing the repercussions and struggles of increasing effort, acquiring skills, assimilating knowledge, networking support, politicking opportunities, overcoming setbacks, managing discouragement, and healing emotions. All this and more awaits them on a journey of giving birth to a doctoral dissertation. Apply your imagination to what awaits God's partners on the path of God's purpose.

To my students, I share a word of wisdom gleaned from many years of leading them through this academic process. This is my word of wisdom for them: "Trust the process and do the next thing."

In biblical terms, to trust the process and do the next thing means to walk in the light you have (I John 1:7). This is what you do when you do not know what to do.

When you do not know what to do, walk in the light you have.

You wait for God. God's people are called on to take the long view. Abraham and Sarah waited for the promised child (Gen. 17). The Israelites waited for release from Egypt (Ex. 2:23). They waited and wandered in the desert and into exile (Deut. 2:14). They waited for the Messiah (Luke 2:28–32). We wait in hope for His return (Acts 1:11).

Waiting on the Lord, putting hope in the Lord, transforms you. So it was for Joseph. He has waited for a dozen years since he was sold into slavery. And, he, like us, waited without knowing when or if there would be a good end. We do not always know God's intentions and strategies. We trust God.

> **Eternal One:** My intentions are not *always* yours,
> and I do not go about things as you do.
> My thoughts and My ways are above and beyond you,
> just as heaven is far from your reach here on earth.
> For as rain and snow can't go back once they've fallen,
> but soak into the ground
> And nourish the plants that grow,
> providing seed to the farmer and bread for the hungry,
> So it is when I declare something.
> My word will go out and not return to Me empty,
> But it will do what I wanted;
> it will accomplish what I determined. (Isa. 55:8–11)

Consider the length of time embedded in God's promise: snow and rain on the mountain melt into streams that flow to the plains.

The water irrigates the ground, plants grow, and seeds are harvested. Seeds are ground into flour, and flour is mixed for baking. The baking produces the promised bread for the hungry.

Through waiting, struggling, hoping, and fretting, a naive teenager is transformed into a confident young man. The boy who ratted out his brothers is not a skilled manager, fit for an empire. The brash teenager in his many-colored coat, who gave little thought to God, becomes the one through whom God reveals history in the making.

Joseph wakes up in his cell on what seems just another morning, another day in confinement. However, it is not just another day. This is the day the Lord has made (Ps. 118:24) to present Joseph to the empire. In the next few hours, the world of Joseph, Pharaoh, and Egypt are also transformed. This is God's day. The time has come. God's partner is ready to lead the empire for the sake of God's purpose. On this day, Joseph will know: God is good. God is in control. God and I are making history.

God reveals His plan. God's plan is brought to reality through Pharaoh's problem. It may have been difficult for Joseph to believe that Pharaoh had a problem. For people in prison, it is almost inconceivable that the high and mighty people are troubled.

Pharaoh has two dreams: first, fat and thin cows, then, plump and shriveled grain. His dream includes the Nile River, the source of life in Egypt. In the morning, troubled Pharaoh sends for his advisers, men of wisdom and magic, but no one understands the meaning of the dreams.[13]

Knowledge is power,[14] and Pharaoh no longer has the knowledge. Only God knows what is going on and what will happen. In the whisper of a dream, God bypasses all the bureaucracy, the

**God leads the empire,
and Pharaoh is unaware.**

gatekeepers, and the palace politics to trouble the king. God leads the empire, and Pharaoh is unaware.

The butler spies an opportunity to curry favor with Pharaoh. With word of the troublesome dream wafting its way through the palace, the self-absorbed butler now remembers Joseph and goes to Pharaoh (Gen. 41:9). His self-serving remembrance plays into God's purpose. God enters Pharaoh's palace "like a thief in the night" (I Thess. 5:2). He pickpockets Pharaoh's power and presents heaven's choice for the new man in charge. Like a chess master moving pieces on the board, God has Pharaoh sending for Joseph. The plan is coming together.

You step into God's moment. Joseph woke up in a prison cell, poorly clothed, unshaven, with the stench of the dungeon. Now, having been "been allowed to shave and change his clothes, he was brought before Pharaoh" (Gen. 41:14). Imagine his thoughts: *Why would Pharaoh want to see me? Could this be God's moment? Or does Pharaoh want my head?*

Joseph, put away your worries; God rules the day. The king of the evil empire, Pharaoh himself, lays bare his ignorance and anxiety before a Hebrew slave. Can you hear God chuckle?

Joseph interprets Pharaoh's dreams: years of plenty followed by years of famine. Joseph may not understand it all, but he sees God as chief actor in Pharaoh's palace. God receives full authority as Joseph, the dreamer, speaks to Pharaoh about dreams:

> I cannot do this, but **God** will answer . . .
>
> **God** is revealing to Pharaoh what He is going to do . . .
>
> As I told Pharaoh, **God** is showing Pharaoh what He means to do *and what will come* . . .

God receives full authority as Joseph, the dreamer, speaks to Pharaoh about dreams.

The doubling of Pharaoh's dream means this future is fixed by **God**, and He will make it happen very soon. (Gen. 41:16, 25, 28, 32, emphasis added)

God's choice, Joseph, commands the attention of the throne room of the empire. The promise to Abraham expands to new dimensions in Joseph: "I am going to put a *special* blessing on you and cause your reputation to grow so that you will become a blessing *and example to others*. I will also bless those who bless you" (Gen. 12:2–3).

You take your place in God's plan. Joseph speaks with confidence. He has no need for excitement, no need for persuasion, and no use of argument. Joseph focuses on God; Pharaoh is irrelevant. The future is out of Pharaoh's hands. The will of heaven has taken over.

Through years of human choices, both good and bad, resentful betrayal and false accusations, wrongful imprisonment and selfish forgetfulness, and, finally, a troubling dream and a self-serving memory, God moves against the powers of this world to establish His purpose.

Everything has led to this dramatic moment. The will of heaven now hangs on one turn of phrase in the mouth of Joseph: "*My advice is that* Pharaoh should select someone who is wise and discerning and put him in charge of the land of Egypt *during this time*" (Gen. 41:33). Joseph's imagination is fully alive and aligned with God's future, a future that is utterly beyond Pharaoh's grasp. Pharaoh plays his part and appoints God's partner to lead the empire: "Since God has shown all of this to you, I can't imagine anyone wiser and more discerning than you. Therefore you will be in charge of my household. All of my people will report to you and do as you say. Only I, because I sit on the throne, will be greater than you. I hereby appoint you head over all of the land of Egypt" (vv. 39–41).

God is good.

God is in control.

And God and Joseph are making history!

SUMMARY: Why Is This Happening to Me?

In this chapter in Joseph's life, he has been both abandoned in prison and honored in the palace. For each event, he might ask, "Why is this happening to me?" There are times we discern the grander purpose and plan of God; there are other times, many times, we cannot grasp why circumstances unfold as they do. In both conditions, our response needs to be the same: seek to know God and seek to know yourself. God will open the textbook of life; trust Him and step into the light you have. But know with certainty your decisions and attitude make a difference. "He that made us without ourselves, will not save us without ourselves."[15]

THINK: Reflection and Conversation

1. This chapter in the life of Joseph covers a wide array of emotions and events. What parts of the chapter resonate with your experience? What do you most identify with in this part of Joseph's story?

2. If we are languishing in prison or walking into the palace, the mind can go wild with imagining. The "what ifs"[16] dance in our heads. What happens when your imagination is fueled by fear? What happens when your imagination is fed by faith? How can we help one another nurture faith-filled thinking?

3. Joseph is the first partner of God placed at a level of high authority in an empire or kingdom (eventually, Israel would be a kingdom). As such, politics is how things get done. Have you observed any political tactics in your workplace, in your family, or even in your church? What happens if you ignore it? What happens if you are obsessed with it? How can you rise above it and still make a difference?

4. There are practical matters concerning not knowing God's plan.
   - When have you found yourself in a figurative prison or palace and wondered what God was doing?
   - How has God used the prison time (time of being stuck, seemingly wasted time) to nurture your soul, give you Himself, and prepare you for what is next?
   - What are some of the lessons you have learned about dealing with conniving and manipulating people (while still holding to your trust in God)?
   - What is your prayer right now concerning what God is teaching you about Himself or yourself?

Looking Ahead: Joseph must think he has arrived; he is in his proper place, manager of all Egypt. Now, the purpose for being in place will be revealed as Joseph faces a need and deeply personal struggle. The brothers turn up in the palace. Old wounds begin to fester.

THE AGONY OF OLD INJURIES

Do I Have to Face This?

I am *completely numb,* totally spent, hopelessly
crushed.
The agitation of my heart makes me groan.
O Lord, You know all my desires;
nothing escapes You; *You hear* my every moan.
My heart pounds against my chest; my vigor is completely drained;
my eyes were once bright, but now the brightness is all gone.
Even my friends and loved ones turn away when
they see this marked man;
those closest to me are no longer close at all.
Those who want me dead lay traps upon my path;
those who desire my downfall threaten—*my end is near*—
they spend their days plotting against me.
Like one who is deaf, my ears do not hear.
Like one who is mute, my tongue cannot speak.
The truth is this: I am like one who cannot hear;
I cannot even protest *against them.*
Still I wait *expectantly* for You, O Eternal One—
knowing You will answer me *in some way,* O Lord,
my True God.

—Psalm 38:8–15

Several decades ago I stepped into the senior pastor position of a church with a long record of success and accomplishment. The church invited me to serve as their leader at a low and difficult time in their history. In the past, they touched many people's lives, expanded mission in the city and around the world, and sent members of the congregation into diverse and fruitful ministries.

At the time of my arrival as pastor, they were hurting and needing a renewal of hope and faith. They needed to remember and revive their partnership with God, just as God's first human partner once did: "Against the odds, Abraham's hope grew into full-fledged faith that he would turn out to be the father of many nations, just as God had promised" (Rom. 4:18).

For Joseph, like his great-grandfather, against all odds, God has done the impossible. For Joseph, the Lord placed him as ruler of Egypt.

I faced a difficult task at the church I pastored. Like Paul's young friend Timothy, my challenge with the church was "to strengthen, *comfort,* and encourage you in your faith" (1 Thess. 3:2). Frankly, I felt overwhelmed. I prayed, consulted, and searched my heart for direction. The advice I received was good. However, looking back, I believe it was safe advice that restricted my thinking to finding a quick win, a sure victory, and a project with certain success.

In opposition to conventional wisdom, I received the best word of advice from a quiet father who had married the sister of the church's leading family. He seldom spoke and never spoke out. He was not the kind of person the church considered for leadership. However, he was a source of deep insight for me.

I made arrangements to visit him and his family in their home. The purpose of the visit was to get acquainted. I also wanted to understand his perspective on the church and his hopes and concerns for the future. Quickly, he pointed to the need for

THE STORY IN SUMMARY

Genesis 41:42–57; 42:1–38; 43:1–15

Pharaoh appoints Joseph in charge of the whole of Egypt. He gives him the symbols of power and authority and a well-connected wife. For seven bountiful years, Joseph buys grain throughout Egypt. When the famine comes, he sells the grain to the people of Egypt as well as starving people from other nations who come for help.

One of the groups of starving people includes Joseph's long lost family. Father Jacob sends the brothers to Egypt to purchase grain. When Joseph meets his brothers, they do not recognize him. He remembers his dream and their cruelty of many years ago and instantly accuses his brothers of spying. Joseph holds one of the older brothers hostage and demands that the others return to their father and bring the youngest brother, Benjamin, to Egypt. When the brothers leave for home, Joseph secretly returns the silver paid for the grain in their bags. The brothers are frightened and believe that God is punishing them because of what they did to Joseph so many years ago.

Back in Canaan, the brothers tell the story to their father, Jacob. Jacob will not allow Benjamin to go to Egypt. His heart continues to grieve because twenty years earlier he was told a wild beast killed Joseph. With Joseph dead, the old man will not risk his youngest son, Benjamin. The lie the brothers told their father lives on in the wound the old man carries every day.

God-inspired vision and a significant challenge. He raised his face and locked my eyes in his gaze as, with quiet intensity, he said, "Pastor, what this church needs is a challenge so big that when it is done people can only say it was God."

IT IS GOOD TO BE JOSEPH!

In the life of Joseph, God had done something so big that we know it was God. The dream of twenty years before, the dream that offered a hint of God, was coming into reality; Joseph was the first lieutenant of the most powerful man in the world, the pharaoh of the Egyptian empire.

God's exceptional deed. Review the reluctant journey of this man. As a seventeen-year-old, Joseph saw sheaves of grain on earth and stars in the heavens bow to him (Gen. 37:5–11).

- Joseph endured the cruelty of his brothers (Gen. 37:13–36), the humiliation of slavery, false accusation, and unjust imprisonment (Gen. 39:1–23).
- He successfully managed his master's home and Pharaoh's prison (Gen. 39:2, 23).
- Further, God gave him insight into the future through dreams, dreams of Pharaoh's household servants (Gen. 40:8) as well as Pharaoh himself (Gen. 41:15–16).

God brought about more than Joseph could hope or imagine (Eph. 3:20). For Joseph, it looked like the sheaves of grain and the stars in the heavens bowed to him; the granaries of Egypt were his, and the courts of Egypt granted his every wish.

The symbols of power. Pharaoh made Joseph second in command of the empire. Seen in terms of a business, Pharaoh owns the business but Joseph is the chief executive officer. He receives a gold chain and a robe, not the multicolored garment of love given by his father, but a vestment of power conferred by Pharaoh himself (Gen. 41:42).[1]

The royal decree. On behalf of Pharaoh, Joseph purchased grain during the seven good years, "more than anyone could measure"

(v. 49). Grain purchased in the time of surplus would be sold during the lean years at premium prices. All of Egypt obeyed Joseph's bidding. Pharaoh "had Joseph ride in the chariot reserved for his second-in-command, and servants ordered everyone, 'Kneel!' as he rode by. So this was how Pharaoh appointed Joseph head over all of the land of Egypt" (v. 43).

A new life. Pharaoh also gave Joseph a wife as an additional trophy[2] of his status and success. She was well connected to a politically powerful family among the Egyptian priesthood (v. 45). Soon, Joseph and his bride produced new life, two sons; the past was over and Joseph's new life began. He named his sons as symbols of his determination to eradicate all ties with the past. The naming of his children indicated the change in Joseph, a change in the way he understood himself and the way he understood God.

First, regarding self-understanding, Joseph turned his back on his birth family; they were dead to him. "Joseph named his firstborn son Manasseh because he said, 'God has made me forget all about my hardship and all of my father's family'" (v. 51). In his mind and heart, he put away the family of his youth; Egypt was his new family.

Second, concerning his awareness of God, he gave the Lord full credit for his new life, his new family, and his new success: "He named the second son Ephraim, because as he said, 'God has made me fruitful in the land of my misfortune'" (v. 52). God brought power and prosperity out of adversity.

A common trap. At last, a good ending! We cheer for Joseph and praise our God. At last, all has worked out for good. Surely, God has completed His plan for Joseph. Something childlike in us is ready to close the book, turn off the light, and

Oh, how tempting to think we are the final product of God's purpose rather than a partner in God's much grander plan.

feel tucked in, safe and warm. The child in us resonates with the stories from our upbringing: "once upon a time"[3] and "they lived happily ever after."[4] Deep within, a voice whispers: Let it be for Joseph, and let it be for me.

Perhaps like you and me, Joseph fell into a common trap that plagues God's partners, the ruse that this must be God's plan because it is working out so well for me. Oh, how tempting to think we are the final product of God's purpose rather than a partner in God's much grander plan. We need to come back to reality; we are a part, a partner, in the eternal working of God's design.

God's plan is not complete. God's plan is not about Joseph; it is about more than Joseph. God was not just working out Joseph's life for Joseph's sake. God has a much larger purpose. Ruling Egypt under Pharaoh's direct authority is only the staging ground for God's efforts. In the next act, God rattles Joseph's world.

The stage is set. Joseph controlled the world supply of grain, "because *by this time* the entire world was in the grip of a severe famine" (v. 57). The world came to Joseph pleading, "Give us each day that day's bread" (Matt. 6:11). At the same time Joseph would painfully learn "forgive us our debts as we forgive those who owe us something" (v. 12).

As famine dried the fields and choked off the supply of food, Joseph faced a flood of family memories that opened old wounds.

OLD WOUNDS

"I can feel the weather changing," she announced to the office staff, who accepted her word as if a meteorologist reported Doppler radar findings. I had to ask, "Do you have a secret way of predicting the weather?"

She told me the story: "When I was a child, I had a nasty spill off my bicycle. I broke a bone in my leg. It took a long time to heal.

It's fine now except when a high-pressure system moves through. Under high pressure, I feel the hurt again."

Joseph fed the world in a time of famine with grain purchased during abundant years and, now, sold in lean years. Meanwhile, back at the sheep ranch where Joseph was born, a high-pressure system of old memories and injuries made its way south toward the Nile valley.

Ruminating on a painful past. In the land of Canaan, Jacob's family suffers hunger with the rest of the world. The brothers are stymied. They do not know what to do. They cannot imagine a solution that would take them out of their small homeland. Father Jacob, whose perspective of the world is much larger, takes over and sends his sons to Egypt to acquire grain. But he would not send his youngest son, Benjamin, "because he was afraid that something might happen to him" (Gen. 42:4).

The brothers' reluctance to travel to Egypt belies a deeper and unresolved wrong. Imagine these ten men packing supplies for the trip; they load the carts, donkeys, and camels. Each one is afraid to mention the ghost in the camp, but the painful memories are fresh again: a plan to kill Joseph, a bargain to sell him into slavery, a blood-stained robe, the lie about a wild animal attack, and a father's unending grief. It was an old wound that had never healed. Finally, they load the silver with which they will purchase grain. Each one remembers silently and alone how "they brought Joseph up out of the pit and sold him to the Ishmaelites for about eight ounces of silver, *the usual price of young male slaves*" (Gen. 37:28).

Joseph's brothers take the first steps on the journey to Egypt. They follow the same trade route over which they saw their younger

Joseph's perfect life crashes at his feet where his brothers bow.

brother carried off in bondage twenty years earlier. What had happened to Joseph? Was he dead, living as a slave in Egypt, or had he been sold up the Nile and deep into Africa? Old memories spawned guilty and fearful emotions.

Enjoying success and serenity today. In Egypt, Joseph's careful plans (Gen. 41:46–49) for Pharaoh's prosperity, as well as his own, yield a high return on investment. Joseph forecasts an increase in the price of grain in direct proportion to the increase in the people's hunger. With careful calculation, he keeps the granaries locked until the people cry out to Pharaoh, who immediately sends them to Joseph (vv. 53–56). He can charge top dollar. In addition to Egyptians, people from neighboring nations pour into Egypt and line up to buy grain from Joseph (v. 57). He negotiates the best price, shores up treaties with allies, and implements sanctions on enemies. Joseph is living the dream of the industrial titans and Wall Street giants; he corners the market on food.

When the past steps into today. Here is the scene: the room is large and lavishly furnished. Joseph occupies center stage in a chair that is several steps above the crowd. To his right and left are accountants, moneychangers, record keepers, and an assortment of lesser bureaucrats. The press of strangers from multiple lands produces a strange, living fresco of costumes, cultures, and odors. Yes, the odors were more than could be overcome by the rich Egyptian perfumes, incense, and floral displays. It had the appearance and smell of money for Joseph.

At first, from a distance, the tightly huddled group of ten men is unremarkable. Joseph glances across the room. Perhaps there is an unconscious faint flicker of familiarity. He dismisses it. As the group draws closer, making their way up the line toward

Joseph is alone in dealing with the injuries of the past.

Joseph, his eye catches them again. Their clothing is reminiscent of another place, another time, and another life.

It is the smell that gives them away, the distinct smell of sheep-herders—a detestable occupation among the Egyptians (Gen. 46:34), but an esteemed lifestyle in the highlands of Canaan, the land promised to Jacob's family. Joseph knows! He steels himself, hiding in his Egyptian persona. Another sale is closed. Joseph looks up to deal with the next buyers. Like a dream materializing (Gen. 42:9), bowing before him are his older brothers. "*When it was their turn,* Joseph's brothers came and bowed down before him with their faces to the ground. The moment Joseph saw his brothers, he recognized them *even though nearly 20 years had passed since last he saw them,* but he treated them like strangers and spoke gruffly to them" (vv. 6–7).

A flash of pain stirred smoldering anger into a cold-blue flame. An old wound, an injury he thought he had put away, rips open anew. Joseph's perfect life crashes at his feet where his brothers bow. Joseph faces a grievance thought long dead. Joseph is alone in dealing with the injuries of the past. This meeting inaugurates a reign of resentment, remorse, and heartache. This is a family affair. Joseph's anger, the brother's guilt, and their father's grief all come to bear on God's purpose.

UNRESOLVED ANGER AND RUTHLESS POWER

With the appearance of his brothers, the Joseph we admire morphs into a different person. He has learned the tradecraft of Egyptian power and politics. We want to imagine him as magnanimous in his treatment of the starving masses that come to him for food. We would prefer to jump to the happy ending of forgiveness and hugs all around. However, the story recorded in Scripture is far more painful and far, far more human.

People of faith shouldn't act like that, but they do. We struggle when we must come to terms with people of faith who act like people of the world, people of the evil empire. I remember sharing a message about dealing with enemies who hurt us. After the service, as I was shaking hands with members of the congregation, a young and naive Christian approached me and said, "Pastor, I understand about forgiving people who hurt you, and I get it when they are people who don't know Jesus. But, if someone in the church ever hurt me, I just don't know if I could handle it."

Here is an awful truth: such is the case with Joseph. He does not behave as we want him to behave. We admire him. We validate the fact that God's hand is on him. Nevertheless, we are dumbfounded by his actions and attitude toward the nation he rules and the brothers who abused him.

Consider the way he leads the Egyptian empire. Joseph cornered the market on food. He bought all grain in response to God's interpretation of Pharaoh's dream—lean years will follow abundant years. This poses the potential for the ultimate insider-trading scheme. We would hope that Joseph would use the inside information to ease the suffering of people. Such is not the case. Joseph profits Pharaoh and Joseph.

Follow Joseph's business strategy for the seven years of famine (Gen. 47:13–26):

- When people are starving, he sells grain at exorbitant prices, leaving the populace in poverty.
- The famine continues. He negotiates the sale of grain in exchange for livestock.
- His next move, having acquired the money and livestock, ties all private property to Pharaoh.

- Hunger continues. He negotiates a 20 percent tax on the food raised from government (Pharaoh and Joseph) seed supplies.
- The people are desperate. They willingly became Pharaoh's slaves rather than starve.

"So Joseph made a law regarding the land of Egypt—which stands to this day—declaring Pharaoh is due one-fifth *of all the land produces*" (v. 26). Joseph enslaving the Egyptians would, no doubt, bring applause from a crowd of ancient Israelites. For our Christian ears, however, we expect compassion from our leaders.

Joseph's ethical commitment is not compassion for starving people but ruthless protection[5] and advancement of Pharaoh and the empire. He takes advantage of people in dire need. When people we trust, people we look to for help, people we count on for goodness and grace, and people of faith take advantage, line their own pockets, and let others suffer for their own advancement, what are we to think and do?

How can people of faith act like that? Here is my answer: I don't know, but from time to time, they do. People we admire in one situation can demonstrate such incongruent behavior in another. People of integrity in one situation become people of duplicity in another. It is not in Joseph we put our trust. We anchor our conviction in God, "Do not put your trust in *the rulers of this world—kings and* princes. Do not expect any rescue from mortal men" (Ps. 146:3).

People of faith should get over old injuries, but they don't. The infamous political theorist Machiavelli observed that people injure

"Do not put your trust in the rulers of this world—kings and princes. Do not expect any rescue from mortal men" (Ps. 146:3).

other people for two reasons—fear or hatred. He wrote a line that describes Joseph and his reaction to seeing his brothers bow before him: "Anyone who believes that new benefits make men of high station forget old injuries is deceiving himself."[6]

When Joseph's brothers bow before him, rage energizes his soul. Nonetheless, like a skillful politician, he hides his emotions and his identity. He gives away nothing. In this way, he controls the situation like a puppet master (Gen. 42:8).

He treats them like strangers, intimidates them, interrogates them, and twists their answers. Joseph accuses them of espionage and then turns to extortion. He demands the nine men remain in prison while one returns home to bring the youngest brother, Benjamin, to Egypt as proof they are telling the truth. He puts all ten in prison for three days (vv. 9–17).

This three days provides Joseph with time to consider his next move. The cool-down period proves helpful. Joseph's position softens: leave one brother in prison and the others return home to fetch Benjamin. Concern enters Joseph's voice as he speaks of the suffering of the rest of their family. This includes Joseph's father and full brother, Benjamin. A thought of lost loved ones tempers his resentment. One brother, Simeon, is arrested, bound before the others, and held as a hostage (vv. 18–25).

I do not care for this portion of Joseph's story. I prefer to ignore it, turn the page, and move on to more present events. But there is something here, something we need to face. Joseph's display of ruthless power rests on two verses: "Although Joseph recognized them, they did not recognize him. He

Perhaps the difficulty in examining Joseph's treatment of his brothers is because his actions and attitude exposes similar motives and imaginings in us.

then remembered the dreams he had *as a young man* regarding his brothers" (vv. 8–9).

He remembered the dreams. He saw his brothers bowing before him. He used God's dream as justification for a personal vendetta. Oh Lord, forgive us.

People of faith suffer if anger is unresolved. Perhaps the difficulty in examining Joseph's treatment of his brothers is because his actions and attitude exposes similar motives and imaginings in us. If you are struggling with resentment in your heart, the words of Jesus can be startling:

> As you know, long ago God instructed *Moses to tell* His people, "Do not murder; those who murder will be judged *and punished." But here is the even harder truth*: anyone who is angry with his brother will be judged for his anger. Anyone who *taunts his friend, speaks contemptuously toward him, or* calls him "Loser" or "Fool" or "Scum," will have to answer to the high court. And anyone who calls his brother a fool may find himself in the fires of hell. (Matt. 5:21–22)

There are times when the anger is right on the surface; you know it is there because you feel it and obsess over it. Such is Joseph's condition. But there was a time, several years ago, when he was certain the past was behind him, when he was confident "God has made me forget all about my hardship and all of my father's family" (Gen. 41:51).

Yet, the resentment persisted, waiting for the moment to rise from dark and hidden caverns in his soul. Here is the good word: God has not abandoned you. He is present, even in the dark places that seem most distant from Him (Ps. 139:8–12). God knows you. He has knit you together. He knows each event that shapes your life, and He knows the hurt you are suffering (vv. 13–21). Trust Him. Let Him take His light into your soul for a full examination.

> Deep hatred boils within me toward them;
> *I am Your friend, and* they are my enemies.
> Explore me, O God, and know the real me. *Dig deeply and discover who I am.*
> Put me to the test and watch how I handle the strain.
> *Examine me to* see if there is an evil bone in me,
> and guide me down Your path forever.
> (vv. 22–24)

UNRESOLVED GUILT AND SHAMEFUL FEAR

I am convinced that food, fun, finances, and family are the four major guilt groups, and family provides opportunities for maximum blameworthiness. The brothers wallowed in their guilt. The journey to Egypt pressed them to reconsider again their evil deeds: abuse of their younger brother, Joseph (Gen. 37:20–21), and deception of their aged father (vv. 32–35).

An unforgiven past gives birth to a fearful future. Guilt acts as a chain that binds the soul in the quicksand of dishonorable days. Guilt functions as blinders on your perspective in life, narrowing vision, options, and possibilities. Cancer destroys the body through the uncontrollable growth of harmful tissue. Guilt destroys your life through the uncontrollable growth of shameful fear.

The harsh treatment ladled on the brothers by the Egyptian ruler (Joseph in disguise) surfaces their guilt. They see more than a cruel ruler of Egypt. They attribute their ill-treatment as payback for their treatment of Joseph: "Now *at last,* we

Guilt destroys your life through the uncontrollable growth of shameful fear.

are paying the penalty for what we did to our brother. We saw his anguish when he pleaded with us, but we wouldn't listen. Now that very anguish has come to us" (Gen. 42:21).

Their shame is further catapulted into agonizing fear by a strange trick Joseph plays on them. Joseph speaks to his brothers through an interpreter, but he, of course, understands everything they say. When the brothers discuss their cruelty to Joseph so long ago, Joseph is moved and must leave the room before he breaks down before them. He then orders that the money they paid for the food be hidden in the sacks of grain the brothers are taking out of Egypt (vv. 23–25).

What is Joseph up to? It is hard to know. Joseph does not even know: his heart is befuddled. The brothers, on the other hand, are frightened. Is the return of the silver a trick? Their collective thought is frightening: "What is God doing to us?" (v. 28).

It is a miserable and fearsome thing to imagine your life in the hands of an angry God. The opening thoughts of Jonathan Edward's famous sermon of 275 years ago certainly apply to the perception of Joseph's brothers as they sit about the campfire looking at the grain and the silver: They are always exposed to destruction; they are always exposed to sudden destruction.[7]

The psalmist paints a soulful portrait of reeling in unresolved guilt:

> Because Your anger *has infected the depths of my*
> *being and stolen my health,*
> my flesh is ill.
> My bones are no longer sound
> because of all the sins I have committed.
> My guilt has covered me; *it's more than I can handle;*
> this burden is too heavy for me to carry. (Ps. 38:3–4)

Unresolved guilt is a slave to a world of retribution. These Hebrew men cannot imagine that God could break beyond their limited perspective. For them, God's purpose is to deal out just deserts, what you have coming, and divine retribution.

They cannot believe or imagine that God can set them free through love, acceptance, and forgiveness.[8] They desperately need grace but are in no position and have no faith to experience it.

Imagine a world without forgiveness. Indeed, that is so much of our world. Forgiveness is a scarce commodity in many corporations, houses of worship, and extended families. Alan Shore, one of the lawyers on the television series *The Practice*, laid the world system bare when he quipped, "To err is human, but to get even? THAT is divine."[9]

Joseph and his brothers live in the world of vengeance and punishment. Sadly, throngs of people scratch out an existence, trying to dodge the crushing blows of ruthless power and shameful fear. Do you remember when you were once under the power of the prince of this world?

> As for you, *don't you remember how you used to just exist? Corpses,* dead *in life,* buried by transgressions, wandering the course of this *perverse* world. *You were the offspring* of the prince of the power of air—*oh, how he owned you,* just as he still controls those living in disobedience. *I'm not talking about the outsiders alone;* we were all guilty of falling headlong for the persuasive passions of this world; we all have had our fill of indulging the flesh and mind, *obeying impulses to follow perverse thoughts motivated by dark powers.* As a result, our natural inclinations led us to be children of wrath, just like the rest of humankind. (Eph. 2:1–3)

Guilt and fear are cleansed in the presence of God. Nobel Laureate Desmond Tutu expressed the need and power of forgiveness:

> Ultimately, you discover that without forgiveness, there is no future. We recognize that the past cannot be remade through punishment . . . There is no point in exacting vengeance now, knowing that it will be the cause for future vengeance by the offspring of those we punish. Vengeance leads only to revenge. Vengeance destroys those it claims and those who will become intoxicated with it . . . therefore, forgiveness is an absolute necessity for the continued human existence.[10]

In a far more personal expression of joy and liberation, the psalmist described souls set free from the chains of guilt:

> How happy is the person whose sin the Eternal will
> not take into account.
> *How happy are those* who no longer lie, *to them-*
> *selves or others.*
> When I refused to admit my wrongs, *I was miserable,*
> moaning and complaining all day long
> so that even my bones felt brittle.
> Day and night, Your hand kept pressing on me.
> My strength dried up *like water* in the summer
> heat;
> *You wore me down.*
>
> *When I finally saw my own lies,*
> I owned up to my sins before You,
> and I did not try to hide my evil deeds *from You.*
> I said *to myself,* "I'll admit *all* my sins to the Eternal,"
> and You *lifted and* carried away the guilt of my
> sin. (Ps. 32:2–5)

UNRESOLVED GRIEF AND FAITHFUL RESIGNATION

In addition to Joseph's resentment and the brothers' guilt, there is one more broken and bleeding member of the family required for God's next move. Jacob, the trickster who wrestled with God, who became Israel the wounded blessing, is an old and broken man. In his declining years, his life is defined by the loss of his beloved Joseph. When his older sons showed him the blood-soaked robe of many colors, he believed their lie and carried the open soulful injury as a suffering widow would later describe her grief, as walking in a circle that has no end:

> I have recently begun to view grief like a series of circles. In the beginning, the circle is tiny, so small that I was merely able to pivot, to spin, unable to move anywhere. There was no leaving the pain of it, the intense horror of the reality. As time drags me with it, the circles gradually widen, they get a bit larger and I find that there are days where I find there is some distance from the pain, some distraction in my responsibilities, in my work, or teaching. But they are circles and by their very nature lead me back to the place of loss and pain I had for a moment stepped away from. There is no escaping it, no healthy way, anyway. I often wish that grief could be linear, that I could just keep walking and walking, leaving it behind me, never to visit it again, never to hurt, to feel, to have to circle back to that gaping hole that sits in the center of myself, that wound that hurts so very, very much.[11]

Jacob opened his broken heart to his family, "'I will go to the grave grieving for my son.' *This is how deeply* Joseph's father grieved for him" (Gen. 37:35).

The darkness of unresolved grief. What happens when you nurse grief for decades? Sorrow and sadness fix your perspective, motivation, and emotions. Existence dissolves into an open wound without blessing: "You have taken from me the one I love and my friend; even *the light of* my acquaintances are darkness" (Ps. 88:18).

With the return of his sons from Egypt, new developments compound Jacob's grief with new pain and frightening prospects. He receives the story of the harsh Egyptian (Joseph is incognito) who holds his son Simeon hostage. Further, the high-ranking official extorts the price of young Benjamin for trading rights in Egypt (Gen. 42:29–35). Smoldering grief explodes in spiteful blame. Jacob accuses his sons, relives the loss of his true love, Rachel, and envisions his death by broken heart: "You have robbed me of my children: Joseph is gone, and Simeon is gone, and now you want to take Benjamin. Everything *and everyone* is against me! . . . I can't let my son go with you. His brother *Joseph* is already dead, and he's all I have left *of Rachel*. If I put him in your care and any harm should come to him on that journey, the sorrow would kill me. *I can't allow* you to condemn this old, gray head to the grave" (vv. 36, 38).

The flicker of remembered faith. I find it all just too much to absorb Joseph's resentment, the brothers' guilt, and now the grief of an old gray-haired man. It makes me want to turn away or at least turn the page and skip to a better ending. But to do so would leave God behind. God is dealing with the anger, fear, and heartbreak. God brings a flicker of faith out of this all-too-human family chaos.

I find myself facing the same temptation when listening to friends share their sad stories of woe and worry. The redoubtable tales are always personal, yet predictable. Hurt people hurt people. I want to skip, jump, fly to the moment of new life, new praise, and a new hope. Nevertheless, God lingers in the sorrow and shame. He lingers because there is a lesson to be learned, a lesson required for the next stage of the journey.

Jesus will not waste the pain.

Faith lives in spite of—and perhaps because of—human suffering in the family. In his heartache, Jacob finds faith. The one who struggled with God and humanity continues the struggle to bring God and his all-too-human family together.

First, faith acts. Despite his sorrow, Jacob initiates both trips to Egypt to buy bread for his starving family (Gen. 42:2; 43:2). Beyond his grief, Jacob still has his eye on the legacy promised from God, the generations yet unborn (Gen. 28:13–15). He knows that God can work beyond the small strip of land his family claims as promise. God is big and mighty and keeps His word.

Second, faith commits. For the return to Egypt, Jacob orders that his sons take the best produce, twice the money, and Benjamin, his beloved, his last connection with Rachel (Gen. 42:38). Jacob has overcome the sorrow in his heart to risk all for the future of God's family.

Third, faith prays. He places the venture in God's keeping: "And may the All-Powerful God grant you mercy from this man, so that he sends back your other brother and Benjamin" (Gen. 43:14). He calls the ancient name, *El Shaddai,* the God-All-Powerful, the Almighty, the God who has promised the future:

- "I am the God-All-Powerful. Walk before Me. *Continue to trust and serve Me faithfully.* Be blameless *and true*" (Gen. 17:1).
- "May the All-Powerful God bless you, make you fruitful, and multiply your descendants so that you will give rise to nation after nation!" (Gen. 28:3).
- "I am the God-All-Powerful. Be fruitful and multiply. You will give rise to a *great* nation; indeed nation after nation will come from you. Kings *and rulers* shall be numbered among your descendants" (Gen. 35:11).

Though faith flickers brightly for a moment, Jacob's next words, words at the close of his blessing, recoil in resignation and pessimism. "As for me, if I am to suffer the loss of my children, then what am I to do?" (Gen. 43:14).

How do we reconcile faith and hopelessness in the same breath? Must we assign our thinking to either the camp of Chicken Little, "the sky is falling,"[12] or the camp of Pollyanna as we "play the glad game"?[13] Life may not be so neatly cataloged. One of my students announced to the class, "I am a consistently disappointed optimist." Does faith always require a positive attitude? Can we believe, yet wince in our unbelief?

We place all our wounds at the feet of Jesus. Jesus invites us to bring our wounded and weary souls to Him: "Come to Me, all who are weary and burdened, and I will give you rest. Put My yoke upon your shoulders—*it might appear heavy at first, but it is perfectly fitted to your curves.* Learn from Me, for I am gentle and humble of heart. *When you are yoked to Me,* your weary souls will find rest. For My yoke is easy, and My burden is light" (Matt. 11:28–30).

Notice that the invitation of Christ is not a way out of the struggle, but a way through the pain.

First, come to me, you who are weary and burdened; I will give you rest. Jesus calls you to come to Him in full honesty and openness. Confess your anger, your guilt, and your grief.

Second, learn from me, I am gentle and humble of heart; you will find rest. Jesus will not waste the pain; He intends for you to learn from Him, learn gentleness and humility of heart. A gentle and humble heart is the next lesson in store for Jacob's family.

SUMMARY: Do I Have to Face This?

The answer to the question is "yes!" The reluctance on our part is natural but harmful. This chapter outlines three sources of inner turmoil: resentment, guilt, and grief. This chapter also suggests three sources of outward turmoil: when people of faith disappoint us, when the lives of faithful people are swallowed up in vengeance, and when acts and words of faith are clouded over with deep pessimism. How you face these inward and outward struggles depends on if you see your life in the hands of an angry God or a loving Savior. Our Savior does not promise escape from struggle, but a way through struggle to a deeper understanding of self and God.

THINK: Reflection and Conversation

1. This chapter in the life of God's family opens the door to the inner life of the family. What we find is difficult to take in. What did you find in this chapter that was most difficult for you? What was most encouraging to you? What did you most identify with?

2. The experience of Joseph, the brothers, and Father Jacob take us to the inner turmoil of the soul. Their struggles involved anger, guilt, and grief. What is your story of inward turmoil? What happened? What helped you get through it? How could someone have better helped you when you were in the midst of your soul's crisis?

3. This chapter suggests that "God lingers in the sorrow and shame. He lingers because there is a lesson to be learned, a lesson required for the next stage of the journey." What lessons have you

learned from your time of battling resentment, dealing with guilt and fear, or suffering from prolonged grief?

4. Consider several practical issues concerning coming to and learning from Jesus when the soul is weary and burdened.

- How would you instruct new believers to bring their weary and burdened hearts to Jesus?
- What is your learning style when you learn hard lessons from Christ? Are you more emotional or intellectual? Do you watch and learn, or act and learn? Do you need to repeat the lesson, or do you learn it the first time?
- For you, personally, what does it mean to take Jesus' yoke upon you?

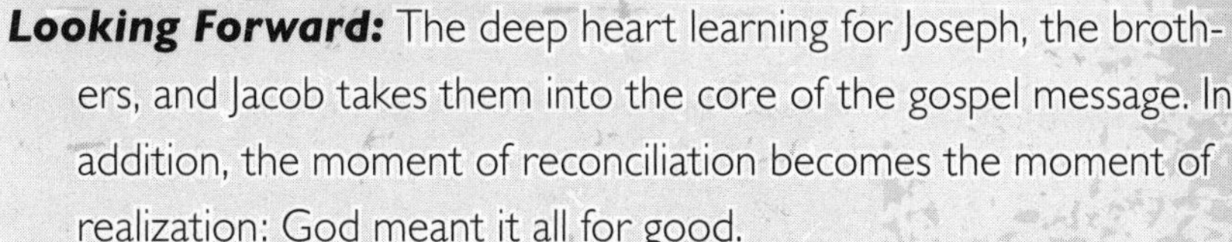

Looking Forward: The deep heart learning for Joseph, the brothers, and Jacob takes them into the core of the gospel message. In addition, the moment of reconciliation becomes the moment of realization: God meant it all for good.

THE GIFT OF DEEP HEALING

What Is My Purpose in Your Plan?

Father, may they clearly know Your will and achieve *the height and depth of* spiritual wisdom and understanding. May their lives be a credit to You, Lord; and *what's more,* may they continue to delight You by doing every good work and growing in the true knowledge that comes from being close to You. Strengthen them with Your infinite power, according to Your glorious might, so that they will have everything they need to hold on and endure hardship patiently and joyfully. Thank You, Father, as You have made us eligible to receive our portion of the inheritance given to all those set apart by the light. You have rescued us from dark powers and brought us safely into the kingdom of Your Son, whom You love and in whom we are redeemed and forgiven of our sins.

—Colossians 1:9–14

I want to share an old and well-known illustration. What makes the story special to me is that I heard it from Dr. Dennis Kinlaw when he held a revival at a church I pastored. He reported the story as he saw it happen at Asbury College.

THE STORY IN SUMMARY

Genesis 43:15–34; 44:1–34; 45:1–15

When the family runs out of grain again, Jacob sends his sons back to Egypt, including Benjamin. He prays for God's blessing but fears the worst.

Joseph receives his brothers at his home. The men bow before Joseph, unwittingly fulfilling the dream of long ago. Joseph is moved to tears when he sees his younger brother, Benjamin. Joseph sends them on their way again, this time secretly returning their silver and hiding his own silver cup in Benjamin's belongings. The men are arrested. Judah pleads for the youngest son as well as the aging father.

Joseph can no longer control himself. He sends everyone out of the room so he can be alone with his brothers. He reveals himself to them. He declares that God has worked through everything to provide a place of rescue for the family. He then kisses his brothers and weeps over them.

A chapel speaker brought a student to the platform. He asked the student to hold an empty glass at arm's length. Carefully, the speaker filled the glass with water.

The speaker then took hold of the young man's arm and began to shake it. Water spilled everywhere, and the students roared in laughter. Turning to the student holding the glass of water he asked, "Why did water spill out of the glass?"

The student, feeling a bit on the spot, replied, "It spilled because you shook my arm."

The speaker pressed a little further. "Listen to my question again: Why did water spill out of the glass?"

Trying to provide a more scientific answer, the young man said, "Because my arm was vibrating?"

"Listen carefully," the speaker repeated. "Why did *water* spill out of the glass?"

By now, everyone in the chapel knew the answer. Water spilled out of the glass because water was in the glass.[1]

Toxic water spilled out of the glass of Jacob's family. Joseph, filled with resentment, used his power and cunning to exact revenge. The guilt swirling within the brothers splattered out in fear and shame. Jacob's grief gave way to deep pessimism. Their old wounds call for deep healing.

A BAD DAY

Daniel Powter's award-winning lyric resonates with us: "You had a bad day."[2] I remember a bad day many years ago.

It was my oldest son's fifth birthday. His grandfather (my dad) wanted to send a special present. I told my father, "This is simple. He wants a two-wheeled bike, but he will need training wheels."

When the bike arrived, the little guy was so excited he could not contain himself. The bike was a beauty, complete with training wheels. The problem was finding the right place to learn to ride the bike. The answer was the quiet cul-de-sac where friends Rod and Cindy Bushy lived.

The next Saturday we went to the Bushys' home for the day. After a lesson and a little help getting started, my boy was off and riding. Rod and I left to play golf while the rest of the family stayed at the house. Their kids and our kids had a ball; at least that was what I expected would happen.

When Rod and I returned from our eighteen holes, instantly I knew something was wrong. All the children, except my son, were sitting on the curb of the cul-de-sac, quietly staring at their feet. I quickly got the story. Rod had a neighbor. He was the kind of neighbor that tests your religion. This neighbor hated dogs, cats, and joyful children. He was angry with life.

Now, all the children knew about the angry man. The kids knew that when the angry neighbor backed his car into the street, it was time to scatter. All the kids knew except my five-year-old son. So when the neighbor backed his car out of the driveway, all the children scattered except my little boy.

The angry neighbor drove his car right behind my little boy as he was enjoying his first day on his first bike. The angry neighbor blasted the horn over and over again and followed the little guy all the way to the curb where my son tumbled over into the grass. He was not hurt, but he was plenty scared.

I went in the house and saw my boy sitting on the couch. "How was the day?" I asked.

He never looked up. "Bad day, Dad. A guy tried to run me over."

On bad days, when anger, fear, guilt, or sorrow overtake you, the Devil whispers his lie in your heart: *It will always be like this.* The lie is the Devil's attempt to overtake your life. If the evil one can trap you in his falsehood, you cannot imagine or believe there is a better day ahead.

I recall a low time in my life, a time when the Devil's propaganda reverberated through my soul: *It will always be like this, always, always, always.* I needed a good word. The word came from a wonderful preacher whose sermon topic was Judas. Judas had a bad day, the worst day of all days. The Devil's lie took hold of Judas: *It will always be like this.* Judas took his own life (Matt. 27:5; Acts 1:18).

When anger, fear, guilt, or sorrow overtake you, the Devil whispers his lie in your heart: *It will always be like this.*

Having told the tragic and familiar story, my minister friend then cupped his hands around his mouth and shouted across the crowd of listeners, "Someone needed to tell Judas the good news, the gospel news—your bad day doesn't have to be your last day."

In grief, anger, and shame, by all human estimation, these were the last days for Jacob's family, for Abraham's legacy. The promise of blessing sank into curses and accusation. The family was stuck in a cycle. "Hate begets hate; violence begets violence; toughness begets a greater toughness."[3] They were chained by the lie: It will always be like this.

HOW TO MAKE WRONG RIGHT

Two wrongs make a right![4] Retaliation is the world's system for setting things right.

The way of vengeance. We witness retaliation throughout the story of Abraham's family. Abraham led the charge, saved Lot, and became a hero in the wars of retaliation (Gen. 14). Sarah was so angry with her servant Hagar, she sentenced the woman and Ishmael to death in the desert, where they would have died had God not intervened (Gen. 21:9–19). Esau threatened to murder his brother, Jacob, who tricked him out of his birthright (Gen. 27:41). Jacob and his father-in-law reached détente, but it was an unsteady peace spying for an excuse to retaliate (Gen. 31:51–53). The sons of Jacob sought vengeance on their younger brother as recompense for his disturbing dreams (Gen. 37:18–20). Twenty years later, Joseph seized the opportunity to settle the score against his brothers (Gen. 42:8–17). This family was awash of the belief that two wrongs make things right.

The way of kindness. A more recent twist on the proverb *Two wrongs make a right* attempts to steer us away from vengeance: two wrongs don't make a right.[5] The proverb provides little comfort if you are the one who has been wronged. The saying leaves you with nothing to do, no course of action, no way to make things right.

However, there is a different way to make a wrong right: "Never let evil get the best of you; instead, overpower evil with the good" (Rom. 12:21). This new way of combating evil is frightening. It requires blessing evildoers, turning your need for vengeance over to God, and treating your enemy with kindness (vv. 14–20). Facing evil armed with nothing but goodness is risky and utterly irrational. This, my friend, is the gospel of Christ, the gospel of reconciliation.

The gospel of reconciliation breaks through from time to time in the story of Abraham's family. The derision between the servants of Lot and the servants of Abraham is ended with goodness. With great generosity, Abraham offered Lot the choice of the best grazing land (Gen. 13:8–9). Again, Abraham interceded for Lot and the righteous people in the cities of Sodom and Gomorrah (Gen. 18:23–33). Through generous gifts, Jacob sought to reconcile with Esau; when they met, Jacob saw in Esau's face the face of God (Gen. 33:1–10).

The gospel of love. The reconciling love we find in Abraham's family foreshadows the full expression of God's love in Jesus Christ. Jesus teaches us to love one another, a difficulty in and of itself. An old rhyme speaks plainly and to the point:

> To live above with saints we love,
> Oh, that will be glory.
> But to live below with saints we know;
> Well, that's a different story![6]

It is surprising, even scandalous, when new believers discover how difficult it can be to love the people with whom they share a life of mutual faith and fellowship. Jesus calls us, commands us, to love one another (John 13:34–35; 15:12, 17).

Jesus also commands us to love our neighbors (Matt. 22:39). This entails love for a stranger, a person in need, and one who may not share our faith (Luke 10:27). This command sums up all the commands of the Old Testament and is greater than all burnt offerings and sacrifices (Mark 12:30–33). This is love for the least, for the ones outside our circle (Matt. 25:34–36). Spiritual author and priest, Henri Nouwen describes the challenge to love a neighbor: "We become neighbors when we are willing to cross the road for one another. . . . There is a lot of road crossing to do. We are all very busy in our own circles. We have our own people to go to and our own affairs to take care of. But if we could cross the road once in a while and pay attention to what is happening on the other side, we might indeed become neighbors."[7]

Love for one another is difficult. Love for a neighbor in need is demanding. However, the most radical thing Jesus ever said went beyond love for each other or for neighbor. Jesus commands that we love our enemies.

> If you're listening, here's My message: Keep loving your enemies no matter what they do. Keep doing good to those who hate you. Keep speaking blessings on those who curse you. Keep praying for those who mistreat you. . . . If you want to be extraordinary—love your enemies! . . . So imitate God and be truly compassionate, the way your Father is. If you don't want to be judged, don't judge. If you don't want to be condemned, don't condemn. If you want to be forgiven, forgive. (Luke 6:27–28, 35, 36–37)

Jesus tells us to pray for those who have done us wrong. He models the prayer in His own prayer: "And forgive us for our wrongs, for we forgive those who wrong us" (Luke 11:4). This is how God intends to restore the world and make Abraham's seed a blessing to all people.[8] The prayer of our Lord is about to come to life in Jacob's family.

THE GOSPEL MAKES THINGS RIGHT

The gospel brings light into darkness. It reveals, clarifies, and makes plain. However, as the dawn approaches, our minds may be more confused before all things are revealed. When the gospel slips up on us, we become disoriented, uncertain, and indefinite.

Before the gospel, we possessed our own convictions and trusted the way of power and death (John 8:44) in the Devil's lie: This is the way it will always be. We were certain we could overcome evil with greater power, cruelty, and intimidation. We have it on good authority that we ought to love those who love us and hate those who hate us (Matt. 5:43). This is rational, reasonable, and the way the world works. We are confident in what we see in the dark. It is frightening how the father of darkness forges glitzy light.

Yet, as the gospel advances, our clarity is clouded. We are not as certain as before. What was so clear in the darkness of thinking that conforms to the pattern of the world becomes uncertain with the dawning of the gospel's brilliance.

Between shadow and light. It was Benjamin who brings the first ray of light to Joseph's angry heart. Upon seeing him, he has his brothers brought to his own home and serves an elaborate feast (Gen. 43:15–34). Then, in contradiction to his display of kindness, Joseph plays another cruel hoax. The money paid for more grain is secretly returned to the sacks of grain. In addition, Joseph has his own silver cup hidden in Benjamin's luggage.

In the morning when the men leave for home, they are only a short way out of the city when Joseph's men surround them and search their belongings. The men are dragged back to Joseph where accusations fly, along with threats of slavery. He particularly threatens the enslavement of Benjamin (Gen. 44:1–15).

The gospel requires us to let go: let go of the anger and the guilt. But to turn loose frightens us. These men have lived with their wounds for so long, it is almost impossible to believe there could be healing. Further, when we live with resentment or shame for years, the injury comes to define us. At a deep level, we cannot imagine our lives without the lingering pain. The pain excuses our behavior, justifies our attitude, and allows us to shift responsibility to others. We are reluctant to turn loose. Indeed, we can only be free through the grace of God.

The gospel dawns. How can we describe the moment the gospel breaks in upon the ugliness of the world? Judah, Joseph's half-brother, opened his heart in a display of anxious love when he "stepped up to Joseph *and begged him for mercy*" (v. 18). He tells a tale of an old father suffering in grief, the death of his beloved son, the loss of the wife of his youth, and, now, the threatened loss of Benjamin. Judah offers to remain as a slave in Egypt if only the young brother can return to his gray-haired father: "For how can I go back to my father without the boy? I couldn't stand to see the terrible suffering this would put him through" (v. 34).

The room is flooded with the desperate account of the family. Joseph can no longer contain himself. He clears the room except for his brothers. He breaks down with such uncontrollable sobbing that all the aristocracy in Egypt whispered the story of Joseph's crying. In that moment, God sweeps in, and the good news of the gospel is revealed in Joseph's revelation:

When the word of the Creator God breaks in, we discover new life, restored relationships, and a hopeful future.

> I am your brother, Joseph, whom you sold into Egypt. Don't be upset or angry with yourselves *any longer* because of what you did. You see God sent me here ahead of you to preserve life. For famine struck this land two years ago, and there are five more years in which there will be no plowing or harvesting. God sent me *here* ahead of you to make sure you *and your families* survive *this terrible ordeal* and have a remnant left on earth. So it wasn't *really* you who sent me here, but God; the same God who made me an advisor to Pharaoh, master of his household, and ruler over everyone in the land of Egypt. . . . Then he kissed all of his brothers *one by one,* cried on their *shoulders as well,* and after that they talked *for a time* together. (Gen. 45:4–8, 15)

Everyone is taken by surprise. The brothers thought Joseph was dead, and now he stands before them. Joseph is stunned by his own awareness of God's sovereign providence. Through human faithfulness and failures, through false accusations and famine, and through prison and Pharaoh's palace, God weaves history for His own purpose.

The full light of God. God breaks in and life is transformed. Through God's kindness and compassion, "*A new day is dawning:* the Sunrise from the heavens will break through in our darkness" (Luke 1:78). When the word of the Creator God breaks in, we discover new life, restored relationships, and a hopeful future.

1) Life. God is the source of life. In the beginning, God spoke and life arose on the planet. God promised an old couple who could not conceive, who were beyond the possibility of conception, that they would produce a son, Isaac. Now, Isaac's grandson, the one sold into slavery, the one thought dead, is alive and ruler over Egypt. "Is anything too difficult for the Eternal One to accomplish?" (Gen. 18:14).

When God called Abraham's family, He had Jesus in mind: "*In these places*, the people who had been living in darkness saw a great light. The light of life will overtake those who dwelt in the shadowy darkness of death" (Matt. 4:16).

Life from God brings forgiveness, freedom, and faithfulness to a grand cause, the restoration of the world under God's rule. After a generation of smug, complacent faith, the hint hidden in the dream has come to full awareness; Abraham's seed fulfills God's purpose.

When you open your life to God's good word, you are lifted into a sacred strategy far greater than you or your particular concerns. You join the movement of God's history. Your life is bigger than you ever dreamed possible.

2) Love. The gospel arrives on a grand scale revealing God's purpose in the world. The gospel also rouses tender intimacy in human relationships: "He kissed all of his brothers *one by one,* cried on their *shoulders as well,* and after that they talked *for a time* together" (Gen. 45:15).

A young friend of mine takes her place in God's purpose by providing an afterschool program for inner city children of poverty. Darnell is a particularly difficult child who attends the program. She is a little girl, eight or nine years of age, filled with rage and fear. It is all she has ever known.

Each day, the program ends by driving the children home and dropping them off one at a time. As each child leaves the van, the staff says together, "We love you." It is a lovely ritual that means a great deal to the staff and the children, with the exception of Darnell.

Life from God brings forgiveness, freedom, and faithfulness to a grand cause, the restoration of the world under God's rule.

"Don't say that to me," she would snap. "You don't love me. Nobody loves me." Her angry reply continued for weeks.

One cold day, deep in November, something changed. "We love you," echoed in the van as the door opened and Darnell stepped out. This time there was no retort from the little girl. For a moment, she gazed at the faces in the van, and then turned to walk away. Before the door could be closed, she turned back, pushed her head inside the vehicle, and declared, "I love you too."

3) Hope. Through the giving of the gospel, we anchor our faith in God who has a purpose for our life that is greater than we can imagine. The gospel's gift opens deep healing through the power of love. Also, we discover a new future on our journey of hope in Christ.

For Abraham's lineage, their hopeful future was in Egypt, the land of Goshen to be precise. Located east of the Nile Delta, the land was perfectly situated for raising livestock as well as growing a family into a nation of people, God's people, the children of Israel (Ex. 1:5–7).

Yet, here is the rub: God's future was not what Joseph, his brothers, or even Jacob imagined. God's future took them on paths and to places they never anticipated. Again I remember the church I pastored many years ago and how we ardently prayed for revival and renewal. People began to attend, find faith, and grow in Christ. The congregation changed in ways we could not envision. I heard an old-timer grumble, "When I prayed for revival, this is not what I had in mind."

It is tempting to pray for the resurrection of Lazarus rather than the resurrection of Christ: "I want my old life back;

It is tempting to pray for the resurrection of Lazarus rather than the resurrection of Christ. It is a temptation to go back to the old life rather than to enter the new life.

I want things the way they used to be; I want the past, just better." It is a temptation to go back to the old life rather than to enter the new life. There are elements in our old life we will maintain. Christ was recognized in His new resurrected body.[9] However, there are dysfunctional elements of the old life that will and must be transformed. God's purposes and plans lead beyond our comfort zone.[10]

THE GOSPEL IS PERSONAL

The meeting between Joseph and his brothers begins in suspicion with everyone holding their cards close. The story ends in reunion, hugs, and kisses. The gospel turned a poker table into a kitchen table. The gospel takes hold personally. Each one persuaded by God's Word responds individually.

Brokenness. Perhaps your response to the light of God is like Joseph, a cool and calculating exterior that must be broken and pried open. Joseph is a seasoned politician and unflappable bureaucrat. Beneath the unruffled exterior, his heart begins to tremble. Note the progress of an opening heart.

- When he saw his younger brother, Benjamin, "Joseph hurried from the room because he was overwhelmed *with affection* for his brother and was afraid he would cry *in front of everyone*. So he went into a private room and wept there" (Gen. 43:30).
- Upon hearing the confession of Judah, "Joseph could no longer keep his composure. The room was crowded with people so he ordered *his attendants:* Send everyone out of the room!" (Gen. 45:1).
- Joseph wanted to keep his emotional revelation to his brothers private, "But he began to cry so loudly that the Egyptians heard it, and the Pharaoh's household heard it too!" (Gen. 45:2).

We may not all have such an emotional response, but for each of us, the gospel enters a surrendered heart, soul, mind, and body (Matt. 22:37).

Uncertainty. The brothers, through Judah's speech (Gen. 44:18–34), throw themselves upon the mercy of Joseph. What follows is a progression of trust and mistrust.

Joseph forgave, and Joseph was changed through the act of forgiveness. He was a different man with his brothers, caring for them and their families. However, the act of forgiveness was received with suspicion from his brothers. The sad tale of anxious uncertainty climaxes years later when Jacob dies.

> When Joseph's brothers began to realize *the implications of* their father's death, Joseph's brothers *began to worry.*
>
> **JOSEPH'S BROTHERS:** What if Joseph still bears a grudge *in some way* against us and decides to pay us back in full for all of the wrong we did to him?
>
> So they sent a message to Joseph.
>
> **JOSEPH'S BROTHERS' MESSAGE:** Your father gave us this instruction before he died. He told us to say to you, "Please, I beg you. Forgive the crime of your brothers and the sins they committed against you. They were wrong to treat you so badly." So please do *what your father asked and* forgive the crime that we, the servants of the God of your father, committed against you. (Gen. 50:15–17)

Joseph cried upon hearing the confession of their fear. In direct application of the story, we must remind each other that we are forgiven, that God's forgiveness is true, and our forgiveness of one another is steady. In a world of pretense and about face, forgiveness must be authentic. To forgive means we no longer judge. Joseph understood: "Am I *to judge* instead of God? *It is not my place.* Even though you intended to harm me, God intended it only for good, and through me, He preserved the lives of countless people, as He is still doing today. So don't worry. I will provide for you *myself*—for you and your children" (Gen. 50:19–21).

Memories. Jacob also dealt with the gospel personally. His faith was renewed when he remembered and relived the wondrous days of the past. He "set out on his journey *to Egypt* with all of his belongings, and when he came to Beersheba, he offered sacrificial gifts to the God of his father, Isaac" (Gen. 46:1). This place, Beersheba, was rich with memory and meaning.

- Jacob's grandfather, Abraham, built a place of worship in Beersheba (Gen. 21:33) and lived there a long time (Gen. 22:19).
- Jacob's father, Isaac, received a vision from God in Beersheba and also built an altar to God (Gen. 26:23–25).
- Jacob himself traveled through Beersheba when he was on the run from his brother, Esau (Gen. 28:10).

With his mind filled with the richness of his own heritage and calling, he heard from God.

GOD: Jacob, Jacob!

JACOB: I'm here. *I'm listening!*

GOD: I am the True God, the God of your father. Don't be afraid to go down to Egypt *and leave the land I promised you,* for I am going to make you into a great nation there. I will go down with you to Egypt, and *one day* I will be the One to bring you back again. *And something else*—Joseph's own

> hands will be the ones to close your eyes *at the time of your death.* (Gen. 46:2–3)

The gospel is universal, for all; the gospel is personal, uniquely delivered to each of us. The word of God broke through the plated armor of Joseph's cool, calculating façade. The message of forgiveness required years to penetrate the deep and debilitating suspicion of the brothers. The vision of heaven continued through the generations of legacy and calling for Jacob. Receiving and living the gospel is not a boilerplate plan but a deeply intimate and personal experience.

THE GOSPEL IS OUR PARTNERSHIP

The members of Abraham's family were the first human partners in God's plan to save the world. When God called Abraham, the plan to send Jesus was already in play. The New Testament author Matthew marks the move from Abraham's family to Jesus. He identified Jesus as a descendent, a son of Abraham. In Jesus, partnership with God enters a new era. In Jesus Christ, we find the final and ideal partner (Heb. 1:1–3). Jesus calls you to believe and become co-heirs and co-partners with Christ (Rom. 8:17). Partnership with God rests on believing the promise, the great yes, in Jesus (2 Cor. 1:20), not in your birth certificate (Matt. 3:9).

Our entrance into partnership with Christ is through the new birth of the Holy Spirit (John 3:7). I want to take you to the moment Jesus offered full partnership to His followers and to us. This is the most dramatic moment in the story of Christ.

Let me set the scene (John 20:19): It is Easter evening in the upper room where the disciples have huddled together in fear. Jesus had died three days earlier. Reports of His risen presence are sporadic and have been met with skepticism. Into this chamber of misgiving, this companionship of anxiety, Jesus appears.

Jesus has just returned from the grave. He has fought and won the greatest of all battles, the battle against sin, death, and the Devil. Jesus has won the decisive victory. The battle continues, but the outcome is certain. The victory is in Jesus.

In this scene, what Jesus says next is the message of His mission.

> **JESUS:** I give you the gift of peace. In the same way the Father sent Me, I am now sending you.

Now He drew close enough to each of them that *they could feel His breath.* He breathed on them:

> **JESUS:** Welcome the Holy Spirit of the living God. You now have the mantle of God's forgiveness. As you go, you are able to share the life-giving power to forgive sins, or to withhold forgiveness. (John 20:21–23)

These reluctant, hesitant, and uncertain disciples receive the call to God's purpose, the gift of God's Spirit, and the message of God's forgiveness. You receive the same call, gift, and message. This is your purpose in God.

You are the gift of peace sent into the world. Peace is not absence but presence. Peace is the presence of wholeness and holiness. Jesus is the presence of peace; you are called to be the presence of peace. Abraham was blessed and a blessing. Jesus sends you with the blessing of making peace: "Blessed are the peacemakers—they will be called children of God" (Matt. 5:9).

Our model is Jesus; as He was sent by the Father, He sends us. If you were to have a spiritual calling card, the words might read:

Peacemaker
Sent by Jesus Christ

However, you are cautiously hesitant. Most often, peacemakers are not sent to restful retreats but to places of conflict and turmoil. Peacemakers are not always welcomed and are sometimes reviled. Peacemaking is not covering over the problems and disparities but exposing them and making them right. It is normal that you should be a bit reluctant to be sent with the peace of Christ into the world. Yet, here is the call—to be sent into the world as Jesus was sent into the world.

You carry the spirit of the living God. You do not take the reluctant journey alone. Along with your calling comes the gift of the Holy Spirit. The Spirit is the presence, the essence of God, as a full member of the Trinity.

Here is a simple way to think of the presence of God's Spirit within you: A twig is not the tree, but everything about the twig is just like the tree. A spark is not the fire, but all that is in the spark is common in the fire. A drop is not the sea. However, taste the drop, and it tastes exactly like the sea.

God takes a drop of Himself, a spark of His life, and places it in you. The Holy Spirit brings the nature of God into your nature. What Jesus did for you on the cross, the Holy Spirit does in you through His presence.

Receiving the gift of the Holy Spirit is taking the yoke of Christ upon you. The Holy Spirit is the Spirit of Christ within us. He gives you rest from today's battles and lessons to prepare you for tomorrow. You have a choice, the yoke of this world or the yoke of Christ. In contrast to the weight of the world, "My [Christ's] yoke is easy, and My [Christ's] burden is light" (Matt. 11:30).

You are entrusted to forgive sin. We are sent into the world as Jesus was sent into the world. We carry the Spirit of Jesus (Acts 16:7; Phil. 1:19) in the Holy Spirit of God. And we are given a message that causes us to tremble. If there is any task in our partnership with God that produces reluctance, it is here, the forgiveness of sin.

In my mother's Bible, the authorized King James Version, it reads, "Whose soever sins ye remit, they are remitted unto them; and whose soever sins ye retain, they are retained" (John 20:23 KJV). To *remit* means to pardon or forgive. To *retain* means to maintain, keep, or remember. The choice to remit or retain changes lives, families, and nations.

A new translation of the Bible that came out during my days in seminary rendered the verse even more striking: "If you forgive anyone's sins, their sins are forgiven; if you do not forgive them, they are not forgiven" (John 20:23 NIV). We are reluctant to take on this responsibility. Nonetheless, the responsibility is ours: "You are able to share the life-giving power to forgive sins, or to withhold forgiveness" (John 20:23).

The responsibility to share or hide the message of God's forgiveness and the choice to forgive or withhold our own forgiveness from others demonstrates God's serious and genuine partnership with us. The commission to forgive others strikes at the heart of sacred partnership. It is in forgiving others that we are set free, even as Joseph was set free from his anger and resentment. In our persistent and consistent forgiving of others, even seventy times seven times (Matt. 18:22), they are set free, even as the brothers of Joseph finally believed the pardon they received.

Consider again the writing of Desmond Tutu. Here, he paints a cosmic canvas of the essential need of forgiveness.

The commission to forgive others strikes at the heart of sacred partnership.

> In forgiving, people are not being asked to forget. On the contrary, it is important to remember, so that we should not let such atrocities happen again. Forgiveness does not mean condoning what has been done. It means taking what happened seriously and not minimizing it; drawing out the sting in the memory that threatens to poison our entire existence. It involves trying to understand the perpetrators and so have empathy, to try to stand in their shoes and appreciate the sort of pressures and influences that might have conditioned them. . . . Forgiving means abandoning your right to pay back the perpetrator in his own coin, but it is a loss that liberates the victim. . . . we will always need a process of forgiveness and reconciliation to deal with those unfortunate yet all too human breaches in relationships. They are an inescapable characteristic of the human condition.[11]

In John's gospel, we meet Jesus: "Look! *This man is more than He seems!* He is the Lamb sent from God, *the sacrifice* to erase the sins of the world!" (John 1:29). At the close of John's gospel, we take up the mission and message of Christ: "You now have the mantle of God's forgiveness. As you go, you are able to share the life-giving power to forgive sins, or to withhold forgiveness" (John 20:23).

A GOOD DAY TO FORGIVE

Forgiveness is something we give to others and something we teach our children. When I discovered what had happened to my little boy the day he learned to ride his bike, I went in the house and found him sitting on the couch. "How was the day?" I asked.

He never looked up. "Bad day, Dad. A guy tried to run me over."

That makes for a bad day. I said, "Let's talk about it."

We went out on the back porch, sat down, and talked. The conversation went something like this:

I asked, "Who was the man?"

"See the fence down there? That's him. That's his fence."

"That man did wrong, didn't he?"

"He is a mean man, Daddy."

"I agree; he is an angry, mean man."

There was a quiet moment between us. Let me explain: my little boy had never been in real danger, but it felt that way. All the folks who lived on the cul-de-sac knew the angry neighbor was unreasonable. All the kids knew to stay out of his way. That is the way it worked in the cul-de-sac.

My little boy learned his first lesson in cul-du-sac rules that day. I was learning with him. I wanted to march over to the crotchety old neighbor and let him have it. There is a right time and a best way to stand for justice. However, at this point and on this day, my little son's heart was my priority.

My friend, Rod, quickly explained that all the neighbors knew reprimanding the neighbor would escalate the problem for everyone. It was apparent that on that day, at least, we were not going to change the neighbor. However, my son and I had to decide how this event would change us. And, that is the deeper question.

Tenderly, I asked my child, "Do we want to be like the angry, mean neighbor?"

"No, we don't want to be like him, Daddy."

I then held my breath and shared words that were as hard for me to speak as for my son to hear: "There's only one way I know to make sure we are not like him. We have to forgive him. That's how we get him out of our hearts."

"Daddy," he looked at me, "Forgive him? Really?"

Forgiveness is not just a moment but a process.

"Yes, honey. We have to learn to stay away from him. But we also have to forgive him."

With the infinite trust that only a four-year-old-just-turned-five has, he said to me, "Okay, Daddy. I will forgive him."

Then my little boy turned toward the fence of the mean, angry neighbor and said, "I forgive you. I forgive you."

Honestly, it took my heart longer to forgive than it did this little child. You see, his heart was pure, and his trust in me was complete. Maybe that is the secret for us as we learn to pray, "Forgive us for our wrongs, for we forgive those who wrong us" (Luke 11:4).

Lord, make my heart pure. Increase my trust in You. Teach me to forgive.

We came in from the porch and had dinner with our friends. Soon, we packed up the bike, backed down the drive, and started out of the cul-de-sac. As we passed the angry, mean neighbor's house, I said to my little son, "Let's do it just one more time, to be sure."

He said, "Okay," strained at the seat belt, looked over at the neighbor's house, and said, "I forgive you." I fought back the tears as I witnessed this pure and trusting child who forgives simply because his father asks him to forgive.

Lord, give me such trust in You that I willingly forgive my enemies.

I know that forgiveness is not just a moment but a process. Forgiveness is like the layers of the onion. We forgive one layer at a time. Jesus wisely told us, "You must forgive not seven times, but seventy times seven" (Matt. 18:22). That means we forgive and forgive again until it is gone from our hearts.

My son was still working on forgiveness when we returned home that night. I asked

Lord, give me such trust in You that I willingly forgive my enemies.

Andrew what story he would like me to read before bed. Without so much as a moment of hesitation he shouted out clear and loud, "Scrooge!" Even though it was only May, I thought it was an excellent choice.

SUMMARY: What Is My Purpose in Your Plan?

The way of the world is to fight the power of evil with greater evil, intimidation, and power—eye for eye, wound for wound. The way of God is to conquer evil with good, with the gift of the gospel in new life, healing love, and a purposeful future. The gospel comes to each person uniquely. The gospel broke through to Joseph's heart with deep emotion. The brothers experienced long suspicion. Father Jacob remembered and relived the legacy of faith. The purpose of the gospel is not served in personal renewal alone; you are called into partnership with God in the restoration of the world. Upon His return from the grave, the first words of Jesus call us to full partnership with Him; He sends us with His peace into the world, His Spirit into the world, and the message of forgiveness. Jesus, the Lamb of God who takes away the sin of the world, now sends us to advance His purpose, the forgiveness of sin. This is God's purpose for us.

THINK: Conversation and Reflection

1. As you review the legacy of Abraham's family—Abraham, Isaac, Jacob, and Joseph—what lessons and insights are most meaningful to you?

2. The gospel brings the power of deep healing, healing from our own sins and healing from the sins of others: "And forgive us for our wrongs, for we forgive those who wrong us" (Luke 11:4). In

a specific and personal way, how has the gospel brought healing to you—healing from your own wrongs and healing from the wrongs of others?

3. How does God's good word most often come to you? Joseph became emotional. His brothers were suspicious. His father remembered. What about you?

4. Consider some practical issues about partnership with God.

- In practical ways, how can we help each other bring the presence of Christ's peace into our own homes, churches, and places of work?
- How do you understand and think about the presence of the Holy Spirit working and guiding your life?
- What is your response, in attitude and action, to your calling, "As you go, you are able to share the life-giving power to forgive sins, or to withhold forgiveness" (John 20:23)? How do you follow this purpose in your home, your work, and your church?
- What place in your life needs the forgiveness of Christ now? How can we help you receive Christ's forgiveness?

NOTES

EPIGRAPH

1. John Wesley, "On Working out Our Own Salvation," *The Works of John Wesley*, Vol. 6 (London: Wesleyan Methodist Bookroom, 1872), 513. Also found at http://wesley.nnu.edu/john-wesley/the-sermons-of-john-wesley-1872-edition/sermon-85-on-working-out-our-own-salvation/.

INTRODUCTION

1. "*Your name will be* Israel because you have wrestled with God and humanity, and you have prevailed" (Gen. 32:28). Throughout his life, Jacob wrestled with God and with his own humanity.

CHAPTER 1

1. Soren Kierkegaard, *Fear and Trembling*, trans. Walter Lowrie. (Princeton: Princeton University Press, 1941).
2. Romans 4:1–3 credits Abraham as righteous with God by faith. Abraham is called "our father in faith" in the Eucharistic prayer of the Roman Canon, recited during the Mass.
3. Your father Abraham anticipated the time when I would come, and he celebrated My coming.

   JEWS: You aren't even 50 years old, yet You have seen *and talked with* Abraham?
   JESUS: I tell you the truth; I AM before Abraham was born. (John 8:56–58)

4. Walter Brueggemann, *Genesis*, Interpretation: A Bible Commentary for Teaching and Preaching (Louisville, KY: John Knox Press, 1982).
5. In Genesis 2–3, Adam and Eve lived in intimate relationship with God but did not participate in God's purpose to restore the fallen world.
6. In Genesis 6–9, Noah served God in harboring a remnant of life on earth.
7. Ray Dunning, *Abraham, The Tests of Faith* (Kansas City: Beacon Hill Press, 2012), 11.
8. Ibid., 13.
9. Mark 1:15; John 1:12, 3:16; Romans 5:8; 10:9–10; Ephesians 2:8; Hebrews 7:25; Revelation 3:20.
10. Albert Edward Day, *The Captivating Presence* (Marble Hill, GA: Enthea Press, 2001), 91.
11. Nehama Liebowitz, *Studies in Bereshit (Genesis)*, (Jerusalem: World Zionist Organization, 1973), 113.
12. Martin Luther's hymn "A Mighty Fortress Is Our God" became the battle song of the Reformation. John Julian, *A Dictionary of Hymnology: Setting forth the Origin and History of Christian Hymns of all Ages and Nations* (New York: Dover Publications, Inc., 1957).
13. A. Carter Shelley, *Preaching Genesis 12–36* (St. Louis: Chalice Press, 2001), 20.

CHAPTER 2

1. The list is adapted from International House Bristol, "Disappointment," accessed June 12, 2014, http://www.ihbristol.com/useful-english-expressions/example/disappointment/7.

2. In Genesis 23:11–16, Abraham must negotiate buying a field to provide a burial site for Sarah.
3. For an excellent discussion of motivation, see Daniel H. Pink, *Drive: The Surprising Truth About What Motivates Us* (New York: Riverhead Books, 2009).
4. See Romans 4:3, 22; Galatians 3:6; the passage is also quoted in James 2:23.
5. See Martin Luther, "Lectures on Genesis: Chapters 15-20," *Luther's Works* (Gen. 15:6). (Saint Louis: Concordia Publishing House, 1999).
6. See D. W. Deal, *Righteousness*, Evangelical Dictionary of Theology (Grand Rapids, MI: Baker Book House, 1990).
7. A recent manifestation of the "believe receive" power in life is in *The Secret*. Faith in commitment to God and His purpose is biblical. The "believe and receive" philosophy puts you in control of your purpose. See http://www.thesecret.TV.

CHAPTER 3

1. *The Stanford Encyclopedia of Philosophy* opens the article on "Promises" with these words: "Few moral judgments are more intuitively obvious and more widely shared than that promises ought to be kept. It is in part this fixed place in our intuitive judgments that makes promises of particular interest to philosophers, as well as a host of social scientists and other theorists. Another feature of promises that make them a topic of philosophical concern is their role in producing trust." Allen Habib, "Promises," *The Stanford Encyclopedia of Philosophy*, accessed July 23, 2014, http://plato.stanford.edu/archives/win2008/entries/promises/.
2. For examples of faith used to describe right doctrine, see 1 Timothy 3:9; Titus 1:13; Hebrews 4:14; and Jude 1:3.
3. We know the names Abraham and Sarah. However, the couple is first introduced in Genesis as Abram (meaning high father) and Sarai (meaning noble woman). In the portion of their story discussed in this chapter, God, as part of the promise, changes their names to Abraham (meaning father of many nations, see Genesis 17:4–5) and Sarah (meaning princess, see Genesis 17:15–16).
4. Kevin Henderson and Ann O'Leary-Kelly, "When Broken Promises Threaten One's Identity: The Impact of Psychological Contract Breach on Self-Identity Threat," *Journal of Organizational Psychology*, Vol. 12 (3/4). (2012): 81–98.
5. James Breig has an interesting article in the *Colonial Williamsburg Journal* (Winter 02–03) on the origin of American proverbs: "Out Damn'd Proverbs." See http://www.history.org/Foundation/journal/Winter02-03/proverbs.cfm.
6. In Genesis 30, the two wives of Jacob each ask Jacob to have children with their servants.
7. In Genesis 16:2–4, Sarah and Abraham scheme to produce a child. They had been promised a child in Genesis 15:4.
8. Brueggemann, *Genesis,* Interpretation, 111. Walter Brueggemann observes, "no moral judgment need be rendered against the alternative device for securing a son, as this may be untested as a proper legal practice elsewhere in the biblical period."
9. Hagar refers to God as *El Roi*, the God who Sees (Genesis 16:8–16). See Walter Eichrodt, *Theology of the Old Testament*, Vol. I (Philadelphia: The Westminster Press, 1961), 183–84.

10. I continue to find Professor Welch's book, *We Really Do Need Each Other*, to be a wonderful source of insight and good sense.
11. Reuben Welch sermon, Eastern Nazarene College (Quincy, MA, 1972).
12. The name *El Shaddai* is used in Genesis 28:3, 35:11, 43:14, and 48:3.
13. Alex Lickerman, "Why We Laugh," *Psychology Today*, http://www.psychologytoday.com/blog/happiness-in-world/201101/why-we-laugh, accessed October 5, 2013.
14. See Romans 2:25–29; Galatians 6:11–15; Colossians 2:11.
15. The earliest citation that I have found comes from the weekly magazine of the US aviation industry. "We must step back and see if the solutions to our problems lie outside the box," *Aviation Week & Space Technology*, accessed November 3, 2013, http://phrases.org.uk/meanings/think-outside-the-box.html.
16. C. S. Lewis, *God in the Dock: Essays on Theology and Ethics* (Grand Rapids: Eerdmans, 1970), 52.

CHAPTER 4

1. The American Chesterton Society, accessed September 9, 2013, http://www.chesterton.org/discover-chesterton/frequently-asked-questions/wrong-with-world/.
2. See the work of Walter Wink, *Engaging the Powers* (Minneapolis: Augsburg Press, 1992).
3. See the work of Manfred F. R. Kets de Vries, *Leaders, Fools, and Imposters* (San Francisco: Jossey-Bass, 1993), 33.
4. Psalm 94 is a song of praise to God, the Avenger.
5. See Christopher Boehm, *Blood Revenge: The Enactment and Management of Conflict in Montenegro and Other Tribal Societies* (Lawrence, KS: University Press of Kansas, 1984).
6. Museo d-e la Nación, Ministerio de Cultura, http://www.mcultura.gob.pe/museo-de-la-nacion-exposiciones.
7. See the online Princeton article, accessed December 2, 2013, http://www.princeton.edu/~achaney/tmve/wiki100k/docs/Nemesis_%28mythology%29.html.
8. See the book by the famed social scientist Phillip Zimbardo, *The Lucifer Effect: Understanding How Good People Turn Evil* (New York: Random House Paperbacks, 2008).
9. See Matthew 21:22; Mark 11:24; John 11:22; 14:13; 15:16; 16:23.
10. American Nutrition Association, "USDA Defines Food Deserts," *Nutrition Digest*, Vol. 36, No. 3, accessed July 23, 2014, http://americannutritionassociation.org/newsletter/usda-defines-food-deserts. (2010)
11. Crimevictims.gov provides an excellent list of resources available for children who have been exposed to violence and criminal behavior.
12. See Matthew 3:2; 4:17; 4:23; Mark 1:15; Luke 4:43; John 3:5.
13. See Psalms 3; 5; 6; 7; 13; 17; 22; 25; 26; 27:7–14; 28; 31; 35; 38; 39; 42–43; 54–57; 59; 61; 63; 64; 69; 70; 71; 86; 88; 102; 109; 120; 130; 140; 141; 142; 143. Hermann Gunkel, *The Psalms: A Form-Critical Introduction* (Philadelphia: Fortress Press, 1967).
14. A. W. Tozer, *The Knowledge of the Holy* (CreateSpace, 1961), 128.

CHAPTER 5

1. *The Desert Wings*, March 3, 1978, reported on Murphy's Laws Site, accessed August 12, 2013, http://www.murphys-laws.com/murphy/murphy-laws.html.

2. For more information on behavior patterns, read *Love Is a Choice* by Dr. Robert Hemfelt, Dr. Frank Minirth, and Dr. Paul Meier (Nashville: Thomas Nelson, 1989).
3. The term *strong-willed woman* evokes strong responses. Consider Dr. Debbie Cherry's book, *The Strong-Willed Wife* (Navpress Publishing Group, 2007). She outlines the positives and negatives of a strong-willed personality.
4. Surprisingly, the Bible has more than thirty verses dedicated to the disgraceful stories and a mere eight verses to the lovely story of the birth of the promised baby, Isaac. We are supposed to learn something from the stories of disgrace, scandal, and shame.
5. Samuel Logan Brengle, *The Soul-Winners Secret* (New York: Salvation Army Printing and Publishing, 1920), 20.
6. Brueggemann, *Genesis,* Interpretation, 186. Brueggemann comments, "Verse 1 sets the test suggesting that God wants to know something. It is not a game with God. God genuinely does not know, and that is settled in Verse 12, "Now I know."

CHAPTER 6

1. Julie Stein, *Exploring Coast Salish Prehistory: The Archaeology of San Juan Island* (Washington: University of Washington Press, 2000).
2. Stories of deception find their way into each generation of Abraham's family. See Genesis 12:14–15, 20:2, 26:7, and 27:19.
3. The women of Abraham's story also share generational vices. See Genesis 21:8–11 and 30:1.
4. The family vice extends to nephews and cousins. See Genesis 13:10–11 and 25:34.
5. For resources on dysfunctional families, see Florence W. Kaslow, *Handbook of Relational Diagnosis and Dysfunctional Family Patterns* (Wiley-Interscience, 1996); David Stoop and James Masteller, *Forgiving Our Parents, Forgiving Ourselves: Healing Adult Children of Dysfunctional Families* (Ventura, CA: Regal, 1997); Blair and Rita Justice, *The Abusing Family* (Insight Books, 1990).
6. P. Greencare, "The Imposter," *Emotional Growth*, Vol. 1. (Madison, CT: International University Press, 1971).
7. William Shakespeare, *As You Like It*, Act 2, Scene 7.
8. Brueggemann, 209. Brueggemann writes, "Jacob is a scandalous challenge to his world because the God who calls him is also scandalous."
9. See also 1 Corinthians 6:8–11; Galatians 5:22–23.
10. See also Matthew 19:30; Mark 9:35, 10:31; Luke 13:30.
11. God completed the reversal of values in Jesus. See John 1:12–13.
12. For Old Testament examples of a reversed value system, see Deuteronomy 10:18, 14:29, 26:12; Psalm 146:9.
13. See Matthew 9:10–13, 11:16–19, 21:32.
14. See John 12:31, 14:30, 16:11.

CHAPTER 7

1. D. W. Winnicott, *Playing with Reality* (New York: Basic Books, 1971).
2. M. Kets de Vries, *Leaders, Fools, and Imposters* (New York: iUniversity, 1993).
3. C. Broderick, *Understanding Family Process: Basics of Family Systems* (Thousand Oaks, CA: Sage Publications, 1993).

4. E. H. Friedman, *Generation to Generation: Family Process in Church and Synagogue* (New York: The Gifford Press, 1985), 15.
5. Ibid., 17.
6. King Abimelech is mentioned in Genesis 20:1–2 and 26:1–7. It is likely that the second king is a descendant of the first.
7. Isaac's love for tasty food is mentioned in Genesis 27:4, 7, 9, 14, 17.
8. Murray Bowen, *Family Therapy in Clinical Practice* (New York: Aronson, 1974), 467–528.
9. See http://www.thebowencenter.org/pages/conceptds.html. On his website, Bowen describes differentiation as follows: "People with a poorly differentiated 'self' depend so heavily on the acceptance and approval of others that either they quickly adjust what they think, say, and do to please others or they dogmatically proclaim what others should be like and pressure them to conform. Bullies depend on approval and acceptance as much as chameleons, but bullies push others to agree with them rather than their agreeing with others. Disagreement threatens a bully as much as it threatens a chameleon. An extreme rebel is a poorly differentiated person too, but he pretends to be a 'self' by routinely opposing the positions of others.

   "A person with a well-differentiated 'self' recognizes his realistic dependence on others, but he can stay calm and clear headed enough in the face of conflict, criticism, and rejection to distinguish thinking rooted in a careful assessment of the facts from thinking clouded by emotionality. Thoughtfully acquired principles help guide decision-making about important family and social issues, making him less at the mercy of the feelings of the moment. What he decides and what he says matches what he does. He can act selflessly, but his acting in the best interests of the group is a thoughtful choice, not a response to relationship pressures. Confident in his thinking, he can either support another's view without being a disciple or reject another view without polarizing the differences. He defines himself without being pushy and deals with pressure to yield without being wishy-washy."
10. Brueggemann, *Genesis*, Interpretation, 143.
11. The phrase "maker of heaven and earth" is used in Psalm 115:15, 121:2, 124:8, 134:3, and 146:6, as well as the great creeds of the church.
12. Jesus declares that "the kingdom of God is near" (Mark 1:15).
13. See Robert Stein, *The Method and Message of Jesus Teachings* (Louisville, KY: Westminster John Knox Publisher, 1994), 11. See also H. Hanegraaff, *Christian Research Journal*, Vol. 27, No. 5. (2004)
14. William R. Noonan, *Discussing the Undiscussable: A Guide to Overcoming Defensive Routines in the Workplace* (San Francisco: Jossey-Bass, 2007). See also Chris Argyris, "Making the Undiscussable and Its Undiscussability Discussable," Public Administration Review, Vol. 40, No. 3, (1980): 205–13.

CHAPTER 8

1. "Like Rodney Said, 'Can't We All Just Get Along?'" *National Public Radio*, accessed July 23, 2014, http://www.npr.org/templates/story/story.php?storyId=97490927
2. Three verses in Romans describe the difference in thinking, faith, and behavior between a follower of Christ and the world: Romans 12:2, 10:9, and 13:12.

3. A secular example of this type of faith is *The Secret*, the book, film, and website, http://thesecret.tv/index.html.
4. Amazon.com, the online bookseller, dedicates a full section to self-help books: http://www.amazon.com/author-rank/Self-Help/books/4736.
5. George J. Holyoake, *English Secularism* (Chicago: The Open Court Publishing Company, 1896), 35.
6. Genesis 30:16, 31:34–35; And Jacob's sons will one day trick him into believing the favored son, Joseph, died (Gen. 37:32–33).
7. Jerry B. Harvey, *How Come Every Time I Get Stabbed in the Back My Fingerprints Are on the Knife?: And Other Meditations on Management* (Jossey-Bass, 1999).
8. Herbert Benson, *The Relaxation Response* (New York: HarperTorch, 1975).
9. Walter Cannon, *Wisdom of the Body* (United States: W. W. Norton & Company, 1932).
10. See Psalm 1:2, 19:14, 38:15, 49:3, 63:6, 77:3, 77:6, 77:12, 104:34, 119:1, 119:23, 119:27, 119:48, 119:78, 119:97, 119:99, 119:148, 143:5, 145:5.
11. Isaac, Jacob's father, was meditating in the fields when he first saw his bride to be, Rebekah (Gen. 24:63).
12. *Waterhole #3*, Directed by William A. Graham. Paramount, 1967.
13. Jacob Needleman, *Money and the Meaning of Life* (New York: Double Day, 1991), 38–40.
14. Patrick Henry Reardon, "The Man Alive," *Touchstone: A Journal of Mere Christianity* (2012), accessed July 23, 2014, http://www.touchstonemag.com/archives/article.php?id=25-05-003-e.
15. For examples, see Genesis 29:31, 32, 33, 35; 30:6, 8, 17, 18, 20, 22, 23, 24, 27, 30; 31:3, 5, 7, 9, 13, 16, 24, 29, 42, 49, 50.

CHAPTER 9

1. The executive training was based on Dr. Quinn's book, *Deep Change: Discovering the Leader Within* (San Francisco: Jossey-Bass, 1996).
2. C-level means a title with the word *Chief* as in Chief Executive Officer (CEO). (As an aside, I was not a C-level executive at my academic institution. You might have called me a D-level person; I was the Director of the Doctor of Ministry Program at Ashland Theological Seminary.)
3. J. R. R. Tolkien, *The Hobbit or There and Back Again* (Houghton Mifflin Harcourt, 1938). A free on-line version is available at http://readanybooks.net/fantasticfiction/The_Hobbit/15583.html. (The quote is found in chapter 6.)
4. The rock and a hard place dilemma is also known as Morton's Fork. "Morton's Fork is a logical dilemma in which people are faced with two equally bad options. You could think of it as being 'between the devil and the deep blue sea,' as the saying goes. Unless the victim of the dilemma manages to find an exception, the outcome of the situation will most probably be undesirable, as there can be no good outcome from any of the choices the victim is faced with. Many people find themselves struggling with Morton's Fork at some point in their lives." Wise Geek, http://www.wisegeek.com/what-is-mortons-fork.htm.
5. William Faulkner, *Requiem for a Nun* (New York: Random House, 1951). Albert Camus turned the story into a stage play in 1956. Senator Obama quoted the

famous line in his "More Perfect Union" speech. Scott Horton's commentary on the Senator Obama's use of the phrase can be found at http://harpers.org/blog/2008/03/the-past-is-not-past-or-is-it/. The phrase was also the subject of a copyright infringement law suite when Sony Pictures used it in the film "Midnight in Paris."

6. *The Time Machine* is a short novel published by H. G. Wells in 1895. The term *time machine* was coined by Wells.
7. Brueggemann, *Genesis,* Interpretation, 268.
8. Robert Coote, "The Meaning of the Name," *Harvard Business Review*, Vol. 65, No. 1, (1972): 137–146. Quote on p. 143.

CHAPTER 10

1. For an excellent list of change resisters, see Roseabeth Moss Kanter, "Ten Reasons People Resist Change," HBR Blog Network, *Harvard Business Review*, http://blogs.hbr.org/2012/09/ten-reasons-people-resist-chang/.
2. The term *change agent* was first suggested in Richard Beckhard, *Organization Development: Strategies and Models* (Reading, MA: Addison-Wesley, 1969), 114.
3. We must not confuse modern Egypt with the Egypt of the Old Testament. Egypt in the Old Testament is a real, historical location and empire. However, Egypt is more; it serves an image of the antithesis of God's kingdom. As an image, Egypt is part of a cognitive map that constructs the identity of God's people. See F. V. Grelfenhangen, *Egypt on the Pentateuch's Ideological Map: Constructing Biblical Israel's Identity* (New York: Sheffield Academic Press, 2002), 7–13.
4. Robert Browning, *Pippa's Song*, in Arthur Quiller-Couch, ed. 1919. *The Oxford Book of English Verse: 1250–1900* (Oxford: Clarendon Press, 1919), No. 718.
5. U.S. Small Business Association, http://www.sba.gov/content/partnership.
6. Brueggemann, *Genesis*, Interpretation, 288–289.
7. The lifestyle of the brothers is characterized in Genesis 34, 37, and 38.
8. For how personal values change, see Anat Bardi and Robin Goodwin, *The Duel Route of Value Change: Individual Processes and Cultural Moderators*, Royal Holloway University of London, http://digirep.rhul.ac.uk/file/476c3e7d-625e-432b-cf15-83f65f388c39/6/Bardi_Goodwin_Value_Change_final.pdf, accessed January 14, 2014.
9. For the symbolism of the monster, see L. J. Swingle, "Frankenstein's Monster and Its Romantic Relatives: Problems of Knowledge in English Romanticism," *Texas Studies in Literature and Language*, Vol. 15 (Spring 1973), 51–65; and Donald G. MacRae, "The Body and Social Metaphor," *The Body as a Medium of Expression* (New York: E. P. Dutton, 1975), 59–73.
10. On the Missional Church, see David J. Bosch, *Transforming Mission: Paradigm Shifts in Theology of Mission* (Maryknoll, NY: Orbis Books, 1991), and Lesslie Newbigin, *The Gospel in a Pluralist Society* (Grand Rapids, MI: Wm. B. Eerdmans Publishing Co., 1989).
11. The proper term for God's visible appearance to Abraham and Jacob is *theophany*. See Bible Study Tools, http://www.biblestudytools.com/dictionaries/bakers-evangelical-dictionary/theophany.html.
12. Charles Spurgeon, "God's Providence," *Metropolitan Tabernacle Pulpit*, Vol. 54 (1909), The Spurgeon Archive, http://www.spurgeon.org/sermons/3114.htm.

13. D. Martin Lloyd-Jones, *Romans, God's Sovereign Purpose*, Vol. 9 (Grand Rapids, MI: Zondervan, 1991), 285.
14. Encyclopædia Britannica, http://www.britannica.com/EBchecked/topic/28270/antinomy.
15. Reported in John Scott, *Romans: God's Good News for the World* (Downers Grove, IL: Intervarsity Press, 1994), 278.
16. God's gift of free choice is from the beginning. For example, God gives Adam a choice of the fruit of the trees (Gen. 2:16), the freedom to name the animals (Gen. 2:19), and the authority to rule over creation (Gen. 1:26, 28) as God's partner.
17. The New Testament admonishes us to wake up. See Romans 13:11, Ephesians 5:14, Revelation 3:2–3.

CHAPTER 11

1. Ben Tracy, "The Economic Ripple Effect Gone Awry," CBS Evening News, http://www.cbsnews.com/news/the-economic-ripple-effect-gone-awry/.
2. Sigal G. Barsade, "The Ripple Effect: Emotional Contagion and its Influence on Group Behavior," *Administrative Science Quarterly*, Vol. 47, No. 4, (2002): 644–75.
3. Sue Black, "Computing Ripple Effect in Software Maintenance," *Journal of Software Maintenance and Evolution: Research and Practice*, Vol. 13, Issue 4, (July/August 2001): 263–79.
4. Brian Wechler, *Village Missions: God's Ripple Effect*, YouTube, http://www.youtube.com/watch?v=c83ptgNO68I.
5. About.com, accessed August 15, 2013, http://urbanlegends.about.com/gi/dynamic/offsite.htm?site=http://www.ime.usp.br/~rbrito/teaching/mack/loo/interessante.html.
6. About.com, accessed August 17, 2013, http://urbanlegends.about.com/library/bl_bill_gates_speech.htm.
7. The Free Dictionary, http://idioms.thefreedictionary.com/fit+for+a+king.
8. The French sociologist, Émile Durkheim, introduced the term *collective consciousness* in his book, *Division of Labor in Society* (1893). For Jacob's family, the division of labor, especially the authority to rule, is the epee-center of their shared concerns, beliefs, and ethical thinking.
9. Brueggemann, *Genesis*, Interpretation, 56.
10. Michael V. Fox, "Wisdom in the Joseph Story," *Vetus Testamentum*, Vol. 51, Fasc. 1, (Jan. 2001): 26–41.
11. David Penchansky, *Understanding Wisdom and Literature: The Nature of Dissonance in the Hebrew Text* (Grand Rapids, MI: Eerdman's Publishing Company, 2012), 18–19.
12. John 12:31, 14:30, 16:11.
13. William Congreve, *The Morning Bride: A Tragedy*, (1697). The quote is spoken by Zara in Act III, Scene VIII.

CHAPTER 12

1. The classic book on stress is from Hans Seyle, *The Stress of Life* (New York: McGraw-Hill, 1956).
2. See http://www.youtube.com/watch?v=j6mxL2cqxrA.
3. The spiritual was first published in *Slave Songs of the United States*, a collection of African American music published in 1867. See also Richard Crawford, *America's Musical Life: A History* (New York: W. W. Norton & Company, 2001).

4. Michael Casey Greene, *Toward God: The Ancient Wisdom of Western Prayer* (Harper Collins, 1989), 103.
5. John Calvin, *The Institutes of the Christian Religion*, Vol. 1, book 1, chapter 1, paragraph 1. (You may download a free copy from the Northwestern Theological Seminary library, Christian Classics Ethereal Library (Grand Rapids, MI), http://www.ntslibrary.com/PDF%20Books/Calvin%20Institutes%20of%20Christian%20Religion.pdf. (The quote is found on page 31 of the download.)
6. In Genesis 40:8, Joseph credits God with the ability to interpret dreams.
7. Cindy E. Hmelo-Silver, "Problem-Based Learning: What and How Do Students Learn?" *Educational Psychology Review*, Vol. 16, Issue 3, (2004): 235.
8. Alan J. Neville, "Problem-Based Learning and Medical Education Forty Years On," *Medical Principles and Practice*, Vol. 18, Issue 1, (2009): 1–9.
9. The term *cupbearer* is also translated as butler (KJV). The cupbearer was highly regarded by the king, fully trusted, and often a personal confidant. We should not think of the aristocratic gentleman's gentleman or valet. For a detailed description, see J. Vergote, *Joseph in Egypt* (Louvain: Publications Universities, 1959).
10. Collin Gautry has written *21 Dirty Tricks at Work*. These are certainly not behaviors to emulate, but you are wise to be aware that others use these tricks. See https://www.learntoinfluence.com/21-dirty-tricks-at-work/.
11. There are many sources on office and family politics. A good place to begin is with Mind Tools, http://www.mindtools.com/pages/article/newCDV_85.htm.
12. See "I Want It Now" from Willy Wonka and the Chocolate Factory, http://www.youtube.com/watch?v=TRTkCHE1sS4.
13. In Genesis 41:1–8, note that King Herod is troubled like Pharaoh in Matthew 2:3.
14. Thomas Hobbes, in his work *Leviathan* (1651), was the first to pen the precise phrase "*scientia potentia est*" (knowledge is power).
15. John Wesley, *The Works of John Wesley*, Vol. 6, p. 513.
16. The phrase "what ifs" is the title of a poem in Shel Siverstein's *A Light in the Attic* (New York: HarperCollins, 1981), 90.

CHAPTER 13

1. The prodigal son received a similar welcome in Luke 15:22 (Gen. 41:42).
2. William Safire's May 1, 1994, article in the *New York Times* traces the modern use of the term *trophy wife*. However, for millennia, women were taken in battle or given as trophies to conquering warriors or ruler.
3. "Once upon a time," Charles Dickens wrote in *A Christmas Carol*, "old Scrooge sat busy in his counting-house." People often use it in a hand-waving, imprecise way to indicate a moment in the past or to imply a fairy tale: "Once upon a time we all believed in the magic of the Fed," the *Independent* headlined a story on December 1, 2007. It's definitely English in origin, though it is hard to say how old it is. The Oxford English Dictionary has examples going as far back as Chaucer's Canterbury Tales in 1385. Askville, by Amazon, http://askville.amazon.com/time-phrase/AnswerViewer.do?requestId=6855906.
4. The closing phrase of a story, "they lived happily ever after," is found in literature all over the world including Albanian, Bulgaria, China, Croatia, France, Germany, Greece,

Israel (modern), Iceland, Italy, Malta, Portugal, Russia, Serbia, Spain, Thailand, and Vietnam. (See http://en.wikipedia.org/wiki/Once_upon_a_time.)

5. Caiaphas, the high priest, displayed the same ethical reasoning when dealing with Jesus: "What you don't understand is that it's better for you that one man should die for the people so the whole nation won't perish" (John 11:50).
6. Nicolo Machiavelli, *The Prince*, chapter 7, paragraph 12 (1515). See http://www.victoria.ac.nz/lals/about/staff/publications/paul-nation/Prince-Adapted2.pdf.
7. Jonathan Edwards, *Sinners in the Hands of an Angry God* (Enfield, CT, July 8, 1741), http://www.ccel.org/ccel/edwards/sermons.sinners.html.
8. See Jerry Cook's book, *Love, Acceptance, and Forgiveness* (Ventura, CA: Regal Publishing, 2009).
9. "Equal Justice," *The Practice*, Season 8, Episode 10 (December 7, 2003).
10. D. TuTu, *No Future Without Forgiveness* (New York: Doubleday, 1999).
11. From the blog *Journeying*. http://gillianb-journeying.blogspot.ca/2012/07/circles.html.
12. The story of *Chicken Little* (Henny Penny) can be found in a collection selected and edited by D. L Ashliman, *The End of the World: The Sky Is Falling* (1999), http://www.pitt.edu/~dash/type2033.html.
13. Eleanor Porter published *Pollyanna* in 1913, and it quickly became a best-selling children's classic. Pollyanna plays the glad game, a challenge to find the good in everything that happens.

CHAPTER 14

1. Dr. Dennis Kinlaw (sermon, Detroit First Church of the Nazarene, Novi, MI, January 1985).
2. See http://www.youtube.com/watch?v=H-aNElsbkM8.
3. Martin Luther King, *The Strength to Love* (1963). The phrase was repeated in the work of Dr. King. See Wolfgang Mieder, *Making a Way Out of No Way: Martin Luther King's Sermonic Proverbial Rhetoric* (New York: Peter Lang Publishing), 337–338.
4. The original saying is "two wrongs infer a right." The saying is from C. Ackers, "The Moral," *The London Magazine*, Vol. 3, (1734): 600.
5. William MacLeod Raine, *The Highgrader*, (New York: Grosset & Dunlap, 1915), 199; see also Clifton Brown, "Boxing Mayweather Is Crowned, but Not Without a Fight," *New York Times* (April 9, 2006). In an ugly fight, Mayweather said he did not return the dirty tactics because "two wrongs don't make a right."
6. The rhyme can be found in Joseph M. Stowell, *Simply Jesus and You: Experience His Presence and His Purpose* (Colorado Springs: Multnomah Books, 2006), 169.
7. J. M. Nouwen, *Bread for the Journey: A Daybook of Wisdom and Faith* (HarperOne, 1996), entry for July 20.
8. Galatians 3:8; see also Genesis 12:2; 18:18; 22:18; 26:4; 28:14.
9. The resurrections of Lazarus and Jesus can be contrasted in John 11:3–44; 20:17, 19; 21:12–15.
10. J. Bardwick, *Danger in the Comfort Zone* (New York: American Management Association, 1991). See also Alasdair White, *From Comfort Zone to Performance Management* (Belgium: White and MacLean Publishing, 2008), 2.
11. D. Tutu, "Without Forgiveness There Is No Future," *Exploring Forgiveness*, pp. 351 –357. (Madison: University of Wisconsin Press, 1998)

ABOUT THE AUTHOR

Dr. Richard Parrott is a professor at Trevecca Nazarene University, teaching leadership studies in the areas of business, education, and Christian ministries. Dr. Parrott is also an ordained elder in the Church of the Nazarene with a quarter century of pastoral ministry. In addition, he was associate professor of Christian Leadership at Ashland Theological Seminary and director of the Doctor of Ministry program, as well as the Founding Executive Director of the Sandburg Leadership Center. His publications include *My Soul Purpose*; *True and Best: Authentic Living*; *When Pastors Pray*; and *Leadership Lessons: Avoiding the Pitfalls of King Saul* (with Dr. Ralph Hawkins). Dr. Parrott resides in Franklin, Tennessee. You may contact the author through his website MySoulPurpose.org.

Thomas Nelson's Refraction collection of books offer biblical responses to the biggest issues of our time, topics that have been tabooed or ignored in the past. The books will give readers insights into these issues and what God says about them, and how to respond to others whose beliefs differ from ours in a transparent and respectful way. Refraction books cross theological boundaries in an open and honest way, through succinct and candid writing for a contemporary, millenial-minded reader.

LEARN MORE AT REFRACTIONBOOKS.COM

NOW AVAILABLE

MARCH 2015

MARCH 2015

APRIL 2015

JULY 2015